P9-CLV-579

Fighting Forces

Fighting Forces

Richard Bennett

BARRON'S

First edition for the United States, its territories and dependencies and Canada published in 2001 by Barron's Educational Series, Inc.

A QUARTO BOOK

All inquiries should be addressed to:
Barron's Educational Series, Inc.
250 Wireless Boulevard
Hauppauge, New York 11788
http://www.barronseduc.com

ISBN 0-7641-5343-9

Library of Congress Catalog Card No. 2001091553

QUAR.FFO

Conceived, designed, and produced by
Quarto Publishing plc
The Old Brewery
6 Blundell Street
London N7 9BH

Project Editor Jean Coppendale
Senior Art Editor Penny Cobb
Designer Pete Laws
Styling and Graphics Grundy & Northedge
Picture Research Image Select International
Proofreader Anne Hildyard
Indexer Pamela Ellis

Art Director Moira Clinch
Publisher Piers Spence

Author's Acknowledgments
I'd like to dedicate *Fighting Forces* to my wonderful mother, Florence. Also, sincere thanks go to my editor, Jean Coppendale, and pictures and design supremo, Penny Cobb. Most of all, I would like to thank my daughter, Katie, who not only helped me greatly, but also put up with me during the writing of this book.

Manufactured by Universal Graphics Pte Ltd., Singapore
Printed by Star Standard Industries (Pte) Ltd., Singapore

9 8 7 6 5 4 3 2 1

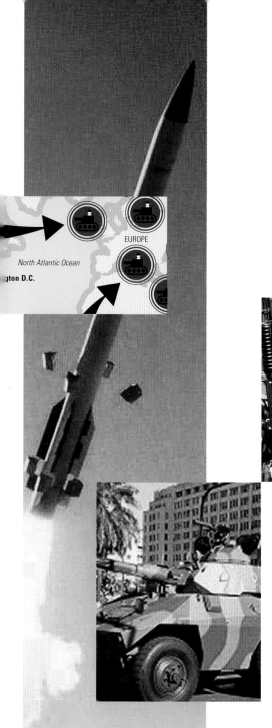

North Atlantic Ocean

.gton D.C.

EUROPE

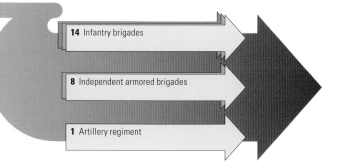

14 Infantry brigades

8 Independent armored brigades

1 Artillery regiment

Contents

Introduction 6

NORTH AMERICA

The United States 10
Canada 26

SOUTH AMERICA

Brazil 32

EUROPE

The United Kingdom 38
France 48
Germany 58
Spain 64
Italy 70
Greece 76

MIDDLE EAST

Saudi Arabia 82
Egypt 88
Iran 94
Iraq 100
Israel 106
Syria 116

ASIA

Russia 122
Turkey 132
India 140
Pakistan 146
China 152
Japan 160
North and South Korea 166
Taiwan 172
Indonesia 178

OCEANIA

Australia 184

Index 190
Credits 192

Introduction

Fighting forces of the twenty-first century

The collapse of Communism in 1991 brought an end to the dangerous, but in retrospect, oddly reassuring simplicities of the Cold War. Western governments and their military forces now stood at a crossroads. Should they take the "peace-bonus" and disarm? Should they downscale and merely remain capable of fighting only as an ally in a U.S.-dominated alliance, or should they develop an independent defense capability? The years that followed have seen a period of sustained change and a great deal of soul-searching by the major armies of the world. Most nations opted to downscale so severely as to emasculate their defense capability in some cases.

Much has been heard of generals being told to trim the fat from their forces or provide "more teeth, less tail." However, informed skeptics remain firmly unconvinced that such political nonsense can mean anything but diminishing the ability of the armed forces to carry out the role assigned to them—the defense of the nation.

Armies are deeply affected not only by political and economic changes, but also by great advances in military technology. Tactics are constantly changing to take advantage of new weaponry. For example, the advent of the helicopter produced a sea change in military operations, from the newly acquired ability to move sizable numbers of assault troops quickly over or around enemy defenses or natural obstacles such as hills, rivers, or jungles, to the enormous tank-killing capability of the U.S. AH-64 or Russian Mi-24 HIND. The missile-firing helicopter has raised considerable doubts over the long-term future of the traditional, 50-ton main battle tank—can this armored monster survive on modern battlefields against heavily armed and agile airborne tank-busters? The answer to this question alone will greatly affect warfare throughout the twenty-first century.

The armies of the major power blocks, NATO and the Warsaw Pact, found it necessary, for much of the last 55 years, to adapt to the prospect of operating large conventional forces under nuclear, biological, or chemical (NBC) warfare conditions. Considerable doubts were expressed about the viability of such forces in these conditions. Huge problems were raised by the necessity of going into battle with tanks totally closed down in the heat of battle, or infantry struggling to fight while smothered in masks and bulky NBC suits. Similarly, other operational shortcomings have never been effectively answered, such as the protection of gunners who remain highly vulnerable while manning their weapons, and vital logistics, fuel supply, and medical services trying to support combat units while under threat from deadly radiation or nerve gas attack.

Weapons of mass destruction

Today, NBC proliferation has spread these problems to an ever-increasing number of countries. The Israeli armed forces not only have a considerable nuclear capability, but also face a number of Arab countries with advanced programs for Weapons of Mass Destruction (WMD). The best known is Iraq, where, despite UN sanctions and repeated attacks on sensitive facilities by Allied forces since 1991, much of Saddam Hussein's chemical warfare and missile capability has been rebuilt, while an Iraqi nuclear bomb may be in existence by the end of 2002.

Iran has a large-scale chemical warfare and missile program, while Syria, with more than 1,000 short-range ballistic missiles, has the most advanced chemical warfare capability in the Middle East. Egypt and a number of other Arab states have warheads

Heavily armed Egyptian troops take up a defensive position in the Sinai Desert, with a B11 107mm anti-tank weapon and AKMS assault rifles.

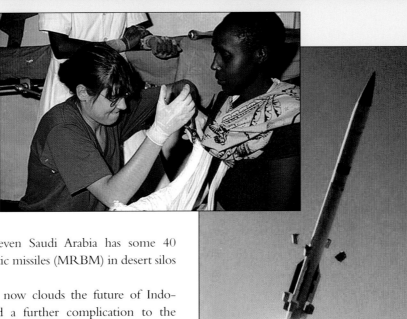

The modern face of Canadian peacekeeping duties worldwide, here a female medical assistant treats an injured Rwandan civilian at a military field hospital.

Very much in the forefront of new technology, the U.S. Patriot-3 will provide a vital defense against ballistic missiles for years to come.

with chemical agents, and even Saudi Arabia has some 40 Chinese medium-range ballistic missiles (MRBM) in desert silos in the north of the country.

The nuclear standoff that now clouds the future of Indo-Pakistani relations has added a further complication to the region's military balance. India, now a leading power, has a potent arsenal of both nuclear warheads and highly capable missile technology. India's ability to project its newfound power beyond its immediate area will be further enhanced by the introduction of long-range missile systems over the next few years. Pakistan has now successfully detonated a nuclear device and has introduced quantities of Chinese short-range ballistic missiles (SRBM). Both India and Pakistan have also pursued a capability in other weapons of mass destruction and have stockpiled a number of chemical warfare agents and possibly biological weapons. India faces not only a future nuclear conflict with Pakistan, but must also accept the possibility that any new confrontation with Communist China may develop along the same lines. Thus India is determined that its future actions will not be constrained by nuclear blackmail. Pakistan in turn looks to an NBC capability as a balance to its powerful neighbor's considerable advantage in conventional forces.

The changing face of warfare

These changes and the advances in electronic warfare, the introduction of computers and information technology, and the end of the Cold War have brought about the largest re-assessment of defense issues in peacetime. Gone is the need for the traditional heavily armored battle groups, trained and equipped for the expected slugging match on the battlefields of Northern Europe. The requirement for large standing forces made up of conscripts has also vanished, to be replaced by the very different demands of the twenty-first century, which require smaller, highly mobile, and fully professional armies. Versatility is increasingly important, as armies need to cope with natural disasters, humanitarian aid, and international peacekeeping operations.

The new battlefield may come to be dominated by the light armored vehicles that will replace the 50-ton main battle tank, for so long the queen of the battlefield. These new vehicles will be suitable for air transportation around the world, and capable of surviving in both rough terrain or in urban battlefields. They will probably have advanced plastic armor, quick-firing guns, and

a range of new missile systems with the added ability to operate closely with swarms of lethal attack helicopters—together with fire support from mobile multiple rocket launchers and self-propelled artillery firing rocket-assisted ammunition. The infantry, appearing increasingly like star-ship troopers, will have state-of-the-art personal weapons, individual communications, image intensifiers, and even be protected by the return of body armor, albeit made of lightweight plastic.

Indeed, the U.S. army is already developing an all-in-one combat suit, which will give its infantry a huge advantage in surviving the unpredictable battlefield environments of the future. These battlefields, unlike anything that has gone before, will be populated with fewer battlefield combatants, as increasingly war is conducted by the technician. The watch-words for armies in the future will increasingly be "Command, Control, Communications, and Intelligence." The army that understands and makes the best use of the advances in electronic warfare and information technology has a winning advantage in the asymmetrical or cyber wars of the new century.

However, despite these advances, it is expected that the traditional tank and other conventional weapons will survive in most armies well into the second half of this century. The privilege of being able to restructure the armed forces to take full advantage of the new technologies will be restricted to a relatively few advanced and, of course, wealthy nations.

The problems and opportunities presented by technological advances are not the only challenges faced by today's military planners. Armies that once trained for a single major combat role must now adapt their tactics and weaponry to a far more

INTRODUCTION

Military terminology can often be a problem for the uninitiated. A few of the main terms and abbreviations used in this book are explained below:

AIFV Armored infantry fighting vehicle.

APC Armored personnel carrier. The difference between an AIFV and an APC is that the infantry dismount from an APC to fight, while the more versatile AIFV allows soldiers to fight while still on board and moving.

Field gun and howitzer The difference between a field gun and a howitzer is that a field gun's shell has a flatter trajectory and usually has the target within sight. A howitzer, however, fires its shell at a high angle and can hit targets "over the hill," or hidden from sight. Many modern artillery pieces are now built as gun-howitzers that combine both abilities.

Ballistic missiles Ballistic means the trajectory has a very high or even exo-atmospheric capability (outside the atmosphere). This gives them a long range, as in the case of the ICBM (Inter-Continental Ballistic Missile).

Guidance Many missiles must "see" their target, as in line-of-sight or wire guided anti-tank missiles, where an operator guides the missile on to the target via an ultra thin wire. Others use infrared homing, as in the case of an anti-aircraft missile, which homes in on the heat signature of a jet fighter, or radar homing, which scans for and then locks on to its target.

MLRS Multiple Launching Rocket System.

Pack This refers to the ability to strip down a howitzer, for example, into smaller loads so that they can be carried on light vehicles or pack animals such as mules in jungle warfare conditions.

Towed Artillery of all types that need to be towed by a vehicle, known as a prime mover—a large six-wheeled truck or tracked carrier.

Self-propelled gun The artillery piece is built onto a tracked chassis and moves under its own power.

TOW Tube launcher, Optically tracked, Wire-guided anti-tank missile.

Manportable A weapon light enough to be carried by one or two men.

Surface-to-air or SAM (Surface-to-Air Missile) is a static or mobile air defense/anti-aircraft weapon.

Surface-to-surface or SSM (Surface-to-Surface Missile) is a bombardment system with ranges of 3 to 30 miles (5 to 50 km). (Beyond that they tend to be called Short Range Ballistic Missiles [SRBM]).

HALO High altitude jumping from an aircraft. Low altitude opening of the parachute.

HAHO High altitude jumping from an aircraft. High altitude opening of the parachute. (Both techniques are used by special forces for covert insertion of forces behind enemy lines or in contested areas).

Killing House Specially constructed building where special forces practice hostage rescue operations or taking out terrorists.

Turkish Nurol armored carriers seen here on patrol while serving with United Nations peacekeeping operations in the Balkans.

complex world. Urban or vertical warfare demands a new type of soldier who must be prepared to fight street-to-street as well as vertically upward, to clear buildings with every room, stairwell, and rooftop defended or booby-trapped. They will fight vertically downward, too, into the sewers, storm drains, underground garages, and subways of urban environments.

Counter-insurgency, or COIN, operations in mountains, jungles, deserts, and plains, against determined local forces, demand yet more new skills. These include dealing not only with difficult terrain, but also extreme weather conditions from arctic blizzards to tropical rain forests. The growth of COIN and counter-terrorist operations has led in turn to dramatic increases in the range and size of special forces, which are still suspect in the eyes of many military traditionalists, not least for the public and media interest shown in their activities.

The army of the twenty-first century will need to be a multi-skilled, quick reacting, highly mobile, suitably armed, and fully professional force. Never before have soldiers had to face so many different and varied forms of opposition. Never before have armies had to adapt to such a wide range of potential operations, terrain, or enemies. The democratic traditions of the very best of today's armies are constantly being tested to the limit, and the resulting strain on the structure and personnel of the fighting forces is enormous.

Time for a change

Not surprisingly, the United States was first to recognize the need to maintain, change, and enhance its national defense in response to the new post-Cold War situation. There has been a constant debate within the U.S. defense community during the last decade over the shape of warfare in the future, the advances in technology, and the bewildering range of potential enemies. The use of low-tech counter-insurgency in many conflicts has left high-tech advanced military forces punching shadows. Much of the debate has therefore centered on the major restructuring and retraining of the U.S. armed forces to deal with this challenge, while still retaining a strategic capability to defend the Western alliance against any resurgence of Russian or Chinese global ambitions.

It is without doubt that only the United States now retains the economic power, the industrial, scientific, and military infrastructure, as well as the political determination to equip, train, and then deploy an army capable of fulfilling the global role that a true superpower would expect of its fighting forces.

How to use this book

Fighting Forces is divided into six regions of the world, and then into countries. Each country follows the same sequence of topics. The introduction outlines the past, present, and future roles of the country's army. Next is a description of the army's operations, its weapons and units, fighting structure, and special forces. Charts and panels detail the armament and manpower capabilities in each country, and show how the different forces are structured.

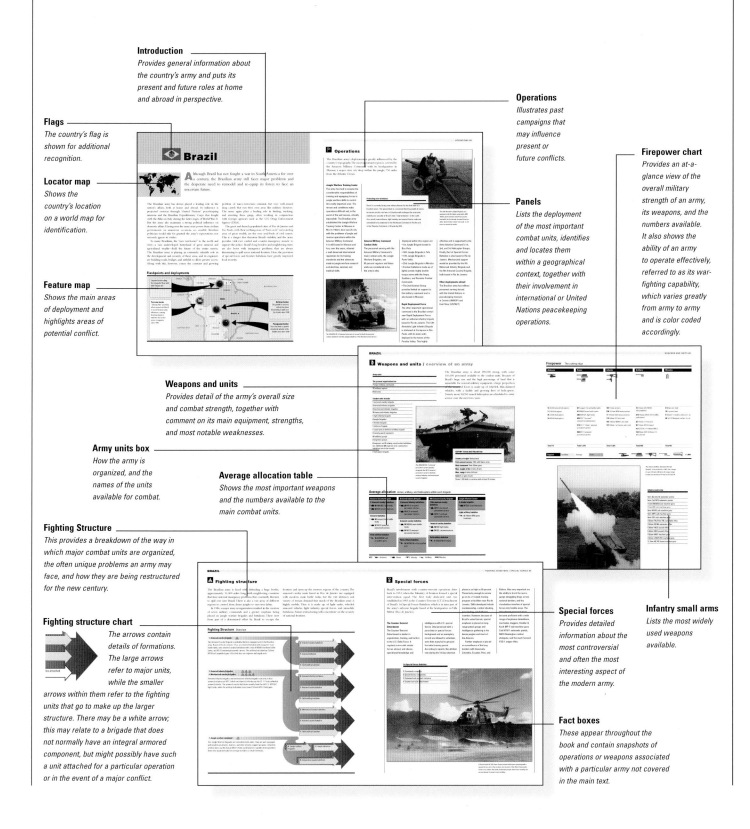

Introduction
Provides general information about the country's army and puts its present and future roles at home and abroad in perspective.

Flags
The country's flag is shown for additional recognition.

Locator map
Shows the country's location on a world map for identification.

Feature map
Shows the main areas of deployment and highlights areas of potential conflict.

Operations
Illustrates past campaigns that may influence present or future conflicts.

Panels
Lists the deployment of the most important combat units, identifies and locates them within a geographical context, together with their involvement in international or United Nations peacekeeping operations.

Firepower chart
Provides an at-a-glance view of the overall military strength of an army, its weapons, and the numbers available. It also shows the ability of an army to operate effectively, referred to as its war-fighting capability, which varies greatly from army to army and is color coded accordingly.

Weapons and units
Provides detail of the army's overall size and combat strength, together with comment on its main equipment, strengths, and most notable weaknesses.

Army units box
How the army is organized, and the names of the units available for combat.

Average allocation table
Shows the most important weapons and the numbers available to the main combat units.

Fighting Structure
This provides a breakdown of the way in which major combat units are organized, the often unique problems an army may face, and how they are being restructured for the new century.

Fighting structure chart
The arrows contain details of formations. The large arrows refer to major units, while the smaller arrows within them refer to the fighting units that go to make up the larger structure. There may be a white arrow; this may relate to a brigade that does not normally have an integral armored component, but might possibly have such a unit attached for a particular operation or in the event of a major conflict.

Special forces
Provides detailed information about the most controversial and often the most interesting aspect of the modern army.

Infantry small arms
Lists the most widely used weapons available.

Fact boxes
These appear throughout the book and contain snapshots of operations or weapons associated with a particular army not covered in the main text.

The U.S. army faces the challenges of the twenty-first century equipped and trained to dominate any future conventional battlefield and with a genuine war-winning capability beyond that of any other nation. The army is in a class of its own, and the gap with the rest of the world is growing rapidly, for no other nation has the technology, money, or the political determination to ensure the maintenance of a professional standing army of the present size and quality of that of the United States.

That determination is also vital to ensure that there is no repetition of the hasty dismantling of the mighty wartime U.S. military machine as happened in 1945–46. This left the U.S. army at the outbreak of the Korean War in 1950, with a force that was once described as largely made up of clerks, cooks, and bottlewashers. A similar mistake occurred in the rapid downsizing of the army following the withdrawal of U.S. forces from Southeast Asia in the early 1970s. While the ending of the Cold War again offered further opportunities for large-scale reductions, the Gulf War of 1990–91, thankfully, created a new awareness among both the U.S. military and

AH64 Apache Armed Helicopters

Country of origin U.S.	
First entered service 1986 with U.S. army	
Main armament 30mm cannon (1,200 rounds)	
8 Hellfire AT Missiles and 38 70mm rockets	
Max. speed 170 mph (284 km/h)	
Max. range 1,150 miles (1,900 km) (ex. tanks)	
Crew 2	
Over 1,000 built, in service with 6 armies	

The heavily armed AH64 Longbow Apache helicopter has a deadly target acquisition and fire control radar added above the main rotor, as well as an impressive array of externally mounted weapons.

Flashpoints and deployments

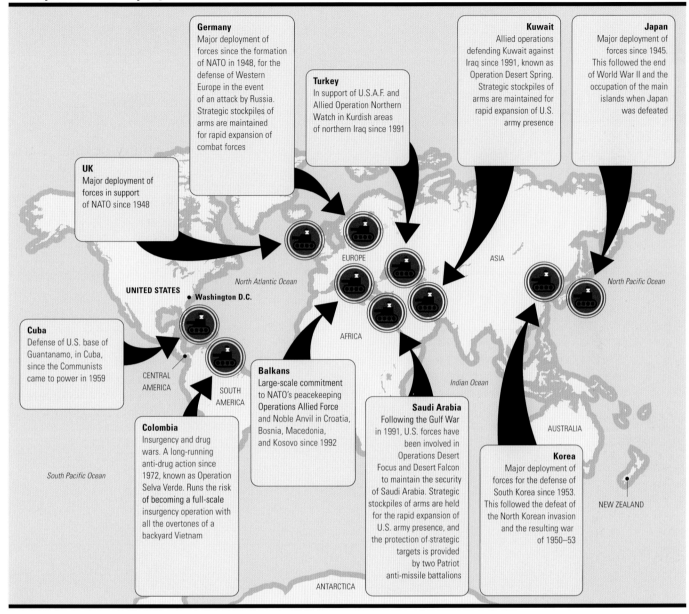

Germany
Major deployment of forces since the formation of NATO in 1948, for the defense of Western Europe in the event of an attack by Russia. Strategic stockpiles of arms are maintained for rapid expansion of combat forces

Turkey
In support of U.S.A.F. and Allied Operation Northern Watch in Kurdish areas of northern Iraq since 1991

Kuwait
Allied operations defending Kuwait against Iraq since 1991, known as Operation Desert Spring. Strategic stockpiles of arms are maintained for rapid expansion of U.S. army presence

Japan
Major deployment of forces since 1945. This followed the end of World War II and the occupation of the main islands when Japan was defeated

UK
Major deployment of forces in support of NATO since 1948

Cuba
Defense of U.S. base of Guantanamo, in Cuba, since the Communists came to power in 1959

Colombia
Insurgency and drug wars. A long-running anti-drug action since 1972, known as Operation Selva Verde. Runs the risk of becoming a full-scale insurgency operation with all the overtones of a backyard Vietnam

Balkans
Large-scale commitment to NATO's peacekeeping Operations Allied Force and Noble Anvil in Croatia, Bosnia, Macedonia, and Kosovo since 1992

Saudi Arabia
Following the Gulf War in 1991, U.S. forces have been involved in Operations Desert Focus and Desert Falcon to maintain the security of Saudi Arabia. Strategic stockpiles of arms are held for the rapid expansion of U.S. army presence, and the protection of strategic targets is provided by two Patriot anti-missile battalions

Korea
Major deployment of forces for the defense of South Korea since 1953. This followed the defeat of the North Korean invasion and the resulting war of 1950–53

UNITED STATES
• Washington D.C.
North Atlantic Ocean
EUROPE
ASIA
North Pacific Ocean
AFRICA
CENTRAL AMERICA
SOUTH AMERICA
Indian Ocean
South Pacific Ocean
AUSTRALIA
NEW ZEALAND
ANTARCTICA

Washington that fine words, without the power to enforce them, are worthless.

The U.S. army has also had to cope with the problems of a fickle civilian population and government officials who are often super-critical of American military forces, yet lack a genuine understanding of both their limitations and their needs. Indeed, that essential lack of understanding was highlighted by the Vietnam War, a war that the army might have won, but which a lack of resolution at home brought to an end before this idea could be tested. The treatment received by the young Vietnam War veterans contrasted sharply with the acclaim given to both the Doughboys and the GI's upon their return from the First and Second World Wars.

While the U.S. army, with its enormous power, is difficult to challenge in conventional terms, its reliance on high technology and its number-counting mentality may make it blind to the threat provided by a very different form of warfare, the low-intensity conflict. In this type of conflict, a conventionally trained, well-armed force can find itself constantly punching shadows with no fixed front-line and often no real idea on whose side a myriad of armed personnel are actually on. The new irregulars who engage in these types of conflicts have little respect for the value of life or human rights, have an attitude that is amoral, indifferent to suffering, usually uncaring of personal danger, have no allegiance to any particular country, and have a fierce determination to bring down the power and authority of both

Army of the future

During 2001–2002, the U.S. army will accelerate the process of establishing the new and more responsive light brigades that will initially use readily available commercial equipment and even borrowed vehicles. The brigades will receive off-the-shelf armored vehicles until such time as the finances are available to procure a new purpose-built family of advanced lightweight and highly mobile vehicles. Flexibility is the watchword and the distinction between heavy and light forces will gradually disappear.

The versatile Hummer jeep. Thousands of these useful vehicles serve with all branches of the U.S. army. They symbolize the innovative use of modern technology to produce new, lighter, airmobile vehicles.

national governments and the international community. In the years to come, the U.S. army is more likely to be found in serious combat with these kinds of individuals, whether they are called guerrillas, terrorists, or insurgents, than with conventionally trained soldiers.

This form of urban warfare, rural insurgency, or international terrorism poses a huge threat, even to an army well practiced in the ways of unconventional warfare. The U.S. army is capable of combat in virtually any terrain, weather, and time of day, with an outstandingly high level of military sophistication, but it has still proved vulnerable to irregulars. Conflicts in Lebanon in 1982–87 and Somalia in 1992–96 are two examples. Even in Southeast Asia, where the U.S. army proved more than competent against the regular North Vietnamese army, it often struggled against the Vietcong guerrillas.

The U.S. army is, however, fortunate to have in place an infrastructure that is able to address this problem, in its Special Forces Command. The Green Berets and the Rangers, with the addition of the 82nd and 101st Airborne Divisions, provide a considerable capability to intervene in regional conflicts. However, there is an enormous gap between theory and practice, and a number of harsh lessons will have to be relearned before the army will be entirely confident of

success in overcoming the threat posed by these unconventional styles of warfare.

On a larger scale, the U.S. army has been restructured since the end of the Cold War, and the new Army XX1 Division is replacing the heavy divisions designed for service on the plains of northern Europe. This unit is more mobile, has increased firepower, and is capable of deployment in any theater of operation. The effective use of high technology, state-of-the-art surveillance, electronic warfare techniques, and advanced strategic and tactical intelligence gathering and analysis, together with the imaginative use of modern information technology has helped to create an army capable of fighting on all levels of the modern asymmetrical battlefield.

The U.S. army of the twenty-first century is truly the world's most outstanding and dominating conventional military force. More than ever before, it is becoming both leaner and meaner.

Leadership is everything

Good leadership is the glue that holds a fighting force together under the stress of battle. The U.S. army has considerable skill in developing comprehensive training programs that ensure that its peacetime officer corps retains the steely cutting edge that leads to success in combat. Physical strength, psychological toughness, and stress management are all included, along with a high level of military competence and a particular emphasis on leadership qualities. The U.S. Military Academy at West Point has a well-deserved reputation throughout the world for excellence in such skills.

A U.S. infantryman wearing disrupted pattern clothing. He has a manpack radio and is equipped with the M16/M203 5.56mm assault rifle and 40mm grenade launcher combination.

Operations

The U.S. army is currently deployed in operations throughout the world. Some of these commitments appear below:

Operation Golden Pheasant, Honduras, involved a brigade of the 82nd Airborne Division that was parachuted into Honduras to deter possible Nicaraguan incursions. There has followed an ongoing program of counter-insurgency and infantry support for the Honduran army, since March 1988.

Desert Falcon, the deployment of two Patriot Anti-Missile Battalions for the protection of strategic sites in Saudi Arabia, has been underway since 1991. Troops from the 10th Mountain, 82nd Airborne, and 3rd Infantry Divisions are rotated to defend the missile batteries.

Joint Guardian reflects the U.S. army's commitment to NATO's Kosovo Force (or KFOR) and has been built around the 2nd Brigade of the 1st Division since 1999.

NATO commitments

The current U.S. army operational deployment also includes a large number of ongoing, major, long-term overseas and NATO commitments. Units for such operations would be drawn from the following U.S.-based and overseas commands:

Forces Command (FORSCOM)

This is the U.S. army's largest command with headquarters at Fort McPherson, Georgia.

1st Corps headquarters at Fort Lewis, Washington (responsible for the area from Alaska to Alabama). Does not have a fixed force structure of assigned divisions, but instead acts as central reservoir of active and reserve components and personnel.

3rd Corps headquarters at Fort Hood, Texas (Army Strategic Command)

• 1st Cavalry (Armored) Division, headquarters at Fort Hood, Texas

• 4th Mechanized Infantry Division, headquarters at Fort Hood, Texas

18th Airborne Corps headquarters at Fort Bragg, North Carolina

• 2nd Armored Cavalry Regiment, headquarters at Fort Polk, Louisiana

• 3rd Mechanized Infantry Division, headquarters at Fort Stewart, Georgia

• 10th Mountain Light Division, headquarters at Fort Drum, New York

• 82nd Airborne Division, headquarters at Fort Polk, Louisiana

• 101st Air Assault Division, headquarters at Fort Campbell, Kentucky

• 18th Aviation Brigade, headquarters at Fort Polk

An outstanding design, the M1 Abrams helped to revolutionize armored warfare. The firepower and great mobility of this main battle tank proved decisive in the Gulf War.

Protection from SCUDs

In late summer of 1991, Saudi Arabia requested immediate assistance from the United States to provide some protection from the threat of Iraqi SCUD Short-Range Ballistic Missiles (SRBM). The United States army quickly deployed two Patriot anti-missile and air defense battalions from Europe, complete with a brigade headquarters. Operation Desert Falcon, as it was called, aimed to protect strategic sites within Saudi Arabia from both air and missile attack. This operation continues today, with units regularly being rotated for duties.

The United States army has a huge commitment to humanitarian relief. Following the devastation caused by hurricane Mitch to Central America in October 1998 (the fourth most severe hurricane ever recorded), the U.S. deployed 1,400 personnel in two major relief operations—the Joint Task Force Bravo to Honduras and Joint Task Force Eagle in El Salvador. Thirty-nine U.S. helicopters flew in support, and the entire relief program did not end until well into February 1999. U.S. forces directly rescued around 700 civilians and brought aid to countless thousands more.

The M2 Bradley armored infantry fighting vehicle proved a versatile and effective companion for the M1 Abrams main battle tank throughout the Gulf War.

The following military commands are administrative and training organizations and do not control operational combat units:
• 1st U.S. Army, headquarters at Fort Gillem, Georgia. Controls the area of continental U.S. east of the Mississippi River
• 3rd U.S. Army, headquarters at Fort McPherson, Georgia
U.S. Central Command
• 5th U.S. Army, headquarters at Fort Sam Houston, Texas. Controls the area of continental U.S. west of the Mississippi River

U.S. Army Europe (U.S.AREUR)
headquarters at Heidelberg, Germany
7th U.S. Army, headquarters at Campbell Barracks, Heidelberg, Germany
• 5th Corps, also with headquarters in the Campbell barracks complex
• 1st Armored Division,

headquarters in Bad Kreuznach, Germany
• 1st Mechanized Infantry Division, headquarters in Wuerzburg, Germany
Southern European Task Force, headquarters, Venice, Italy

U.S. Army Pacific (U.S.ARPAC)
headquarters at Fort Shafter, Hawaii
U.S. Army Alaska, headquarters at Fort Richardson, Anchorage
• 172nd Infantry Brigade headquarters at Fort Wainwright, Fairbanks
U.S. Army Hawaii, headquarters at Schofield Barracks, Oahu
• 25th Infantry Division, headquarters at Schofield Barracks, Oahu
U.S. Army Japan headquarters at Camp Zama
1 corps headquarters only, no assigned combat units

8th U.S. Army, South Korea, headquarters at Yongsan, Seoul
• 2nd Infantry Division, headquarters at Camp Red Cloud, Uijongeu
• 6th Air Cavalry Brigade, headquarters at Camp Humphreys, Pyongtaek

U.S. Army Central Command (U.S.CENTCOM)
headquarters at MacDill AFB, Florida. Controls units in the Middle East (ARCENT) with air defense units in Saudi Arabia. 1 brigade headquarters and prepositioned equipment for 1 armored brigade in Kuwait and prepositioned equipment for 1 armored brigade in Qatar

U.S. Army Southern Command (U.S.SOUTHCOM)
headquarters at Fort Buchanon, Puerto Rico. This command has no major combat units permanently attached
• Joint Task Force Bravo, headquarters at Soto Cano AB, Honduras

The U.S. army continues to face an enormous number of potential conflicts, but the main emphasis will remain on those in the Middle East and a possible resumption of the Gulf War with Iraq. The other area is Korea, where the U.S. army continues to be deployed in support of the South Korean (ROK) army after 50 years, and this emphasis would appear to be ongoing for the immediate future.

Weapons and units / overview of an army

The present U.S. army has 471,500 personnel, including 71,500 women, with some 220,000 personnel available for front-line service.

The U.S. army continues to be equipped with leading-edge weapons and equipment, ensuring a considerable ability to react to any challenge, and to dominate any battlefield. Understanding the opportunities offered by the latest high technology, the U.S. has achieved an unassailable lead among the armed forces of the world. This lead is sure to be increased by the unwillingness of its allies, and the inability of potentially hostile states, to either understand or adequately respond to the challenges of asymmetrical or cyber warfare, or indeed to the advanced technologies that are likely to be involved in the conflicts of the twenty-first century.

AH64 Apache Armed Helicopters

Country of origin U.S.

First entered service 1986 with U.S. army

Main armament 30 mm cannon (1,200 rounds)

8 Hellfire AT Missiles and 38 70 mm rockets

Max. road speed 170 mph (284 km/h)

Max. range 1,150 miles (1,900 km) (ex. tanks)

Crew 2

Over 1,000 built, in service with 6 armies

Army units

The present organization has

3 army headquarters

3 corps

1 airborne corps headquarters under whose command are

2 armored divisions

1 mechanized infantry division

2 light infantry divisions

1 air assault division

1 airborne division

5 aviation brigades

3 armored cavalry brigades

6 artillery brigades

1 independent infantry battalion

1 airborne task force

In addition there are

9 Patriot

2 Avenger air defense missile battalions

Average allocation Armor, artillery, and helicopters within each brigade

Infantry small arms

9mm Beretta M9 automatic pistols

5.56mm M16 series automatic rifles

5.56mm M4 carbines

7.62mm M21 sniper rifles

7.62mm M60 series machine guns

5.56mm M249 Minimi machine guns

12.7mm M2 HB heavy machine guns

Armored Division	Mechanized Division	Air Assault Division	Airborne Division
467 M1A1/2 Abrams main battle tanks	**467** M1A1/2 Abrams main battle tanks	No attached armor	No attached armor
600 M2A3 Bradley armored infantry fighting vehicles	**536** M2A3 Bradley armored infantry fighting vehicles	**18** 105mm M102/M119 towed airmobile artillery	**18** 105mm M102/M119 towed airmobile artillery
144 155mm M109/M109A6 Paladin self-propelled artillery	**144** 155mm M109/M109A6 Paladin self-propelled artillery	Each battalion in the aviation brigade will have:	Each battalion in the aviation brigade will have:
108 M106 107mm self-propelled mortars	**108** M106 107mm self-propelled mortars	**15** AH-1/AH-6 Apache Longbow attack helicopters	**15** AH-1/AH-6 Apache Longbow attack helicopters
18 227mm M270 MLRS multiple rocket launchers	**18** 227mm M270 MLRS multiple rocket launchers	**33** OH58D Kiowa Warrior/RAH-66 Comanche helicopters	**33** OH58D Kiowa Warrior/RAH-66 Comanche helicopters
Each battalion in the aviation brigade will have:	Each battalion in the aviation brigade will have:	**24** UH60 Blackhawk support helicopters	**24** UH60 Blackhawk support helicopters
15 AH-1/AH-64 Apache Longbow attack helicopters	**15** AH-1/AH-6 Apache Longbow attack helicopters	**9** EH60 electronic warfare helicopters	**9** EH60 electronic warfare helicopters
33 OH58D Kiowa Warrior/RAH-66 Comanche helicopters	**33** OH58D Kiowa Warrior/RAH-66 Comanche helicopters		
24 UH60 Blackhawk support helicopters	**24** UH60 Blackhawk support helicopters		
9 EH60 electronic warfare helicopters	**9** EH60 electronic warfare helicopters		

KEY Airborne   Armor   Infantry   Artillery   Missiles

Firepower   The cutting edge

Airborne	Armor	Infantry	Artillery	Missiles

511 AH1S

743 AH64A/D

54 AH6 attack helicopters

809 UHIH/V

1,395 UH60/MH60

466 CH/MH47D/E

468 OH58A/C

385 OH58D (194 are armed)

136 TH67

2 RAH66 support helicopters

66 EH60A electronic counter-measures (ECM) helicopters

47 C12C/R

88 C12D/J

3 C20

48 C23A/B

11 C26

2 C31

1 C37

2 C182

2 O2

1 PA31

45 RC12D/H/K

12 RC12P/Q

2 T34

22 UC35

4 UV18A

2 UV20A fixed-wing aircraft

7,900 M1A1/A2 Abrams main battle tanks

110 TPZ-1 Fuchs armored reconnaissance

6,710 M2/3 Bradley armored infantry fighting vehicles

15,200 M113A2/A3 armored personnel carriers

345 81mm M252

896 120mm M120/121 mortars

1200+ 84mm AT4 anti-tank

458 105mm M102

418 M119

715 155mm M198 towed

2,512 155mm M109A1/2/6 self-propelled

1,075 227mm MLRS multiple rocket launchers

20,000 Dragon

332 Javelin anti-tank

1,380 TOW (on HMMWV vehicles)

523 TOW (on M901 vehicles)

6,720 TOW (on M2/3 armored vehicles)

5,000+ Stinger manportable surface-to-air

785 Avenger

99 Linebacker (Stingers mounted on vehicles)

485 Patriot towed surface-to-air

Total 5,327	Total 29,920	Total 2,441+	Total 5,178	Total 35,324+

Support	Excellent	Average	Poor		= 1,000

◭ Fighting structure

The U.S. army has altered both the size and the organization of its main fighting forces units many times since 1945. However, the downsizing and fundamental restructuring that has taken place since the end of the Cold War has created a significantly different army. The cumbersome armored and mechanized divisional formations of the last 40 years are being phased out. In their place the combined arms, fully integrated brigade is to be the future main combat unit within the new multi-capable Heavy Division, the first of which will be fully operational by 2001.

The U.S. army intends to develop a force that is deployable, agile, and versatile; one that is lethal and capable of dominating every crucial point within its operational task as well as being serviceable and logistically sustainable at all times. It will be equipped with digital communications, enhanced command and control and intelligence, upgraded Abrams and Bradley fighting vehicles, and Apache Longbow and Comanche combat helicopters. It is intended that the new formations will remain the standard structure until at least 2010.

The U.S. army, long in the forefront of military technology and strategy, has accepted the immense challenge of preparing for the future wars of the twenty-first century. With this restructuring it has established a true war–fighting capability.

M1M-104 Patriot, an advanced airmobile surface-to-air and anti-missile system that proved effective against Iraqi SCUDs during the Gulf War, seen here in desert conditions.

The mainstay of the U.S. field artillery battalions, the 155mm M109A6 self-propelled gun. A highly effective weapon, it has replaced all other self-propelled artillery.

The humble battalion

While attention is rightly paid to the mighty division or brigade, the ordinary battalion is at the cutting edge of actual combat. The U.S. Light Infantry Battalion, for example, has only three rifle companies and a headquarters company and so is an austere unit. Even so, its firepower is considerable with several hundred M16 automatic rifles, 18 M60 machine guns, 65 M203 grenade launchers, 18 Dragon and 4 TOW anti-tank missile launchers, 6 60mm and 4 81mm mortars. Twenty-seven Hummer jeeps and 15 motorcycles provide the battalions with transport.

The devastating firepower of the M270 multiple launch rocket system is clearly shown. It carries 12 rockets, with a total of 644 M77-shaped charge warheads per rocket.

Fighting Structure Overview

2 Armored divisions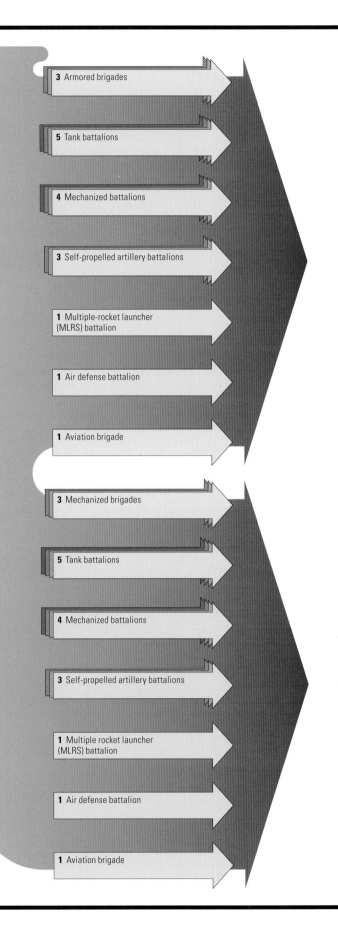
2 Mechanized divisions

The organization of these formations is very similar to the armored battalions; they have M1A1/2 Abrams main battle tanks, TPz-1 Fuchs armored reconnaissance vehicles, and both the M2/3 Bradley armored infantry fighting vehicles and the M113A2/3 (or variants) armored personnel carriers. The divisional artillery has battalions equipped with 155mm M109A2/6 self-propelled guns, a battalion of MLRS (multiple rocket launcher systems), and an air defense battalion with Avenger (vehicle mounted Stingers) surface-to-air missiles or Linebacker combined 25mm gun and four Stinger surface-to-air missiles. Both divisional structures incorporate an aviation brigade with AH-1S or AH-64 combat helicopters, units of combat engineers with bridge layers and mine clearing equipment, and a considerable signals, intelligence, electronic warfare, and NBC (nuclear, biological, and chemical) warfare capability.

The Theater High-Altitude Area Defence (THAAD) missile is the only anti-missile system expected to be capable of engaging the full spectrum of theater class ballistic missile threats by 2005.

3 Armored brigades

5 Tank battalions

4 Mechanized battalions

3 Self-propelled artillery battalions

1 Multiple-rocket launcher (MLRS) battalion

1 Air defense battalion

1 Aviation brigade

3 Mechanized brigades

5 Tank battalions

4 Mechanized battalions

3 Self-propelled artillery battalions

1 Multiple rocket launcher (MLRS) battalion

1 Air defense battalion

1 Aviation brigade

1 Air assault division

This airmobile unit is tasked to move nine air assault battalions with the three artillery battalions with 105mm M102/M119 light field guns in a very short time. The aviation lift capability provided by two assault helicopter battalions, command and transport battalions supported by three attack helicopter battalions with AH-1S and AH-64, makes this possible. The assault battalions are heavily equipped with infantry support weapons, including TOW and Dragon anti-tank guided weapons systems, Stinger manportable surface-to-air missiles, and 120mm M120/1 mortars. The operational and the strategic value of this unit are enormous.

1 Airborne division

This elite force of nine airborne battalions is the U.S. Army's "shock troops," capable of deployment in most parts of the world. Well-equipped and superbly trained, this force is often the first one in.

This division includes three artillery battalions with 105mm M102/M119 and 155mm M198 towed guns, an air defense battalion with Avenger (vehicle mounted Stingers) surface-to-air missiles or Linebacker 25mm gun, and four Stinger surface-to-air missiles. It also provides close air support from an air cavalry battalion with missile-armed combat helicopters.

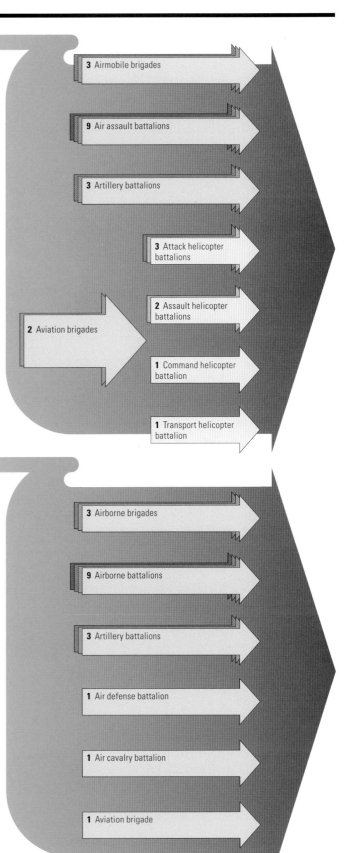

3 Airmobile brigades

9 Air assault battalions

3 Artillery battalions

3 Attack helicopter battalions

2 Assault helicopter battalions

2 Aviation brigades

1 Command helicopter battalion

1 Transport helicopter battalion

3 Airborne brigades

9 Airborne battalions

3 Artillery battalions

1 Air defense battalion

1 Air cavalry battalion

1 Aviation brigade

Special forces

For some years the U.S. army lagged behind many of the other leading armies in not having a dedicated anti-terrorist force. And although the Blue Light, a small Counter Revolutionary Warfare (CRW) unit drawn from 5th Special Forces Group (airborne) was assigned an anti-terrorist role, it was not until the formation of Delta Force that the U.S. army finally had a genuine anti-terrorist capability.

The Javelin is a manportable, fire-and-forget, anti-tank missile system, which is intended to replace the Dragon in U.S. army service. It has a range of 1½ miles, (2.4 km), twice that of the Dragon, and it will further enhance the capability of U.S. special forces.

Democracy returned

Following the breakdown in civil order on the island of Grenada in the West Indies, and the threat it posed to foreign nationals, U.S.-led forces invaded on October 25, 1983. SEAL units had previously made covert landings to collect intelligence about possible Cuban forces supporting the government, and at 05.34 the first rangers began dropping on the runway at Salines. Within hours, the airfield was secure, and elements of the 82nd Airborne Division were able to deploy. Within four days, opposition had been suppressed, hostages released, and Grenada was on the way back to democracy.

A U.S. soldier on special operations wearing disruptive pattern fatigues. He has an M16 rifle and an advanced image intensifying scope.

Delta Force

The 1st Special Forces Operational Detachment, otherwise known as Delta Force, is the United States first dedicated national intervention, counter-revolutionary warfare, and aggressive special operations unit. It was activated in November 1977 and was largely the brainchild of Charles Beckwith, an experienced

Freedom for Panama

U.S. special forces, and in particular the Rangers, were involved in an unusually delicate and difficult special operation in Panama during 1989–90. Operation Just Cause had as its key objective the removal of President Manuel Noriega. A JSOTF (Joint Special Operations Task Force), which included the 75th Ranger Regiment, army special forces units, and SEALS carried out a range of covert operations that brought about Noriega's eventual downfall.

special forces officer who had served with the British 22nd Regiment Special Air Service during the 1960s.

Delta Force was originally organized and trained along SAS lines, but soon developed a very distinct ethos and character of its own, with the initial intake being from the 10th Special Forces Group (airborne) at Camp Dawson, West Virginia. To these

men, a few U.S. Army Rangers and volunteers were added from other special forces groups, and in May 1978 the first 73 trainees made it into the newly operational force.

Delta's first major operation was the attempted rescue of the hostages held by Iranian militants in the occupied U.S. embassy in Tehran on April 25, 1979. Whatever may be said

about the standard of the overall planning and execution of this operation (which has deserved severe censure), criticism cannot be similarly aimed at Delta's training and planning, which was meticulous and would have stood a good chance of success in other circumstances.

Delta Force has gone on to be used in special forces operations as part of Operation Urgent Fury,

the U.S. invasion of Grenada in 1983, and during Operation Just Cause, the U.S. invasion of Panama in December 1989. Here, it successfully carried out Operation Acid Gambit, the rescue of the U.S. citizen Kurt Muse, who was being held hostage in the Carcel Modelo Prison.

In the Gulf War of 1990–91, it was covertly deployed within

The UH60 Black Hawk helicopter replaced the ubiquitous UH-1 Huey in the 1980s. The workhorse of the U.S. army, the Black Hawk is regularly used for heliborne insertion and special operations.

Restore Hope

Operation Restore Hope saw numerous special forces units deployed in support of UN relief operations in Somalia in December 1992. Soldiers from the 2nd Battalion, 5th Special Forces Group (airborne), previously deployed in Kenya, joined up with SEALS already in Mogadishu, the capital of Somalia. The overall success of the special forces in bringing much needed aid to a stricken country has been overshadowed by the events of October 3–4, 1993, when they became involved in the fiercest urban firefight since the Vietnam War.

The U.S. army's highly secretive Intelligence Support Activity (ISA) draws some of its personnel from the U.S. Navy's famous SEAL 6 unit, seen here deploying an assault craft in heavy surf.

Iraq itself, tracing and destroying SCUD missile launchers. And as part of Task Force Ranger, the U.S. intervention in Somalia in 1992–93, Delta Force personnel were called upon to carry out difficult and dangerous clandestine operations within rebel-held areas of the capital Mogadishu. Delta Force has also seen considerable service during the recent Balkan wars of 1992–2000, in operations to track down and capture suspected war criminals in Croatia, Bosnia, and Kosovo.

The Delta Force headquarters is at Fort Bragg, North Carolina.

Its training is of the very highest standard, providing personnel with extraordinary levels of physical fitness, mental toughness, and motivation. All aspects of modern special forces techniques are practiced regularly until they become instinctive. They include combat shooting, sniping, the House of Horror, Delta's own version of the SAS Killing House, hostage rescue, anti-hijacking, VIP protection, heliborne insertion, HAHO (High Altitude High Opening) and HALO (High Altitude Low Opening) parachuting, unarmed combat, combat swimming, demolition, and sabotage. The unit is given training to survive and operate effectively in all combat environments: jungle, desert, arctic, mountain, riverine, urban, and built-up city areas. The force trains and operates regularly with other similar units from around the world, in particular the British SAS, German GSG9, French GIGN, and the Israeli *Sayeret Matkal*.

It has access to a huge range of high-technology surveillance, electronic warfare, communications, and intelligence equipment, and is also provided with the finest logistic, communications, and transport back-up possible from the U.S. Army, U.S. Air Force, U.S. Marine Corps, U.S. Navy, and other Federal agencies. It liaises closely with the Central Intelligence Agency and other organizations within the U.S. government's intelligence community.

The Delta Force has access to a complete arsenal of U.S. and foreign weapons and explosives, favored arms being the 7.65mm PPK, 9mm P7 and Browning HP automatic pistols, 9mm MP5 and 9mm Uzi sub-machine guns, 5.56mm M16A1 automatic rifles and the CAR-15 carbine version, Remington 40XB sniper rifles, .5 Barrett M82 long-range sniper rifles, H&K 21 machine guns, 7.62mm M60 machine guns, 40mm M79/M203 grenade launchers, and an eye-popping array of unusual and exotic weaponry.

The Delta Force provides the United States with a first-rate national intervention anti-terrorist force, but it is only part of a much larger special forces community.

ISA (Intelligence Support Activity)

The U.S. army has a highly covert unit, called the ISA (Intelligence Support Activity), which draws its personnel from the U.S. Navy SEALs and the army's own special forces. With some 200 personnel, it is tasked to provide clandestine intelligence for special operations, including pathfinder units, and also to provide guides armed with local knowledge. It provides intelligence, including communication specialists, for deep penetration missions of a small team of commandos.

SEAL 6

The U.S. Navy's SEAL 6 unit, established in November 1986, actually forms part of the Delta Force. Similar in operation and training to the British Royal Marine's Commachio unit, it is tasked to protect off-shore oil installations and other highly classified potential terrorist targets, and has developed a close working relationship with both the British SAS and the Royal Marines Special Boat Squadron (SBS).

The Special Operations Command

The Special Operations Command, formed in 1980, controls a range of units that includes five regular and four reserve special forces groups which are better known by their nickname, the Green Berets. These groups provide highly effective elite infantry, more in the style of the French Foreign Legion's specialist 2nd Regiment than that of the British SAS.

The Green Berets

This group was created during the Korean War (1950–53), with the 10th Group (airborne). It was the first unit to be raised by Colonel Aaron Bank at Fort Bragg, North Carolina. He adopted the Green Beret in honor of the British World War II Commandos. The Green Berets have given honorable service in many campaigns, the most famous being Vietnam, and the latest being Colombia where they are training the Colombian army to combat not only the FARC, anti-government guerrillas, but also their drug-cartel paymasters.

By 1969, seven such special forces groups had been formed, the 1st, 3rd, 5th, 6th, 7th, and 10th.

And, although there has been some downsizing, there are today four operational groups:
• 1st headquarters at Fort Lewis, Washington State (with one battalion in Okinawa, Japan)
• 5th headquarters at Fort Bragg, North Carolina
• 7th headquarters at Fort Benning, Georgia
• 10th headquarters at Fort Devens, Massachusetts (with one battalion at Bad Tolz, in Germany)

Hope lost

The disastrous events in Mogadishu, Somalia, on October 3–4, 1993 will stay with the U.S. special forces indefinitely. What had begun as a relatively straightforward military operation was to end with 99 elite U.S. special forces personnel trapped in a hostile area of Mogadishu and with a Black Hawk helicopter shot down. The U.S. troops finally shot their way out to safety, but at the expense of numerous civilian casualties. The appalling sight of dead U.S. soldiers being dragged around the dusty streets by screaming mobs traumatized the United States, and also served to highlight how vulnerable the sophisticated military machine can be to the most simple of insurgencies.

A UH-60 Black Hawk helicopter deploying airmobile forces in a quick insertion operation, typical of the Green Berets or Rangers.

Canada

The Canadian army (officially called the Canadian Land Force Command) is a well-trained, motivated, professional force, but at present it is still defining a role for itself (beyond its support of NATO and its peacekeeping role with the UN). And in order to maintain the highest standards of efficiency, the army must continue to convince Canadian government policy-makers to provide necessary budgets for new weapons and maintain the current infrastructure.

The Canadian army is a force capable of supporting the civilian community in times of emergency, such as extreme weather conditions. But in recent years, Canadian forces have also had to deal with internal threats from organizations such as the FLQ (Front de Liberation du Quebec), and growing problems of ethnicterrorism with the threat of violence from Native Canadians over unresolved historic disputes about land ownership and rights.

In addition, there is an increased threat of international terrorism, usually aimed at the United States, and the fact that many terrorist groups now look upon Canada as a safer base for their future operations. These are major reasons for the creation of enhanced Canadian Special Forces and far greater surveillance of, in particular, militant Islamic groups.

With a growing restlessness within Canada, the threat of global terrorism, and a continuing demand for high quality personnel for United Nations' peacekeeping missions, it seems likely that Canada's red maple leaf flag will continue to be conspicuous throughout the world in the new century.

Flashpoints and deployments

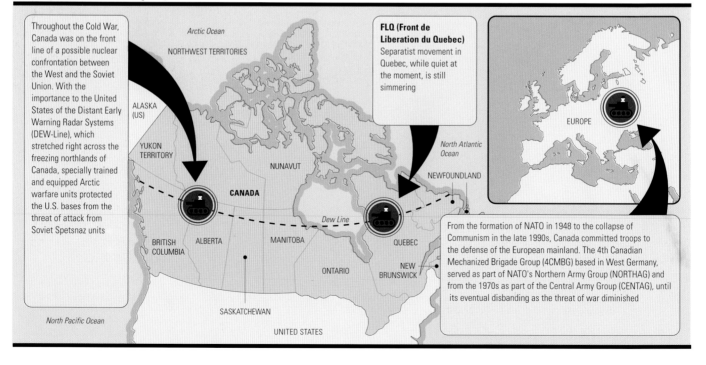

Throughout the Cold War, Canada was on the front line of a possible nuclear confrontation between the West and the Soviet Union. With the importance to the United States of the Distant Early Warning Radar Systems (DEW-Line), which stretched right across the freezing northlands of Canada, specially trained and equipped Arctic warfare units protected the U.S. bases from the threat of attack from Soviet Spetsnaz units

FLQ (Front de Liberation du Quebec)
Separatist movement in Quebec, while quiet at the moment, is still simmering

From the formation of NATO in 1948 to the collapse of Communism in the late 1990s, Canada committed troops to the defense of the European mainland. The 4th Canadian Mechanized Brigade Group (4CMBG) based in West Germany, served as part of NATO's Northern Army Group (NORTHAG) and from the 1970s as part of the Central Army Group (CENTAG), until its eventual disbanding as the threat of war diminished

Arctic Ocean
NORTHWEST TERRITORIES
ALASKA (US)
YUKON TERRITORY
NUNAVUT
CANADA
Dew Line
BRITISH COLUMBIA
ALBERTA
MANITOBA
ONTARIO
SASKATCHEWAN
QUEBEC
NEW BRUNSWICK
NEWFOUNDLAND
North Atlantic Ocean
EUROPE
North Pacific Ocean
UNITED STATES

Operations

The Canadian army has long been considered one of the most professional and well-trained land forces, and has been deployed for combat and peacekeeping missions throughout the world many times over the last 55 years. Today's army is deployed largely as a result of its commitments to NATO and the United Nations. The Canadian army has a commitment to provide a single infantry battalion group for the NATO Immediate Action Group in Europe within three weeks. It is also committed, if required, to provide a full battle group that will consist of an infantry battalion, one armored squadron, a mechanized infantry company, and an artillery battery, to the United Nations within 90 days.

1st Canadian Division

The 1st Canadian Division based in Kingston, Ontario, while committed to NATO, is a "skeleton" formation retaining only a small headquarters staff. The Canadian forces have a commitment to NATO to provide ten more active infantry battalions in an emergency, and these would become the combat element of the 1st Division in wartime.

Canada's overseas commitments include Kosovo and Bosnia in the former Yugoslavia.

Regular combat formations

The army deploys its regular combat formations in four regions:

Land Force Western Area based in Edmonton, Alberta with
• 1st Canadian Mechanized Brigade Group
Land Force Central Area based in Toronto, Ontario with
• 2nd Canadian Mechanized Brigade Group
Land Force Quebec Area based in Montreal, Quebec with
• 5th Group-Brigade Mecanise du Canada
Land Force Atlantic Area based in Halifax, Nova Scotia with
• one armored squadron and one infantry battalion

Other deployments abroad

Canadian forces continue to meet their long-standing commitments to the United Nations and NATO. Its forces are presently serving with:
• Operation KINETIC FYR in Macedonia KFOR (NATO Kosovo Force), since 1994
• Operation TOUCAN in East Timor (UNTAET), since 1999
• UNDOF (United Nations Disengagement Observation Force), Golan Heights Operation
• DANACA Israel-Syria, since 1974
• UNDP-CMCC (United Nations Development Program-Cambodian Mine Clearing Center), helping to clear over 6,000,000 mines since 1991
• Operation PALLADIUM, this is presently Canada's largest overseas operation with over 1,200 personnel in Bosnia as part of NATO's SFOR (Standing Force) peacekeeping mission, since 1997
• UNFICYP (United Nations Peacekeeping Force-Cyprus) named Operation SNOWGOOSE. Canada provided one infantry battalion between 1964–1993, but at present they are acting only as observers

Weapons and units / overview of an army

The Canadian army has a strength of 20,900, including 1,600 women, with about 9,000 personnel in combat formations. The army is compact and well-equipped with a good variety of modern weapons. The armored units will be improved when all the 114 Leopard C1/2 are upgraded to C1A5 standard, and about 400 M113 armored personnel carriers are similarly upgraded. Many of the armored vehicles listed are in fact either in operational reserve or in store. The combat units are supported by a substantial engineering, medical, and logistics capability. However, the army lacks a dedicated airborne force and all aviation support is controlled by the Air Force (Air Command).

Army units

The present organization has

1 divisional headquarters (cadre only)
1 operational task force headquarters
3 mechanized infantry brigade groups
1 independent air defense regiment
1 independent engineer support regiment

A Canadian armored unit equipped with the German built Leopard C1 main battle tank armed with a British 105mm gun.

Average allocation Armor, artillery, and helicopters within each brigade

Mechanized Infantry Brigade Groups

Armored regiment

- **38** Leopard C1/2 medium battle tanks
- **26** M113 armored personnel carriers
- **26** Cougar reconnaissance
- **24** M113/TOW ATGW self-propelled

2 Infantry battalions

- **126** M113 armored personnel carriers
- **26** Cougar/Coyote reconnaissance

1 Light infantry battalion

- **126** Grizzly/Bison armored personnel carriers
- **26** Cougar/Coyote reconnaissance

1 Field artillery regiment

- **18** M109A4 155mm self-propelled guns

Air defense artillery battery

- **24** Javelin/Starburst surface-to-air missile launchers

Independent air defense artillery regiment (attached at divisional level)

- **18** ADATS surface-to-air missile launchers

Cougar Armored Reconnaissance Vehicle

Country of origin	Canada (Swiss design—Piranha)
First entered service	1983 with Canadian army
Main armament	90mm or 25mm with AT missiles
Max. road speed	60 mph (100 km/h)
Max. range	400 miles (670 km)
Crew	3 with up to 6 infantrymen
Large numbers in service with 4 countries (inc. U.S.M.C.)	

A Grizzly wheeled armored personnel carrier crossing a bridge at Camp Wainwright, Alberta. The turret armament is one 12.7mm and one 7.62mm machine gun.

KEY 🛩 Airborne   🛡 Armor   🔫 Infantry   🔧 Artillery   🚀 Missiles

Firepower The cutting edge

Airborne	**Armor**	**Infantry**	**Artillery**	**Missiles**
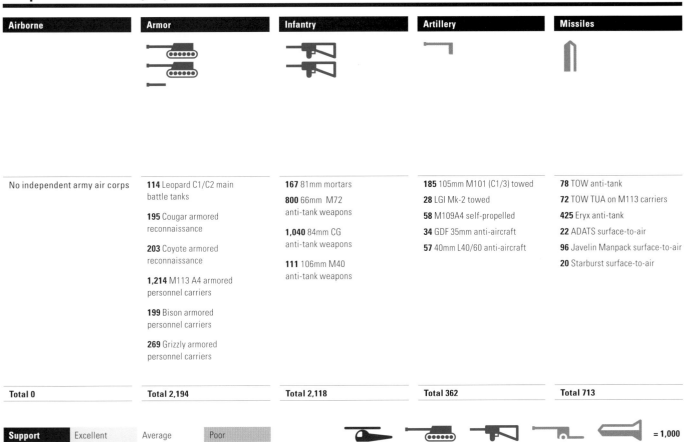				
No independent army air corps	**114** Leopard C1/C2 main battle tanks	**167** 81mm mortars	**185** 105mm M101 (C1/3) towed	**78** TOW anti-tank
	195 Cougar armored reconnaissance	**800** 66mm M72 anti-tank weapons	**28** LGI Mk-2 towed	**72** TOW TUA on M113 carriers
	203 Coyote armored reconnaissance	**1,040** 84mm CG anti-tank weapons	**58** M109A4 self-propelled	**425** Eryx anti-tank
	1,214 M113 A4 armored personnel carriers	**111** 106mm M40 anti-tank weapons	**34** GDF 35mm anti-aircraft	**22** ADATS surface-to-air
	199 Bison armored personnel carriers		**57** 40mm L40/60 anti-aircraft	**96** Javelin Manpack surface-to-air
	269 Grizzly armored personnel carriers			**20** Starburst surface-to-air
Total 0	**Total 2,194**	**Total 2,118**	**Total 362**	**Total 713**

Support	Excellent	Average	Poor		= 1,000

Infantry small arms

9mm FN Browning automatic pistols
9mm P14 automatic pistols
7.62mm C1A1 automatic rifles
7.62mm C3 sniper rifles
7.62mm C2A1 light machine guns
7.62mm C6/MAG GP machine guns

The Cougar is the wheeled fire support vehicle variant of the Grizzly. It is equipped with the complete Alvis Scorpion turret mounting, a 76mm gun and a 7.62 co-axial machine gun.

⟁ Fighting structure

For the last 50 years, the Canadian army has maintained mechanized units that are only to reinforce NATO's presence in Europe, and arctic-warfare trained infantry units that simply provide an effective early warning system for their U.S. partners. Canada's dealings with the U.S. have always been considered its most vital military relationship.

Some considerable restructuring and downsizing has recently taken place, leaving the Canadian forces with mechanized infantry brigades that are well-equipped, highly mobile, and capable of fulfilling their assigned roles. However, there is now an increasing move to provide specialist units to help maintain internal security and counter-terrorism. The concern is that this may create future manpower shortages for the mechanized brigades within what is already a relatively small fighting force.

Fighting Structure Overview

1 Task force headquarters (divisional-size force) ⟁

Each group has an armored regiment equipped with Leopard C1/2 main battle tanks and reconnaissance units with Cougar and Coyote armored vehicles.
Each infantry battalion is fully mechanized with M113 armored personnel carrier variants, including the M113 TOW/TUA anti-tank guided weapon system carrier. The light infantry has a mix of Grizzly and Coyote armored vehicles. The field artillery has U.S.155mm M109A4 self-propelled guns. The air defense battery has Javelin surface-to-air missiles. Each mechanized brigade has an engineer regiment, and attached signals and logistics companies.

3 Mechanized infantry brigade groups

- **1** Armored regiment
- **2** Infantry battalions
- **1** Light infantry battalion
- **1** Field artillery regiment
- **1** Air defense artillery battery
- **1** Engineer regiment

1 Independent air defense artillery regiment

1 Independent engineer support regiment

🎖 Special forces

Canada's previously limited anti-terrorist capability had long been the responsibility of the police. But with the spread of international terrorism, this duty has been passed to the military and is now provided by the highly effective Joint Task Force-2.

Joint Task Force-2
- Three operational squadrons
- Several specialist detachments
- One command group
- One training group

Canada's Joint Task Force-2 is the armed forces elite counter-terrorist and special operations unit based at the Dwyer Hill Training Center in Ontario. It was activated in April 1993, and

was taken over from the Royal Canadian Mounted Police (RCMP) Special Weapons Squads, who had traditionally been responsible for all anti-terrorist activities in Canada. The facilities at Dwyer Hill include a DC 10 airplane and a range of other vehicles, including a bus and a multi-story building for hostage rescue training. Other facilities include a Close Quarter Battle (CQB)

building, state-of-the-art shooting range, gymnasium, and an Olympic-sized swimming pool.

Training includes marksmanship, combat shooting, combat swimming, explosives, ordnance disposal, intelligence gathering, communications, unarmed combat, strength and stamina, heliborne insertion, mountaineering, arctic warfare, HAHO (High Altitude High Opening), and HALO (High Altitude Low Opening) parachuting.

Joint Task Force-2 use a range of weapons including SIG Sauer P226/229 and Browning HP automatic pistols, Canadian C7 assault rifles, C8 carbines,

Canadian C3A1, SIG Sauer-3000 and Heckler & Koch PSG-1 sniper rifles, with Heckler & Koch MP5 and Canadian C9A1 sub-machine guns.

The force is commanded by a lieutenant colonel with some 250 highly trained and motivated soldiers. They are organized into specialist two- or four-man teams, that come under the operational control of a 25–30-man squadron. The Joint Task Force is very secretive and keeps much information about its size, weapons, exact roles, and missions confidential. Although this unit is supposedly trained only as a counter-terrorist force, it is in fact a special operations unit tasked to perform the same range of missions as the Special Air Service, Delta Force, French GIGN, or German GSG-9. In fact, they operate closely with those units in cross-training and shared intelligence.

Although described as a domestic orientated unit, it is understood that members of the Joint Task Force-2 were deployed in Rwanda and Uganda in 1994, Bosnia in 1994, Yugoslavia in 1995, Bosnia/Haiti/Zaire in 1996, and Kosovo in 1999. In fact, the force is clandestinely deployed on each and every large-scale peacekeeping mission that the Canadian armed forces undertake.

Canada's Joint Task Force-2 have used the Swiss-designed Cougar reconnaissance vehicle to give them fast and high mobility light armored support during operations in the Balkans.

Tough training

Joint Task Force-2 has developed a fearsome reputation for its tough training and equally difficult entry qualifications. Applicants are thoroughly vetted and initial selection is based on "Cooper's Test," which is used primarily by both the British SAS and U.S. Delta Force. This is followed by about five weeks of intensive training. It has been reported that fully qualified personnel from the U.S. Rangers and French Foreign Legion have failed this selection course.

Brazil

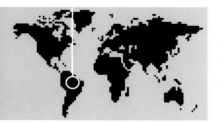

Although Brazil has not fought a war in South America for over a century, the Brazilian army still faces major problems and the desperate need to remodel and re-equip its forces to face an uncertain future.

The Brazilian army has always played a leading role in the nation's affairs, both at home and abroad. Its influence is projected overseas through United Nations' peacekeeping missions and the Brazilian Expeditionary Corps that fought with the Allies in Italy during the latter stages of World War II. But the army also maintains a strong political influence on domestic affairs. Having seen the army seize power from civilian governments on numerous occasions, no sensible Brazilian politician would take for granted the army's expectations, nor seriously ignore its wishes.

To many Brazilians, the "new territories" to the north and west—a vast, undeveloped hinterland of great mineral and agricultural wealth—hold the future of the entire nation. The Brazilian army is playing an extremely valuable role in the development and security of these areas, and its engineers are building roads, bridges, and airfields to allow greater access. Along with this, however, comes the constant and growing problem of narco-terrorism; criminal, but very well-armed drug cartels that run their own areas like military dictators. The army again plays a leading role in finding, tracking, and arresting these gangs, often working in conjunction with foreign agencies such as the U.S. Drug Enforcement Agency (DEA).

The great and densely populated cities of Rio de Janeiro and São Paulo, with their seething mass of "have-nots" surrounding areas of great wealth, are the very seed-beds of civil unrest. This is a danger that threatens Brazil's stability, and the army provides vital riot control and counter-insurgency muscle to support the police. Brazil's long borders and neighboring states are also beset with insurgency problems that are always threatening to spill across national frontiers. Here, the provision of special forces and frontier battalions have greatly improved local security.

Flashpoints and deployments

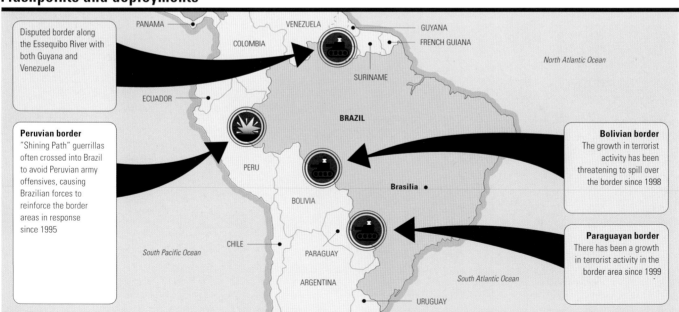

Disputed border along the Essequibo River with both Guyana and Venezuela

Peruvian border
"Shining Path" guerrillas often crossed into Brazil to avoid Peruvian army offensives, causing Brazilian forces to reinforce the border areas in response since 1995

Bolivian border
The growth in terrorist activity has been threatening to spill over the border since 1998

Paraguayan border
There has been a growth in terrorist activity in the border area since 1999

⚑ Operations

The Brazilian army's deployment is greatly influenced by the country's topography. The most important region is covered by the Amazon Military Command with its headquarters in Manaus, a major river city deep within the jungle, 750 miles from the Atlantic Ocean.

The elite Brazilian Jungle Brigades are equipped with the Italian airportable M56 105mm pack howitzer which has proved invaluable in the densely forested Amazon delta. Easily broken down into loads, it can even be carried by mules.

Jungle Warfare Training Center

The army has had to assume the considerable responsibilities of training and equipping forces in jungle warfare skills to control this vastly important area. The terrain and conditions make operations difficult and, in the worst of the wet season, virtually impossible. The Brazilian army established the Jungle Warfare Training Center in Manaus in March 1964 to deal specifically with the problems of jungle and riverine operations within the Amazon Military Command. It is still based in Manaus and has, over the years, attained a well-deserved international reputation for its training standards and the advances made in jungle warfare research and doctrine, survival, and medical skills.

Protecting new territories

Brazil is currently facing new military threats for the first time in a hundred years. The government is concerned that the growth of narco-terrorism and the civil war in Colombia will endanger the economic viability and security of Brazil's vital "new territories" in the north. As a result, new airborne, light cavalry, and special forces units are scheduled to be stationed in the Northeast Command in Recife and in the Planalyo Command in Brasilia by 2003.

Amazon Military Command Combat Units

The personnel serving with the Amazon Military Command's main combat units, the Jungle Warfare Brigades, are 85 percent regulars and these units are considered to be the army's elite.

Deployed within this region are:
- 1st Jungle Brigade based in Boa Vista
- 16th Jungle Brigade in Tefe
- 17th Jungle Brigade in Porto Vellio
- 23rd Jungle Brigade in Maraba
- Frontier battalions made up of lightly armed, highly mobile troops serve with the Ampa, Southern, and Roraima Frontier Commands
- The 2nd Aviation Group provides limited air support to this military command and is also based in Manaus

Rapid Deployment Force

The other important operational command is the Brazilian army's own Rapid Deployment Force with an airborne infantry brigade based in Rio de Janeiro. The 12th Airmobile Light Infantry Brigade is stationed at Cacapava in São Paulo, with its main units deployed in the towns of the Paraiba Valley. This highly effective unit is supported by the Army Aviation Command's 1st, 2nd, and 3rd Helicopter Groups. Finally, the 1st Special Forces Battalion is also based in Rio de Janeiro. Mechanized support would be provided by the 9th Motorized Infantry Brigade and the 5th Armored Cavalry Brigade, both based in Rio de Janeiro.

Other deployments abroad

The Brazilian army has military personnel serving abroad with the United Nations in peacekeeping missions in Croatia (UNMOP) and East Timor (UNTAET).

The ENGESA EE-9 Caseavel armored car is used by both the armored cavalry battalions and the jungle battalions of the Brazilian armed forces.

☝ Weapons and units / overview of an army

Army units

The present organization has

7 major military commands

12 military regions

8 divisions

Combat units include

1 armored cavalry brigade

3 armored infantry brigades

4 mechanized infantry brigades

10 motorized infantry brigades

1 light infantry brigade

4 jungle brigades

1 frontier brigade

1 airborne brigade

1 coast and air defense artillery brigade

3 cavalry guard regiments

10 artillery groups

2 engineer groups

8 engineer and **2** railway construction battalions
(an additional **24** engineer and construction
battalions are to be raised)

1 helicopter brigade

The Brazilian army is about 189,000 strong, with some 110,000 personnel available to the combat units. Because of Brazil's huge size and the high percentage of land that is unsuitable for normal military equipment, a large proportion of the armored forces is made up of wheeled, thin-skinned vehicles, with a sizable and growing fleet of helicopters. Twenty more SA350 armed helicopters are scheduled to enter service over the next two years.

The ENGESA EE-11 armored personnel carrier operates alongside the M113 armored personnel carrier in both the armored infantry and mechanized cavalry brigades.

GDF-001 Towed Anti-Aircraft Gun

Country of origin Switzerland

First entered service 1961 with Swiss army

Main armament Twin 35mm guns

Max. height of fire 3 miles (6 km)

Max. range 5 miles (9.5 km)

Crew 3 on gun mount

Some 1,700 built, in service with at least 20 armies

Average allocation Armor, artillery, and helicopters within each brigade

Armored Cavalry Brigade

2 Armored cavalry battalions

- **48** M41B/C light tanks
- **24** EE9 reconnaissance

Armored battalion

- **58** Leopard main battle tanks
- **52** M113 armored personnel carriers

Field artillery battalion

- **18** M7/M108 self-propelled guns

Armored Infantry Brigade

2 Armored infantry battalions

- **20** M113 armored personnel carriers
- **15** EE11 armored personnel carriers

Armored cavalry battalion

- **30** M60A3 main battle tanks
- **26** M113 armored personnel carriers

Field artillery battalion

- **18** M7/M108 self-propelled guns

Mechanized Cavalry Brigade

2 Mechanized cavalry battalions

- **40** M113 armored personnel carriers
- **15** EE11 armored personnel carriers

Armored cavalry battalion

- **48** M41 light tanks
- **24** EE9 reconnaissance

Field artillery battalion

- **4** 105mm M101 towed

Jungle Warfare Center

4 Jungle brigades

- **16** EE9 reconnaissance

Light artillery battalion

- **12** 105mm M56 pack howitzers

KEY ⬛ Airborne   ⬛ Armor   ⬛ Infantry   ⬛ Artillery   ⬛ Missiles

Firepower   The cutting edge

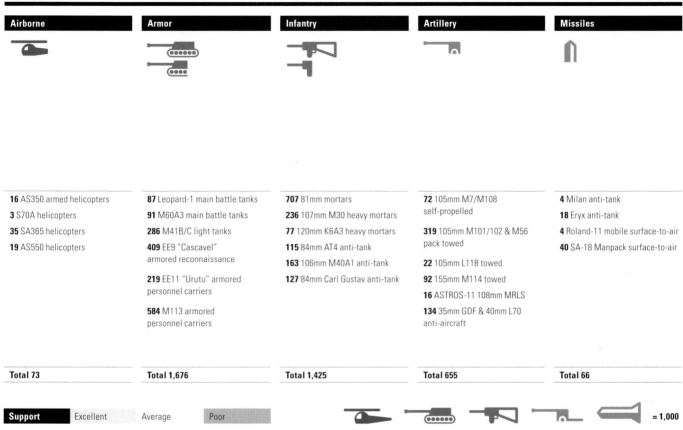

Airborne	Armor	Infantry	Artillery	Missiles
16 AS350 armed helicopters	**87** Leopard-1 main battle tanks	**707** 81mm mortars	**72** 105mm M7/M108 self-propelled	**4** Milan anti-tank
3 S70A helicopters	**91** M60A3 main battle tanks	**236** 107mm M30 heavy mortars	**319** 105mm M101/102 & M56 pack towed	**18** Eryx anti-tank
35 SA365 helicopters	**286** M41B/C light tanks	**77** 120mm K6A3 heavy mortars	**22** 105mm L118 towed	**4** Roland-11 mobile surface-to-air
19 AS550 helicopters	**409** EE9 "Cascavel" armored reconnaissance	**115** 84mm AT4 anti-tank	**92** 155mm M114 towed	**40** SA-18 Manpack surface-to-air
	219 EE11 "Urutu" armored personnel carriers	**163** 106mm M40A1 anti-tank	**16** ASTROS-11 108mm MRLS	
	584 M113 armored personnel carriers	**127** 84mm Carl Gustav anti-tank	**134** 35mm GDF & 40mm L70 anti-aircraft	
Total 73	**Total 1,676**	**Total 1,425**	**Total 655**	**Total 66**

Support   Excellent   Average   Poor   = **1,000**

The Astros (Artillery Saturation Rocket System), first produced in 1981, has a range of up to 38 miles (60 kms); the longer range rockets are produced in Iraq as the Sajil-60.

Infantry small arms

9mm Beretta-92 automatic pistols
9mm Colt M73 automatic pistols
11mm MB50/53 sub-machine guns
11mm M3 sub-machine guns
9mm M1972 sub-machine guns
9mm MPK sub-machine guns
9mm URU sub-machine guns
7.62mm FAL/Para-FAL automatic rifles
7.62mm M1969 automatic rifles
5.56mm HK33 assault rifles
5.56mm MD2 assault rifles
7.62mm M971 machine guns
7.62mm UIRAPURU machine guns
12.7mm M2 HB heavy machine guns

◭ Fighting structure

The Brazilian army is faced with defending a huge border, approximately 10,000 miles long, with neighboring countries that have internal insurgency problems that constantly threaten to spill over into Brazil. There is also a vast array of different regions to control, from dense jungles to vast river deltas.

In 1986, a major army reorganization resulted in the creation of seven military commands and a greater emphasis being placed on jungle warfare brigades and battalions. These now form part of a determined effort by Brazil to occupy the frontiers and open up the western regions of the country. The armored cavalry units based in Rio de Janeiro are equipped with modern, main battle tanks, but the vast distances and variety of terrain demand that much of the Brazilian army is highly mobile. Thus it is made up of light tanks, wheeled armored vehicles, light infantry, special forces, and airmobile battalions. Future restructuring will concentrate on the security of national frontiers.

Fighting Structure Overview

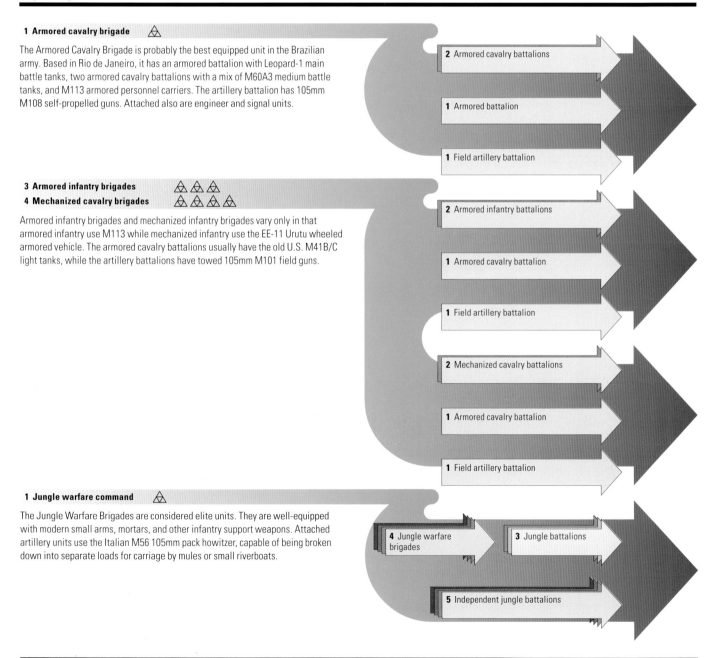

1 Armored cavalry brigade ◭

The Armored Cavalry Brigade is probably the best equipped unit in the Brazilian army. Based in Rio de Janeiro, it has an armored battalion with Leopard-1 main battle tanks, two armored cavalry battalions with a mix of M60A3 medium battle tanks, and M113 armored personnel carriers. The artillery battalion has 105mm M108 self-propelled guns. Attached also are engineer and signal units.

2 Armored cavalry battalions
1 Armored battalion
1 Field artillery battalion

3 Armored infantry brigades ◭ ◭ ◭
4 Mechanized cavalry brigades ◭ ◭ ◭ ◭

Armored infantry brigades and mechanized infantry brigades vary only in that armored infantry use M113 while mechanized infantry use the EE-11 Urutu wheeled armored vehicle. The armored cavalry battalions usually have the old U.S. M41B/C light tanks, while the artillery battalions have towed 105mm M101 field guns.

2 Armored infantry battalions
1 Armored cavalry battalion
1 Field artillery battalion
2 Mechanized cavalry battalions
1 Armored cavalry battalion
1 Field artillery battalion

1 Jungle warfare command ◭

The Jungle Warfare Brigades are considered elite units. They are well-equipped with modern small arms, mortars, and other infantry support weapons. Attached artillery units use the Italian M56 105mm pack howitzer, capable of being broken down into separate loads for carriage by mules or small riverboats.

4 Jungle warfare brigades
3 Jungle battalions
5 Independent jungle battalions

Special forces

Brazil's involvement with counter-terrorist operations dates back to 1953, when the Ministry of Aviation formed a special intervention squad. The first truly dedicated unit was established in 1983 as the Counter-Terrorist (CT) Detachment of Brazil's 1st Special Forces Battalion, which is in turn part of the army's airborne brigade based at the headquarters in Villa Mittor (Rio de Janeiro).

The Counter-Terrorist Detachment

The Counter-Terrorist Detachment is similar in organization, training, and tactics to the U.S. Delta Force. It regularly trains with similar forces abroad, and shares operational knowledge and intelligence with U.S. special forces. Only personnel with a parachute or special forces background and an exemplary record are allowed to volunteer, even then many fail to get past the initial training period. According to reports, the attrition rate during the 14-day selection phase is as high as 90 percent. Those lucky enough to survive go on to a 13-week training program at facilities near Rio de Janeiro. Skills developed include marksmanship, combat shooting, parachuting, and heliborne insertion. However, because of Brazil's varied terrain, special emphasis is placed on long-range patrol groups and intelligence gathering in the dense jungles and rivers of the Amazon.

Further emphasis is placed on surveillance of the long borders with Venezuela, Colombia, Ecuador, Peru, and Bolivia. Also very important are the ability to track the narco-gangs smuggling drugs across national borders, and the clandestine insertion of special forces into hostile areas. The detachment personnel must become proficient with a wide range of explosive demolitions, machetes, daggers, Heckler & Koch MP-5 sub-machine guns, Colt M1911 automatic pistols, M870 Remington combat shotguns, and the much favored PSG-1 sniper rifles.

1st Special Forces Battalion

1 Commando company	
2 Special forces companies	
1 Command and support company	
1 Counter-terrorist detachment	

A French-built AS-332 Super Puma assault helicopter operating with a special forces unit in the northern rain forests of the Brazil-Venezuelan border area, where the native Yanomami people have been resisting the encroachment of modern road-building.

The United Kingdom

Only 45 years ago, the British army was a largely conscript, national service force, deployed in NATO's front line throughout Germany as the British Army on the Rhine (or BAOR). In many ways it was still a post-colonial army scattered in garrisons and far-flung outposts across much of the world, with little changed since the 19th century.

The biggest and most fundamental changes began in 1964–66, following the end of conscription and the establishment of a volunteer army. The old War Office, which had been responsible for the army, was replaced by a Ministry of Defense, which was finally able to bring together the interests of all three services (the army, the navy, and the air force). This was soon followed by the withdrawal of British forces from the newly independent African colonies.

Then, there was the British retreat from east of Suez in 1967–68. With the exception of the garrison in Hong Kong (which survived until the handover of sovereignty to China in 1997), the British army left its positions in Singapore, Malaysia, and Aden. The army was now primed to become a highly professional force largely committed to its NATO role with very few deployments outside the European theater of operations—that is, until it was called upon to prove its

capabilities in the Falkland Islands in 1982. There, the British army once again managed to snatch victory from the jaws of defeat with a very close-run triumph over the Argentine forces following their invasion of the islands.

Since 1969, the British army has had to deal with a full-fledged insurgency in its own backyard—Northern Ireland. At times, there have been as many as 15 infantry battalions

British anti-tank capability will be greatly strengthened with the delivery of 67 AH-64D Apache attack helicopters over 2001 to 2003.

Challenger-1 is Britain's premier main battle tank. Armed with a rifled 120mm gun, this vehicle proved a formidable opponent for Iraq's Russian armor in the Gulf War.

Future of the armored corps

The front-line strength of the British army has been built around its armored corps since the end of World War II. And for the whole of the Cold War period, heavily armored units were deployed with the British Army on the Rhine (BAOR) in West Germany. However, the decade following the collapse of Communism has seen a considerable reduction in the number of tanks in the British army. The future is uncertain, but a mixture of fast, heavily armed, and airportable vehicles, and missile-armed attack helicopters, should allow a return to a highly mobile form of warfare.

Flashpoints and deployments

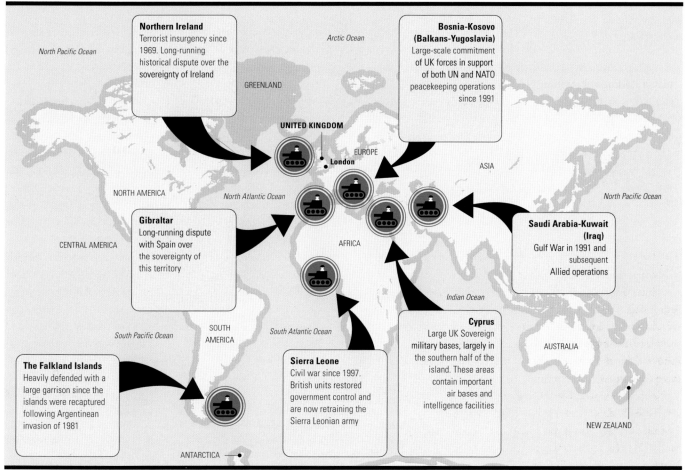

Northern Ireland
Terrorist insurgency since 1969. Long-running historical dispute over the sovereignty of Ireland

Bosnia-Kosovo (Balkans-Yugoslavia)
Large-scale commitment of UK forces in support of both UN and NATO peacekeeping operations since 1991

Gibraltar
Long-running dispute with Spain over the sovereignty of this territory

Saudi Arabia-Kuwait (Iraq)
Gulf War in 1991 and subsequent Allied operations

The Falkland Islands
Heavily defended with a large garrison since the islands were recaptured following Argentinean invasion of 1981

Sierra Leone
Civil war since 1997. British units restored government control and are now retraining the Sierra Leonian army

Cyprus
Large UK Sovereign military bases, largely in the southern half of the island. These areas contain important air bases and intelligence facilities

deployed in the province, and this drain on an already over-stretched manpower base continues today without any immediate signs of relief. Northern Ireland, or Ulster, was also the background against which the British army created the most highly developed anti-terrorist capability in the world. The army maintains computerized databases of suspects, advanced surveillance and monitoring systems, new and imaginative explosives-sniffing and bomb-disposal equipment, and many clandestine operational techniques developed by secretive units such as the 14th Intelligence Company or the Special Air Service.

The end of 1991 and the collapse of Communism in Russia saw the dismantling of the heavily mechanized British Army on the Rhine, and only a single armored division now remains in Germany. The 1990s were also a period of considerable change in the structure of the British army within the UK, with the traditional military districts being replaced by new "regenerative" divisions, which are effectively only administrative and training units. The operational capability has also been reduced to one under-strength mechanized division, an air assault brigade, and special forces command.

The British army that marches into the new millennium remains a highly professional and extremely well-trained force. However, with its many commitments to NATO, the United Nations, and its remaining overseas bases, the army finds itself short of manpower, vital equipment, and active combat units. It has sadly lacked the support and understanding of Britain's political parties and has been let down on numerous occasions in the interests of petty political expediency. The Ministry of Defense and the procurement agencies have regularly allowed many important weapons, support, and communications programs to miss delivery dates. The result is that second-rate equipment is used.

It is a testament to the professionalism and dedication of the British army that despite this background of ineptitude they prove themselves capable, time after time, of successfully carrying out the military tasks asked of them.

⊞ Operations

The British army is presently considered to be overextended, with its commitments being far too great for its current strength, particularly its infantry units. Formations are tasked to play a leading role within NATO's Rapid Reaction Corps (or ARRC), which has two main operational divisions earmarked for service. Still further strain is placed on the British army's limited resources by the Allied Command Europe (or ACE) Mobile Force, which requires the commitment of an infantry brigade group, and by its involvement with both the United Nations and NATO's many peacekeeping operations. Defense of overseas territories from the Falkland Islands to Gibraltar and support of Commonwealth defense forces also continue to reduce available manpower.

Northern Ireland

The biggest drain of all, for the last 30 years at least, has been the ongoing insurgency in Northern Ireland. This particular operation at present ties down 12 major infantry units in the form of 5 battalions as the garrison, 1 committed reserve battalion and 6 more infantry battalions that are rotated on temporary service in the province. In addition, 6 home defense battalions and an engineer regiment make up the strength of this command.

Balkan peacekeeping

UK forces were deployed in the former Yugoslavia in 1992. Initially these forces were part of the United Nations Protection Force (UNPROFOR), but from December 20, 1995 onward, command has been in the hands of the NATO Implementation Force (IFOR, later changed to SFOR in 1999). The UK committed some 5,000 troops to UNPROFOR, but over 10,000 to IFOR/SFOR, amounting to some 10 per-cent of Britain's front-line strength.

Current operational deployments

The current operational deployment of British forces keeps Headquarters for Land Command at Erskine Barracks, Wilton, near Salisbury. It replaced the previous Headquarters UK Land Forces in the restructuring that took place in April 1995. There are also two ready divisions, both of which are committed to NATO.

1st (UK) Armored Division HQ at Herford (Germany)
• 4th Armored Brigade HQ at Osnabruck
• 7th Armored Brigade HQ at Bergen
• 20th Armored Brigade HQ at Paderborn

3rd (UK) Mechanized Division HQ at Bulford, Wiltshire
• 1st Mechanized Brigade HQ at Catterick
• 12th Mechanized Brigade HQ at Aldershot
• 19th Mechanized Brigade HQ at Colchester, Essex

To be reinforced in the NATO ARRC role by the Italian army's ARIETE Armored Brigade

There are three regenerative divisions, which would form the basis of extra operational units in a major conflict.

2nd Division HQ at Edinburgh and responsible for the UK north of the Humber, and has:
• 15th Brigade HQ at York
• 51st Highland Brigade HQ at Perth
• 52nd Lowland Brigade HQ Edinburgh

Challenger-1 main battle tank with the British armored regiment serving with NATO's KFOR peacekeeping operation in the Yugoslav province of Kosovo during 1999–2000.

Committed West Africa

The bitter civil war that began in Sierra Leone in West Africa in March 1991 has destroyed much of the former British colony, and by 2000 was reported to have caused the deaths of more than 50,000 civilians. It was not until the United Nations, spearheaded by British units, entered the conflict in late 1999 that some semblance of control was reasserted. Considerable retraining of Sierra Leonian forces by British units has rebuilt a national army, and Britain is committed to maintaining forces in the country for as long as necessary.

4th Division HQ at Aldershot is responsible for central and southeast UK and has
- 2nd Brigade HQ at Shorncliffe, Kent
- 49th Brigade HQ at Chilwell, Nottingham
- 145th Brigade HQ at Aldershot

5th Division HQ at Shrewsbury is responsible for the UK in the west, midlands, northwest, and Wales, and has
- 42nd Brigade HQ at Preston
- 43rd Brigade HQ at Exeter
- 143rd Brigade HQ at Shrewsbury
- 16th Brigade HQ at Brecon

16th Air Assault Brigade HQ at Colchester has
- 1st Parachute Battalion,
- 2nd Parachute Battalion
- 3rd Parachute Battalion; with in addition the 1st Royal Irish Regiment, now trained in the airmobile role

Northern Ireland Command HQ Lisburn
- 3rd Brigade HQ at Portadown
- 8th Brigade HQ at Londonderry
- 39th Brigade HQ at Belfast with the 107th (Ulster) Brigade based in Lisburn

Other deployments abroad

British army personnel are deployed in a wide variety of operations with attachments on training or support duties in Belize (training), Canada (training), Cyprus (two infantry battalions), Falkland Islands (one infantry company), Germany (one armored division), Gibraltar (liaison), and Nepal (training). The British are with NATO in peacekeeping operations in Bosnia (SFOR-11, Standing Force) since 1994 with a brigade group, and in Yugoslavia (KFOR, Kosovo Force) since 1999 with an armored brigade. They are also involved with the UN in peacekeeping operations in Cyprus (UNFICYP) since 1974, East Timor (UNTAET) since 1999, Georgia (UNOMIG) since 1975, and Sierra Leone (UNOMSIL) since1997.

Heavily equipped British infantry serving with NATO in Kosovo. The weapon is the L85A1 5.56mm individual weapon which has replaced the 7.62mm FN L1A1 or SLR (self-loading rifle) in front-line service.

CH47 Chinook helicopters of the British Royal Air Force are used to transport airmobile battalions and their heavier equipment.

Weapons and units / overview of an army

The current strength of the British army is 113,900, including 6,380 women, with some 65,000 personnel available for front-line service.

The present structure of the British army is complicated and rather unsatisfactory. There are far too few flexible, rapid reaction combat units, but there is a large and sophisticated logistics, engineer, and support capability quite out of keeping with the army's front-line strength. Today's British army, while still one of the world's most professional and respected forces, is increasingly short of modern weapons, particularly in air defense, modern command, and control. It is also falling behind in many other important areas of the new technologies.

Army units

The present organization has

1 land command headquarters

3 divisional headquarters (replacing the old military district commands)

1 support command in Germany

Main units include

1 armored division

1 mechanized division, the ARRC corps, a joint helicopter command

1 air defense brigade

14 infantry brigade headquarters (only three are operational in Northern Ireland, the rest are training/administrative, mixed regular and territorial army)

British infantry armed with 5.56mm L86A1, the standard light support weapon that has replaced the MAG L7AI machine gun in most units.

Challenger Mk-1/2 Main Battle Tanks

Country of origin UK

First entered service 1984 with British army

Main armament 120mm rifled gun (50 rounds)

Max. road speed 34 mph (56 km/h)

Max. range 270 miles (450 km)

Crew 4

Over 800 built, in service with 2 armies

Average allocation Armor, artillery, and helicopters within each brigade

Armored Division	Mechanized Division	Northern Ireland Command	Air Assault Brigade
250 Challenger main battle tanks	**95** Challenger main battle tanks	No attached armored fighting vehicles or artillery	Armor and artillery attached as required
100 Scimitar armored reconnaissance	**200** Warrior armored infantry fighting vehicles		
350 Warrior armored infantry fighting vehicles	**450** Saxon armored personnel carriers		
300 AFV432 armored personnel carriers	**150** AFV432 armored personnel carriers		
52 155mm AS90 self-propelled artillery	**100** 155mm AS90 self-propelled artillery		
24 Lynx attack helicopters	**24** 227mm MLRS multiple rocket launchers		
10 Gazelle support helicopters	**10** Lynx attack helicopters		
	5 Gazelle support helicopters		

KEY ⬎ Airborne ⬏ Armor ⬐ Infantry ⬑ Artillery ◁ Missiles

Firepower   The cutting edge

Airborne	Armor	Infantry	Artillery	Missiles

144 SA341

110 Lynx AH1/7/9 attack helicopters

14 Chieftain

410 Challenger

192 Challenger-2 main battle tanks

11 Scorpion light tanks

332 Scimitar

138 Sabre

11 Fuchs armored reconnaissance

726 Warrior

11 AFV432 armored infantry fighting vehicles

748 AFV432

529 Spartan

609 Saxon

1,390 Saracen armored personnel carriers

2,093 51mm light mortars

543 81mm L16 mortars (including 110 on armored carriers)

600+ 94mm LAW80 anti-tank

166 105mm L118/9

3 M56 PACK

44 155mm FH70 towed

179 155mm AS90 self-propelled

63 227mm MLRS multiple rocket launchers

755 Milan TOW

60 Swingfire (on Striker armored vehicles) anti-tank

135 HVM

24 Rapier self-propelled surface-to-air

80 Rapier towed

147 Starstreak

374 Javelin manportable surface-to-air

Total 254	Total 5,121	Total 3,236+	Total 455	Total 1,575

Support	Excellent	Average	Poor						= 1,000

The British 105mm L118/119 light gun howitzer can be easily transported by helicopter, towed, or broken down in pack loads. Over 400 serve in the U.S. armed forces such as the M119AI.

Infantry small arms

9mm HP automatic pistols
9mm P226 automatic pistols
9mm MP5 sub-machine guns
5.56mm L85A1/SA80 automatic rifles
5.56mm M16A1 automatic rifles
7.62mm L96A1 sniper rifles
.50 Barrett 86A1 sniper rifles
.338 LCR sniper rifles
5.56mm L86/LSW machine guns
7.62mm L7A1/MAG/GPMG machine guns
12.7mm M2 HB heavy machine guns

THE UNITED KINGDOM

▲ Fighting structure

The British army was radically restructured following the collapse of Communism in 1991. Swept away were the traditional, heavily armored and mechanized divisions tasked with defeating an assault by massed Soviet tank forces on the plains of Western Germany. These have been replaced by two modern, slimmer ready divisions, well-equipped, more mobile, and with a high war-fighting capability. While both of these divisions are earmarked to form part of the Allied Rapid Reaction Corps (ARRC), NATO's premier Strategic Response Formation, they also retain the flexibility to be deployed on other national or international rapid response tasks.

The Air Assault Brigade (formed 1999–2000) has been structured to quickly project itself deep into hostile territory. Based on the experience gained with the now-disbanded Air Mobile and Parachute Brigades, this elite and highly maneuverable unit significantly enhances the British army's ability to react to a developing crisis with both speed and force.

Fighting Structure Overview

1 Armored division ▲

This division is based in Germany and its three armored brigades each operate Challenger-2 main battle tanks and Warrior armored infantry fighting vehicles. The brigade artillery regiment has 155mm AS-90 self-propelled guns. Divisional troops include a reconnaissance regiment with Scimitar armored reconnaissance vehicles, and three or four field artillery regiments with 105mm L118/9 guns. An air defense regiment has Javelin/Starstreak surface-to-air missiles and four engineer regiments with armored bridge-layers and mine-clearing equipment. The divisional artillery can be reinforced from the UK with Rapier surface-to-air missiles and MLRS (multiple rocket launching systems).

1 Headquarters Northern Ireland ▲

With three infantry brigades and an additional locally raised brigade, this command has in total some nine infantry battalions either permanently based in Ulster or on a tour of duty, and a further six battalions from the Royal Irish Regiment available for peacekeeping duties. This command has no armored fighting vehicles or artillery attached and uses mostly a variety of wheeled light armored vehicles, commonly known as pigs.

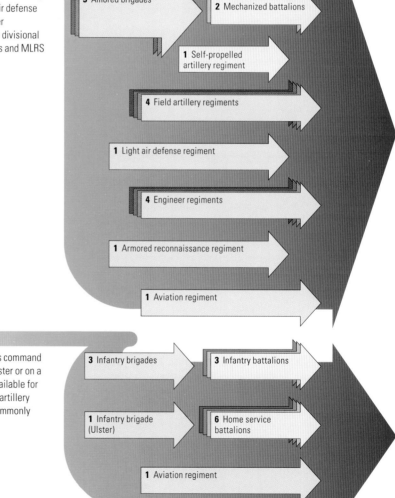

One of over 300 Scimitar, 30mm cannon armed, light combat vehicles providing the reconnaissance capability of the heavily armored units.

Air assault force

The 16th Air Assault Brigade based at Colchester in southeast Britain will provide the army with its main rapid reaction intervention force. Its complement includes three parachute battalions, the Royal Irish (Airmobile) Regiment, a Pathfinder platoon, the 7th Royal Horse Artillery, 23rd Engineer Regiment, and two attack helicopter regiments, the 3rd and 4th. Other units will include the 13th Air Assault Support Regiment, 216th Signal Squadron, and the 156th Royal Military Police Company.

1 Mechanized division (the only operational division in the UK)

Based in the UK, this division gives Britain a force available for duties beyond the NATO area. The mechanized brigades have both the Warrior armored infantry fighting vehicles and the wheeled Saxon armored personnel carriers, and a regiment of Challenger-2 main battle tanks. Divisional troops include three field artillery regiments with towed 105mm L118/9 guns; the air defense regiments which have both Rapier and Javelin/Starstreak surface-to-air missiles, and a regiment of MLRS (multiple rocket launching systems). The reconnaissance regiment has Scimitar armored reconnaissance vehicles, signals, and engineer regiments, and an aviation regiment with Lynx and Gazelle combat helicopters. This division, if deployed with NATO's Allied Rapid Reaction Corps, will be reinforced by the Italian *Ariete* armored brigade.

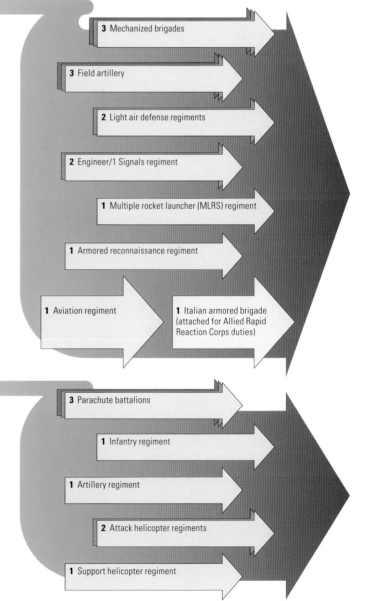

3 Mechanized brigades

3 Field artillery

2 Light air defense regiments

2 Engineer/1 Signals regiment

1 Multiple rocket launcher (MLRS) regiment

1 Armored reconnaissance regiment

1 Aviation regiment

1 Italian armored brigade (attached for Allied Rapid Reaction Corps duties)

1 Air assault brigade

This brigade comprises three battalions of the elite paras and an airmobile-trained infantry battalion supported by an artillery regiment of 105mm towed L118/9 guns. These assault units are heavily equipped with infantry support weapons, in particular the Milan anti-tank guided weapon system. Mobility is provided by two aviation regiments with Lynx and Gazelle combat helicopters, while 18 RAF Chinook and 18 Puma helicopters supply further transport support, which is sufficient to move the entire airmobile battalion in one airlift operation.

3 Parachute battalions

1 Infantry regiment

1 Artillery regiment

2 Attack helicopter regiments

1 Support helicopter regiment

Special forces

In 1942, the British army formed the first Special Air Service (SAS), which would eventually become the role model for most of the world's special forces. Although the idea was temporarily abandoned in 1946, the changing nature of conflict quickly proved the necessity of such highly specialized forces.

22nd Regiment (SAS)

In 1952, the 22nd Regiment, Special Air Service was formed as a temporary measure during the Malaysian emergency. Based on the operational skills developed by the SAS units in World War II, the 22nd quickly proved its capability in operations against the Communist terrorists and went on to become an established regular unit.

The continued need for special forces units in British territories around the world soon became apparent, and the 22nd SAS was deployed to Oman, Dhofar, Aden, Kuwait, and many other areas in Africa and Asia. High-visibility operations, such as the successful storming of the Iranian embassy in London in May 1980 to free 90 hostages held by a group of Iranians opposed to the new Islamic government in Tehran, have ensured the SAS lasting—and largely unwanted—fame.

The SAS were also involved in many other clandestine operations, often in support of foreign governments, throughout the next 10 years. However, some operations during the Gulf War of 1991 failed, mainly due to a lack of sufficient basic equipment available to the operational squadrons deployed to Saudi Arabia. Considerable efforts have been made since to ensure that the SAS is now better funded and equipped for for future large-scale operations.

The 22nd SAS has gone on to achieve honor in innumerable anti-terrorist operations and in Bosnia and Kosovo from 1994–2000. However, concern has been expressed that the effectiveness of the 22nd SAS has been reduced by the high level of public interest in this unit. The unit has also been undermined by the willingness of ex-members of the regiment to write publicly about their experiences, and by the over-recruitment of parachute regiment personnel. This has come at the expense of more traditional, technically oriented volunteers from the engineers, signals, intelligence, and elite infantry corps.

Today, the 22nd Regiment Special Air Service remains one of the prime anti-terrorist and hostage rescue units in the world. It has its headquarters at the Duke of York Barracks in West London, where its Crisis Alert Unit is based. Its main training base and depot has recently moved to new accommodations outside the city of Hereford in the western area of England.

Organization

It is presently organized into five operational units: A Squadron, B Squadron, D Squadron, G (Guards) Squadron, and R (Reserve) Squadron. The original C Squadron was made up of Rhodesian recruits and this was disbanded in the 1960s. Each squadron has four operations squads of 16 men each, which are in turn divided into four 4-man specialist units known as the Boat, Air, Mountain, and Mobility troops. Each squadron takes turns for a six-month period to act as the Crisis Alert Unit, or Counter Revolutionary Warfare (CRW) squadron, sometimes known as the

Embassy siege

One of the most publicized special forces operations in history was the assault on the Iranian Embassy in London in 1980. Twenty-six hostages had been taken by Iranians opposed to Ayatollah Khomeini's new regime. At 19.23 hours on May 5, the sixth day of the siege, the immediate reaction Pagoda troop of the 22nd SAS Regiment's Counter Revolutionary Warfare group launched Operation Nimrod. Eleven minutes later, the embassy had been cleared, 25 hostages survived, and all but one of the terrorists did not.

Heavily equipped Land Rovers based on SAS World War II experience in the western deserts of Egypt. They are armed with .5 Browning M2 heavy machine guns.

Death on the rock

In late 1987, Britain's security service, MI5, received intelligence that an IRA active service unit was planning to bomb a major target in Gibraltar. MI5 managed to identify the members of this unit, and MI5 watchers—including members of the SAS—tracked them to Spain. On March 6, 1988, the IRA team drove into Gibraltar. The MI5 watchers assumed that they were armed and carrying the bomb. Once in Gibraltar, two SAS teams moved into action and, due to a misunderstanding, opened fire, killing all three of the IRA team. None had been armed and no bomb was found.

A parachute brigade trooper armed with a 7.62mm MAG L7AI general purpose machine gun.

Special Project Team. It has its own communications support in the form of the 264th (SAS) Signals Squadron, which provides secure links for worldwide operations.

The 22nd SAS is further strengthened by the addition of two territorial units. The first is the 21st (Artists Rifles) Regiment SAS. This is the oldest SAS unit, having been established in 1946 as a reserve unit, and it currently recruits highly trained personnel in Southern England. It acts as a mirror unit for the 22nd SAS, but with an additional emphasis on intelligence gathering.

The second territorial unit is the 23rd SAS, which recruits largely in the north of England and Scotland. This unit keeps alive the skills developed by the highly secretive World War II organization, MI-9, and carries out combat rescue, escape and evasion, prisoner-of-war rescue or interrogation, and clandestine intelligence gathering.

Both the 22nd SAS and the territorial units demand an extraordinary level of physical fitness, stamina, and technical ability from their personnel. They are trained in the Killing House, close-quarter battle, combat shooting and combat swimming, explosives, sabotage, sniping, heliborne-insertion, desert, mountain, arctic and jungle warfare and survival, languages, camouflage, parachuting using paravanes, HALO (High Altitude Low Opening) and HAHO (High Altitude High Opening), hostage rescue, defensive driving, as VIP bodyguards, and much more. They have at their disposal a huge range of British and foreign weapons and explosives, including many used by the world's terrorists. These include 5.56mm M16AI automatic rifles, 5.56mm L85AI (SA80) automatic rifles, 5.56mm G41 sniper rifles, 7.62mm L99A1 sniper rifles, 12.7mm Barrett M82A2, 5.56mm FN Minimi machine guns, Remington 870 combat shotguns, 7.62mm L7A1 machine guns and 94mm LAW anti-tank rocket launchers, Milan anti-tank missiles, M203 40mm grenade launchers, and Stinger manportable surface-to-air missiles.

The 22nd Regiment SAS will, if it is properly supported and equipped, remain at the pinnacle of the world's special forces units.

France

F rance has had a long-term, somewhat schizophrenic relationship with NATO, which continues to play a major role in the country's defense thinking. While playing a leading role in the NATO alliance's recent peacekeeping missions in Bosnia and Kosovo, France is also currently pursuing a pivotal position within the new European Rapid Reaction Force. In addition, the French army provides substantial forces that are always ready to respond to purely national interests.

Along with most of NATO's forces, France restructured its large, heavily armored, and largely conscript standing army following the collapse of Communism in 1990–91. This has resulted in a reduction of manpower and a determined and long-overdue move away from universal conscription toward a smaller, largely professional army. No longer tasked to fight huge tank battles in defense of West Germany, the new French army is a flexible, all-arms, integrated, rapid reaction combat force, capable of fulfilling a multitude of roles.

Again, like much of Western Europe, France has a growing internal security problem, particularly with Islamic groups, in southern France and in many large cities. There is also the continuing risk of conflict in the Basque region, where the

Basque terrorist group ETA still maintains arms supply and support networks. In addition, the French army is regularly called upon to supply forces to many of its former colonies in response to military coups, rebellions, or the simple breakdown of civilian control. To help deal with these responsibilities, France maintains Europe's largest and best-equipped national

Ending the draft

In 1996, the French government finally made the decision to end conscription, having accepted that France was no longer in danger of being invaded. Some generals were unhappy at losing a system that had been in existence since 1789. Those in favor, however, argued that the French army's mission was to protect national interests abroad, and that this would be best done by a smaller force of professional soldiers.

An impressive display of 54-ton Leclerc main battle tanks. This vehicle has unequalled mobility and a highly effective 120mm main gun.

Flashpoints and deployments

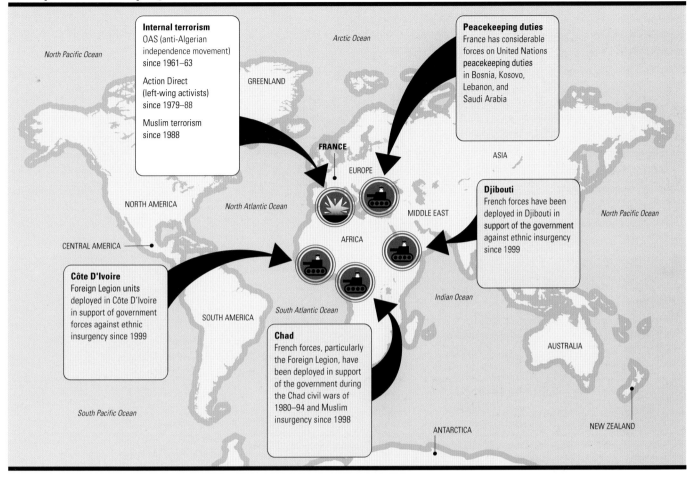

Internal terrorism
OAS (anti-Algerian independence movement) since 1961–63

Action Direct (left-wing activists) since 1979–88

Muslim terrorism since 1988

Peacekeeping duties
France has considerable forces on United Nations peacekeeping duties in Bosnia, Kosovo, Lebanon, and Saudi Arabia

Djibouti
French forces have been deployed in Djibouti in support of the government against ethnic insurgency since 1999

Côte D'Ivoire
Foreign Legion units deployed in Côte D'Ivoire in support of government forces against ethnic insurgency since 1999

Chad
French forces, particularly the Foreign Legion, have been deployed in support of the government during the Chad civil wars of 1980–94 and Muslim insurgency since 1998

North Pacific Ocean

Arctic Ocean

GREENLAND

FRANCE

EUROPE

ASIA

North Pacific Ocean

NORTH AMERICA

North Atlantic Ocean

MIDDLE EAST

AFRICA

CENTRAL AMERICA

SOUTH AMERICA

South Atlantic Ocean

Indian Ocean

AUSTRALIA

South Pacific Ocean

ANTARCTICA

NEW ZEALAND

Rapid Reaction Force with dedicated airborne, marine, mountain warfare, and airmobile brigades.

The famed Foreign Legion brigade, while still fulfilling its traditional colonial role, now also provides elite infantry and specialist counter-terrorist units.

More and more, the French army is viewing itself as a fire brigade that responds quickly to support the internal security forces and also deals with national and international terrorism. In addition, it provides garrisons for French territories overseas, and peacekeeping forces within its former colonial states in Africa, South America, and the South Pacific. It also supports United Nations missions and NATO, and fulfills an important role in the new European Rapid Reaction Force.

The futuristic uniform and equipment of a French special forces trooper. He is wearing vision-enhancing goggles and carrying a FAMAS automatic rifle.

Operations

The French army's recent operational deployments have been dominated by a combination of NATO peacekeeping missions, commitments to the United Nations, and a large number of low-intensity operations in French-speaking ex-colonial states in Africa and the South Pacific. The demands placed upon the army by each of these very different conditions have created a highly flexible operational structure with an emphasis on multiple-role rapid reaction forces.

Reliance upon the traditional divisional formation as the main operational combat unit is no longer viable to meet the challenges of the twenty-first century. As a result, a decision was made in the mid-1990s to restructure the French army's operational capability. Starting in 2002, the division will be replaced by four Forces General Staff (EMF) with headquarters in Nantes, Besançon, Limoges, and Marseilles. These active operational headquarters will provide a responsive and flexible command capability to allow for the most effective use of rapid reaction forces and the new multiple-role integrated combat brigades.

The French army has a four-fold commitment to the new European Rapid Reaction Force, to the Franco-German Combat Brigade, to providing a full-sized mechanized division made up of brigades that are independent of NATO (unless there is a crisis), and to providing a flexible and rapid response to national operational missions.

French forces deployed in Kosovo with a Panhard VBL lightweight reconnaissance vehicle.

The end of an empire

Soon after the French army's humiliating withdrawal from Indochina in 1954, it found itself involved in the Algerian War of Independence. This war lasted until 1962, when France finally admitted defeat, but not before its soldiers became so estranged from their own government that they rose in revolt led by senior officers in the Algerian garrison. Algeria gained independence in 1962, and France finally lost the remnants of its empire.

The VAB is the standard French armored personnel carrier and is noted for its simplicity, mobility, and high degree of operational habitability.

Rapid reaction forces

The primary combat unit in the future will be the brigade, and currently operational are

- 11th Parachute Brigade based in Toulouse
- 4th Airmobile Brigade based in Essey les Nancy
- 6th Light Armored Brigade based in Nimes
- 9th Light Marine Brigade based in Nantes
- 27th Mountain Infantry Brigade based in Varces

Conventional backup

This highly capable rapid reaction force is backed up for conventional operations by units tasked to the new European force and NATO

- 2nd Armored Brigade based in Orléans
- 7th Armored Brigade based in Besançon
- 1st Mechanized Brigade based in Chalons-sur-Champagne
- 3rd Mechanized Brigade based in Limoges
- Franco-German Combat Brigade in Mullheim, Germany

Special forces

The French army's operational capabilities are further enhanced by powerful and effective special forces, including the Foreign Legion with the 2nd Regiment as part of the 6th Light Armored Brigade, and two further regiments—the 1st in Aubagne and the 4th in Castelnaudery.

Other deployments abroad

The French army's current operational deployments include forces based in the Antilles (West Indies), French Guiana (South America), Mayotte and La Réunion (Indian Ocean), New Caledonia and Polynesia (Pacific), Chad, Côte D'Ivoire, Djibouti, Gabon, and Senegal (Africa).

Units or military observers committed to the United Nations and other peacekeeping operations are serving in

- Bosnia (SFOR, NATO)
- Croatia (SFOR, NATO)
- East Timor (UNTAET)
- Egypt (UN MFO)
- Georgia (UNOMIG)
- Iraq/Kuwait (UNIKOM)
- Lebanon (UNIFIL)
- Saudi Arabia (SOUTHERN WATCH)
- Sierra Leone (UNAMSIL)
- Western Sahara (MINURSO)
- Yugoslavia (KFOR, NATO)

The Milan-2 anti-tank missile is guided throughout its 1.4-mile range by an electronic flash-lamp system. It is now in service with over 40 armies.

A colonial-style intervention

In 1978, units of the Foreign Legion were deployed to Africa to the former French colony of Chad. Initially, this was an internal security operation, but by 1980 the conflict had escalated, and it became known that Libya was supplying weapons to the northern rebels. By 1983, additional French units were needed to defeat a sizable intervention by Libyan troops. The Legion units were only withdrawn after the 1984 cease-fire had ensured that Colonel Ghadaffi could not overthrow the Chad government.

The Mistral highly portable fire and forget surface-to-air missile system has a lethal reputation. Over 600 have been fired under operational conditions, with a 92 percent kill rate.

The French army has a strength of 169,300, including 9,150 women, with some 90,000 personnel in combat formations.

The French army will continue to maintain and enhance a considerable rapid reaction capability. An effective and well-equipped armored force will be strengthened by an additional 207 Leclerc main battle tanks, as well as upgrades for some 300 AMX10 armored infantry fighting vehicles (AIFV). They will be well-supported by combat engineering, armored bridge laying, and mine-clearing units. Comprehensive medical facilities and substantial logistical support provide the French army with a real war-fighting capability.

Army units

The army is in the process of a major reorganization that will allow for deployment of

2 armored brigades

2 mechanized infantry brigades

2 light armored brigades

1 mountain infantry brigade

1 airborne brigade

1 air mobile brigade

2 artillery brigades

1 engineer brigade

1 signals brigade

1 intelligence and electronic warfare brigade

The Foreign Legion adds

1 armored regiment

1 parachute regiment

5 infantry regiments

2 engineer regiments

The marines (effectively under army control) have

24 regiments

Special operations forces provide

2 parachute regiments

2 helicopter units for special operations and electronic warfare

Average allocation Armor, artillery, and helicopters within each brigade

Armored Brigades	**Mechanized Infantry Brigades**	**Mountain Infantry Brigade***	**Airborne Brigade***	**Airmobile Brigade**
2 Armored regiments	**Armored regiments**	**Armored cavalry regiment**	**Armored cavalry regiment**	**3 combat helicopter regiments**
48 Leclerc main battle tanks	**48** AMX30B2 main battle tanks	**48** ERC90F4 reconnaissance	**48** VBL MII reconnaissance	**50** SA341/2 attack helicopters
52 AMX10PC armored infantry fighting vehicles	**52** AMX10PC armored infantry fighting vehicles	**52** AMX10PC armored infantry fighting vehicles and VBL MII reconnaissance	**52** AMX10PC armored infantry fighting vehicles	**Support helicopter regiment**
16 AMX10RC reconnaissance	**16** AMX10RC reconnaissance			**50** SA532/330 transport helicopters
2 Armored infantry regiments	**Armored infantry regiment**	**3 Infantry regiments**	**4 Parachute regiments**	
56 AMX10PC armored infantry fighting vehicles	**56** AMX10PC armored infantry fighting vehicles	**52** VAB armored personnel carriers	**52** VAB armored personnel carriers	
16 VAB/HOT anti-tank guided weapons self-propelled	**16** VAB/HOT anti-tank guided weapons self-propelled	**Artillery support regiment**	**Artillery support regiment**	
Self-propelled artillery regiment	**Amored PC infantry regiment**	**32** TR-F-1 155mm towed	**32** TR-F-1 155mm towed	
48 AU-F-I 155mm self-propelled	**60** VAB armored personnel carriers			
Air defense batteries	**16** VAB/HOT anti-tank guided weapons self-propelled			
24 Roland/Mistral self-propelled surface-to-air missiles	**Self-propelled artillery regiment**			
	48 AU-F-1 155mm self-propelled			
	Air defense batteries			
	24 Roland/Mistral self-propelled surface-to-air missiles			

Over 3,500 AMX-30 and variants have been built for the French army or for export since 1966. This highly successful tank is only 36 tons and is armed with a combination of a 105mm main gun with a co-axial 20mm cannon.

KEY ⊶ Airborne ⊶ Armor ⊷ Infantry ⊷ Artillery ⊲ Missiles

*Rapid reaction forces

Firepower   The cutting edge

Airborne	Armor	Infantry	Artillery	Missiles

154 SA341F attack helicopters

155 SA342M attack helicopters

30 SA342AATCP attack helicopters

4 AS532 reconnaissance helicopters

27 AS532 transport helicopters

128 SA330 transport helicopters

199 Leclerc main battle tanks

635 AMX30B2 main battle tanks

337 AMX10RC armored reconnaissance

192 ERC90F4 "Sagaie" armored reconnaissance

899 VBL M11 armored reconnaissance

713 AMX10P/PC AIFV

3,900 VAB armored personnel carriers

363 RT-F1 120mm mortars

9,850 89mm Manpack anti-tank

9,690 APILAS Manpack anti-tank

105 155mm TR-F-1 towed

273 155mm AU-F-1 self-propelled

774 20mm 53T2 anti-aircraft

61 227mm multiple launching rocket system (MLRS)

780 Eryx anti-tank

1,384 Milan anti-tank

135 HOT on VAB carriers anti-tank

69 Hawk surface-to-air

113 Roland-1/2 Mobile surface-to-air

30 Mistral surface-to-air

Total 498   Total 6,875   Total 19,903   Total 1,213   Total 2,511

| **Support** | Excellent | Average | Poor | | = 1,000 |

The highly mobile Roland-2 surface-to-air missile system provides effective air defense for mechanized units of the French army.

Infantry small arms

9mm MAB PA15 automatic pistols
9mm MAB PAP F1 automatic pistols
9mm MAT1949 sub-machine guns
5.56mm FA MAS automatic rifles
5.56mm FA MAS G2 automatic rifles
7.5mm FR FI/F2 sniper rifles
7.5mm AAT52 FI machine guns

◮ Fighting structure

With the downsizing of its large armored and mechanized divisions following the end of the Cold War, France is creating a professional army with smaller, highly mobile rapid reaction formations. The national mission of the army, as stated in a recent defense review, is to project French power abroad more effectively.

This has been made possible by the restructuring of the light armored, airmobile, parachute, mountain, special forces, and Foreign Legion brigades into well–equipped, self–sufficient, integrated fighting units. They have improved command and control, new armored vehicles, self-propelled artillery, missile systems, logistics, and helicopter support. These are the brigades the French army has committed to NATO, the new European Rapid Reaction Force, UN peacekeeping duties, and to the many French garrisons still stationed around the world.

Fighting Structure Overview

2 Armored brigades ◬ ◬

The armored regiments have Leclerc main battle tanks, and a mix of ERC-90F4, AMX-10RC, or VBL M11 armored reconnaissance vehicles. The armored infantry have AMX-10PC armored infantry fighting vehicles and VAB armored personnel carriers, as well as modern small arms and infantry support weapons (including Milan or Eryx), and HOT anti-tank guided weapon systems on VAB armored vehicles. The artillery regiment has 155mm AU-F-1 self-propelled guns. Air defense units have Roland-1/2 or Mistral surface-to-air missiles.

- **2** Armored regiments
- **2** Armored infantry regiments
- **1** Self-propelled artillery regiment
- **1** Engineer regiment

2 Mechanized infantry brigades ◬ ◬

Apart from the AMX-30B2 main battle tanks in the armored regiment, these brigades show a high degree of standardization of both armored vehicles and other equipment.

- **1** Armored regiment
- **1** Armored infantry regiment
- **1** Armored personnel carrier infantry regiment
- **1** Self-propelled artillery regiment
- **1** Engineer regiment

A French infantry unit wearing disruptive pattern fatigues and armed with the 5.56mm FAMAS F1 bullpup-style automatic rifle.

Unique specialization

The 11th Airborne Division, together with its two full-sized brigades, has an interesting range of specialized units that provide this formation with an outstanding ability to intervene in a wide variety of military situations quickly and effectively. These units include the 1st Regiment of Hussar Parachutists (a light armored cavalry regiment), 1st Regiment Parachute Infantry (RPI), Detachment d'Intervention Nautique (marine para-commando), the 35th Parachute Artillery Regiment, and the 17th Parachute Engineer Regiment.

RAPID REACTION FORCES

Although these are effectively specialized infantry units, both the mountain and airborne brigades have armored cavalry regiments with ERC-90F4 or AMX-10RC armored reconnaissance vehicles and an artillery support unit with towed 155mm TR-F-1 guns and 120mm RT-FI mortars. The air mobile brigade has three combat helicopter regiments flying SA341 and SA342 attack helicopters, and a support helicopter regiment of SA532 and SA330.

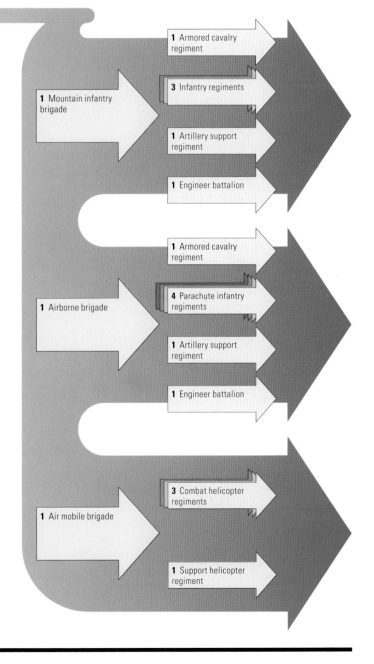

1 Mountain infantry brigade

1 Armored cavalry regiment

3 Infantry regiments

1 Artillery support regiment

1 Engineer battalion

1 Airborne brigade

1 Armored cavalry regiment

4 Parachute infantry regiments

1 Artillery support regiment

1 Engineer battalion

1 Air mobile brigade

3 Combat helicopter regiments

1 Support helicopter regiment

🎖 Special forces

The French have a long tradition of specialist elite units, such as the world-renowned Foreign Legion. Today, France can call upon a wide range of special forces units provided by both the armed forces and the national police.

African rescue (1)

The Foreign Legion's famed 2nd REP (parachute regiment) took part in one of its bloodiest and most brilliant campaigns on May 13, 1978, in Kolwezi in Zaire. Around 400 Legionnaires parachuted into the region and defeated a force of 4,000 heavily armed rebels, cleared an area within a 185 mile radius, and safely evacuated the civilians. Having killed over 250 rebels for the loss of five Legionnaires, the regiment was safely back at its home base in Corsica by June 4.

The 1st Parachute Infantry and Marine Regiment

The 1st Parachute Infantry and Marine Regiment is the French army's primary special operations unit. Known as the Black Berets, they are very similar to the Special Air Service. Indeed, they owe many of their traditions to the Free French Special Air Service units which served with such distinction during World War II.

The 1st Parachute Unit is an extremely effective and well-equipped force. Its main missions are intelligence gathering, direct action, special operations, and counter-terrorism.

Training includes marksmanship, combat shooting, unarmed combat, combat swimming, desert, mountain and amphibious warfare, heliborne-insertion, para-gliding, HAHO (High Altitude High Opening), HALO (High Altitude Low Opening), and a wide range of clandestine and intelligence-gathering techniques. Personnel are trained to use most weapons and have a stock of standard service, commercially bought, and captured terrorist weapons that includes hundreds of makes of rifles, sub-machine guns, automatic pistols, machine guns, grenades, and explosives.

The 1st Parachute Unit is supported by ALAT (Special Operations Aviation Unit) with two special operations helicopter squadrons—the first with Puma and Cougar transports and the second with Gazelle gunships. It is now part of the Special Operations Command, formed in the aftermath of the Gulf War in 1991 and designed to ensure full cooperation between the various special forces units and their parent services.

Special Scout Team of the 2nd REP

The Special Scout Team of the 2nd REP (Legion Parachute Regiment) is a particularly experienced and effective counter-terrorist unit. Its personnel are specially trained in hard skirmishes, sabotage of hard value targets, long-range reconnaissance and patrol, prisoner-of-war (POW) rescue, psychological warfare, deep clandestine penetration behind enemy lines, and the elimination of terrorist targets.

GIGN

GIGN (Intervention Group of the National Gendarmerie) was formed in 1974 and has never had more than 100 personnel. GIGN has always been inventive and effective, and has a reputation for being one of the world's busiest and finest counter-terrorist units. It has taken part in over 1,200 operations world-wide and is trained to act effectively in a myriad of situations. Training includes every technique from HALO (High Altitude Low Opening) to parachuting into the sea in full scuba gear.

Special forces firepower: a legionnaire from the famed 1st Parachute regiment holding a 12.7mm Barrett long-range sniper rifle.

African rescue (2)

France's premier HRU (hostage rescue unit) is the GIGN, and one of its best known operations was in February 1976 when it rescued 29 out of the 30 children being held by terrorists aboard a school bus in Djibouti, in northeast Africa. Thanks to the long-range shooting skills of the French marksmen, the terrorists were taken out before they killed most of the children.

A special forces soldier camouflaged and armed with a heavy Barrett 12.7mm sniper rifle.

To even be considered for GIGN, personnel must have five years of experience with an exemplary record. Training then takes 10 months, and as many as 90 percent of volunteers fail to make the grade.

A special forces combat swimmer in black wet suit armed with a MAS automatic rifle.

Germany

The German army was hugely affected by both the national reunification in 1990 and the collapse of Soviet Communism in 1991. Not the least of the army's problems was the difficult absorption of the once powerful East German army, with its different weapons, training, and traditions. That this was achieved successfully was a great credit to both the West and East German armed forces.

In search of a new role, Germany has thrown its undoubted influence into re-creating NATO as an active peacekeeping force within Europe. It was a founding partner in Europe's own Rapid Reaction Force, and has developed a new willingness to see the rehabilitated, reunited nation as a central player within the geopolitical structure of a post-Cold War Europe.

This attitude has quickly extended to the acceptance that this new role for Germany will require an army that is not only highly trained and motivated, but also well-equipped with mobile, integrated, and multiple-role combat formations. It must also have a determination and ability to project its forces beyond national boundaries and outside Europe.

As a result, the German army has been radically downsized and restructured in an attempt to create new, flexible, high mobility units required by this strategy. However, there is some doubt as to whether the surgery has in fact been too

severe, leaving the present German army's combat capability dangerously eroded.

While the German army has a reputable military tradition, it now also has a new role decreed for it by a united Germany within NATO, and by the European Rapid Reaction Force. It has established a long-lasting military link with France, and continues to be highly supportive of U.S. aspirations for NATO. However, it seems to lack the wholehearted support of the German people. Without this, the German army risks relegation to a secondary status, quite inappropriate for a country with the strongest economy in Europe and a geographical position that sits firmly across the geostrategic center of the continent.

Flashpoints and deployments

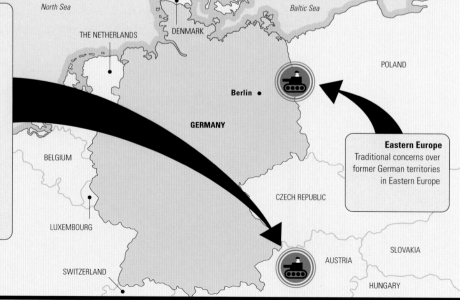

Peacekeeping duties
German forces are now playing an increasingly important role in peacekeeping operations throughout the Balkans and it is expected that a unified Germany will play a leading and influential role in the new European Rapid Reaction Force. The old West German army was on the front lines throughout the Cold War, with the Berlin airlift in 1948, the East German revolt in 1953, the Hungarian revolution in 1956, the Berlin crisis in 1962, and the invasion of Czechoslovakia in 1968 all taking place alarmingly close to Germany's eastern border. Unification with East Germany in 1989, the collapse of Communism, and the subsequent break-up of a number of Eastern European states in the 1990s have proven sufficient reminders for the new Germany to continue its support of a strong and militarily determined European Union.

Eastern Europe
Traditional concerns over former German territories in Eastern Europe

North Sea
Baltic Sea
THE NETHERLANDS
DENMARK
POLAND
Berlin
GERMANY
BELGIUM
CZECH REPUBLIC
LUXEMBOURG
SLOVAKIA
FRANCE
AUSTRIA
SWITZERLAND
HUNGARY

Operations

The deployment of the West German army from 1955 to 1990 was simple—its goal was to stop or delay the expected Warsaw Pact armored invasion of Western Europe. Beyond that, the West German army had little or no interests.

The heavily armored divisions trained and waited, but in 1991, with the sudden collapse of the Communist threat, it quickly became apparent that the whole reason for the structure of the army, its major formations, and its deployment had been terminally undermined.

The present German army has been downsized and partly reorganized, but without a genuine external threat or an

obvious role to fulfill, it has proven quite a difficult task to create a viable combat force. However, the army is currently trying to establish itself in roles that will allow it to play an influential part in the new Europe. It has begun a major restructuring of its forces, and is redeploying combat units to meet revised operational requirements.

The KRK *(Kriesen Reaktions Krafte)*

Part of the German army consists of the KRK (or Rapid Reaction Force), which receives training priority and equipment, and whose units are kept at a high state of readiness for operations outside Germany.

This force comprises:
• *1st Airborne Mechanized Brigade (KRK) based in Fritzlar.* This unit also forms the Crisis Reaction Force (CRF) and is the only KRK unit kept on immediate readiness.
• *12th Armored Brigade (KRK) based in Amberg*

• *21st Armored Brigade (KRK) based in Augustdorff*
• *31st Airborne Brigade (KRK) based in Oldenburg*
• *37th Light Infantry Brigade (KRK) based in Frakenburg*
• *Franco-German Combat Brigade (KRK) based in Mullheim*

The HVK *(Haupt Verteidigungs Krafte)*

The remaining units are under the HVK (or Main Defense Force), which are held at much lower states of readiness, and would require considerable mobilization before they gained a true war-fighting capability.

Other deployments abroad

The German army is committed to providing operational combat units to NATO's Allied Rapid Reaction Corps (ARRC), as well as the new European Rapid Reaction Force. The increasing willingness to commit forces outside its national boundaries led to the first such operational use of a modern German combat unit in June 1999, when armored troops crossed the border into

Kosovo as part of NATO's KFOR peacekeeping mission. German forces are now serving with NATO in Bosnia (SFOR), and with the United Nations in Georgia (UNOMIG), and in Iraq/Kuwait (UNIKOM).

Lightning rescue

On October 13, 1977 a Lufthansa 737 airliner with 91 passengers on board was hijacked by four terrorists. The airplane eventually landed in the Somali capital of Mogadishu. On October 17, 29 members of the GSG-9 HRU (hostage rescue unit) aided by two experienced British SAS troopers stormed the airplane, killing all four terrorists and safely rescuing the hostages. The GSG-9 team had only arrived at 17.30 hours and by 03.13 hours they were already on the long return flight back to West Germany.

The German army's powerful Leopard-2 main battle tanks are armed with a stabilized 120mm smooth bore gun.

⬣ Weapons and units / overview of an army

Army units

The present organization has

The Army Forces Command has

1 airmobile force command (divisional-sized)
2 airborne brigades
1 commando brigade
1 army aviation brigade
1 electronic warfare brigade
3 Corps Commands have between them a total of
4 armored divisions
2 armored infantry divisions
1 mountain division

The present strength of the German army is 221,000, including 3,000 women, with some 120,000 personnel available for front-line duty. Although the number of active combat units has been drastically reduced, and some of the remaining formations downsized, there has been a move to upgrade both the quality and reliability of equipment and to raise the combat readiness of the remaining front-line units.

Heliborne assault with some of the German army's fleet of 108 CH53G helicopters.

Average allocation Armor, artillery, and helicopters within each brigade

Airmobile Force Command

Airborne brigade

No vehicles

Airborne brigade (Crisis Reaction Force—CRF)

- **41** SPz-2 reconnaissance
- **180** TPz-1 armored personnel carriers

Commando special forces brigade

No vehicles

Army aviation brigade

- **200** PAH-1/HOT attack helicopters
- **50** CH53G/UHID support helicopters

Armored Division

Armored brigade

- **23** Leopard-2 main battle tanks
- **123** Marder-3 armored infantry fighting vehicles
- **41** SPz-2 reconnaissance
- **50** M113 armored personnel carriers

Armored infantry brigade

- **41** Leopard-1/2 main battle tanks
- **180** Marder-2/3 armored infantry fighting vehicles
- **41** SPz-2 reconnaissance
- **90** M113 armored personnel carriers

Armored cavalry battalion

- **41** SPZ-2 reconnaissance
- **41** Marder-2/3 armored infantry fighting vehicles
- **30** M113/TPz-1 armored personnel carriers

Artillery regiment

- **72** 155mm M109A3G self-propelled guns
- **9** multiple launching rocket systems

Leopard-2 Main Battle Tank

Country of origin Germany
First entered service 1992 with German army
Main armament 120mm smoothbore gun (42 rounds)
Max. road speed 42 mph (67 km/h)
Max. range 325 miles (523 km)
Crew 4
Several thousand built, in service with 5 armies

The next generation of German self-propelled artillery is illustrated by the 155mm PzH-2000. It has a range of up to 25 miles (40 km) with assisted ammunition.

KEY ⬥ Airborne ⬥ Armor ⬥ Infantry ⬥ Artillery ⬥ Missiles

Firepower   The cutting edge

Airborne	Armor	Infantry	Artillery	Missiles

204 PAH1 (BO-105 attack helicopters armed with HOT anti-tank missiles)

145 UH1D

108 CH53G

90 Bo-105M support helicopters

800 Leopard-1A3/4/5

1,782 Leopard-2 main battle tanks

409 Spz-2 Luchs

114 TPz-1 Fuchs armored reconnaissance

2,120 Marder-2

133 Wiesel armored infantry fighting vehicles

917 TPz-1 Fuchs

2,109 M113 armored personnel carriers

394 120mm Brandt

515 Tampella mortars

18 105mm GebH

143 M101

192 155mm FH70 towed

571 155mm M109A3

49 PzH2000 self-propelled

78 110mm LARS

154 227mm MLRS multiple rocket launchers

1,145 20mm Rh202 towed air defense

380 35mm Gepard self-propelled air defense

1,606 Milan manportable anti-tank

157 HOT (on Jaguar armored carriers)

210 TOW (on Wiesel armored carriers) self-propelled anti-tank

300 Stinger manportable surface-to-air

143 Roland self-propelled surface-to-air

Total 547	**Total 8,384**	**Total 909**	**Total 2,730**	**Total 2,416**

Support	Excellent	Average	Poor						= **1,000**

Infantry small arms

9mm P1/P7 automatic pistols
7.62mm G3 automatic rifles
4.7mm G11 assault rifles
5.56mm G50 automatic rifles
7.62mm PSG1 sniper rifles
9mm MP2 (Uzi) sub-machine guns
9mm MP5SD sub-machine guns
7.62mm MG3 machine guns

This 8 x 8 Luchs armored reconnaissance vehicle provides the German army with high mobility and is armed with a 20mm cannon.

◭ Fighting structure

The modern German army was created in 1956 to fight the expected huge armored battles following a Soviet invasion of Western Europe. After the collapse of the Communist threat, the German army faced not only the absorption of its old enemy the HVA, or East German army, but also the need to find a viable role for itself. There has been a considerable downsizing of overall strength, with a restructuring of major units to allow Germany to fulfill its new role as a major contributor to both NATO and the new European Rapid Reaction Forces.

There has also been a determined effort to create smaller, but well-armed armored infantry brigades, fully integrated with self-propelled artillery and attack helicopters. These brigades, along with the highly trained specialist airborne and mountain brigades, make up the newly restructured German army—leaner, more specialist, professional, and ultimately providing a far more effective fighting force.

Fighting Structure Overview

1 ARMY FORCES COMMAND Airmobile Force Command (divisional headquarters) ◭

This is a divisional-sized force with an airborne/airmobile brigade heavily equipped with mortars, anti-tank guided weapon systems, manportable surface-to-air missiles, and modern small arms. The second similarly equipped airborne brigade is tasked as the Crisis Reaction Force (or CRF). It also has a Commando Special Forces Brigade highly trained in both counter-terrorist and counter-insurgency operations, and an Army Aviation Brigade with five helicopter regiments equipped with PAH-I (Bo-105 with HOT anti-tank guided weapons), attack helicopters, and a mix of UH-ID, CH-53G, and Bo-105M support helicopters. A support brigade and a specialist SIGINT (Signals Intelligence) and ELINT (Electronic Intelligence) brigade complete the force.

- 1 Airborne brigade
- 1 Airborne brigade (Crisis Reaction Force—CRF)
- 1 Commando special froces brigade
- 1 Army aviation brigade → 5 Aviation regiments
- 1 Signals intelligence (SIGINT/ELINT) brigade
- 1 Support brigade

4 Armored divisions ◭ ◭ ◭ ◭

These once extremely powerful formations have been scaled down to only one armored brigade, equipped with Leopard-2 main battle tanks. The single armored infantry brigade is now equipped with Marder A2/3 armored infantry fighting vehicles and the armored cavalry battalion is equipped with SPz-2 Luchs and TPz-1 Fuchs wheeled armored vehicles. The divisional artillery regiment has both 155mm M109A3G self-propelled guns and the MLRS (Multiple Rocket Launching System), while air defense is provided with a mix of Gepard Twin 35mm guns and Roland surface-to-air missiles. There is a considerable number of divisional support units, including combat engineers and signals.

- 1 Armored brigade
- 1 Armored infantry brigade
- 1 Armored cavalry battalion
- 1 Artillery regiment
- 1 Engineer brigade

Special forces

The German army has a number of *Fernspah*, which are passive Long Range Reconnaissance and Patrol (LRRP) units. Members are selected from airborne brigades and trained at the world famous NATO LRRP school in Weingarten. Only standard service weapons are issued, and as a result of the German army's well-known disapproval of special operations, or any specialist force that hints at the elitist attitudes of the pre-1945 German army, these units keep quite a low profile. In fact, the main counter-terrorist units belong to the para-military Border Guards rather than the army.

GSG-9

The Federal Police Ministry formed GSG-9 *(Grenzschutz-gruppe-9)* as a direct result of the humiliating failure of the German anti-terrorist groups at the 1972 Munich Olympics. The inept police response to the Black September Terrorists led to the death of innocent athletes and officials. A decision was quickly made to ensure that Germany would have an effective counter-terrorist organization and, because the German army had again proved unwilling to create elite units, the para-military Border Guards were chosen in 1973 to host the new unit. However, GSG-9 has benefited from having an undefined role as a military unit under Federal Police control. Its highly skilled personnel not only have the power of arrest, but they can also conduct long-term clandestine operations, infiltrate terrorist groups, and carry out surveillance and counter-terrorist operations in any environment.

GSG-9 recruits only volunteers from the Border Guards and ex-army personnel. The training is extremely thorough and GSG-9 has a higher proportion of graduates than most similar organizations, due to the greater demands made on the personnel's intellectual abilities through the combination of special forces and detective work. But rigorous screening still ensures that there is an 80 percent drop-out rate. Cross-training is conducted with other NATO elite units and some graduates attend the international LRRP school at Weingarten. Training includes HALO (High Altitude Low Opening) and LALO (Low Altitude Low Opening), scuba diving, combat swimming, demolition and explosives disposal, mountain warfare, skiing, and heliborne insertion.

Based at a state-of-the-art center at Saint Augustin Center near Bonn, the GSG-9 operate in five-man teams and use a wide variety of weapons including Austrian Steyr AUG assault rifles, PSG-1 sniper rifles, and MP5/SD3 silenced sub-machine guns.

Diplomatic protection

Following the occupation of the U.S. Embassy in Tehran in 1979, the GSG-9 found itself deeply involved in preventative protection as members of a highly specialized unit advising on the strengthening of security at West German embassies in Tehran, Beirut, and Cairo. Later, GSG-9 personnel were regularly sent on assignments to embassies in Latin America, Africa, and Asia, and eventually GSG-9 created a large, professional VIP protection capability.

German airborne soldiers parachuting from a pair of Bell UH-1 helicopters.

Spain

Spain has long been one of Europe's major military powers, but it suffered a slow and serious decline in the twentieth century. The bitter and bloody civil war of 1936–39, followed by the isolation brought about by General Franco's dictatorship, left the Spanish army with little more than a large infantry force armed with a collection of museum pieces.

However, after the resumption of democratic government in 1977, a considerable effort was made to rebuild the army. After careful restructuring, today's Spanish forces are barely recognizable from just a few years ago. In 1982, Spain became a member of NATO, and the definition of the national defense policy became a key question. The Spanish government eventually settled on three main areas of involvement: the Atlantic Alliance (in the form of NATO), the Western European Union with its additional military capability, and the bilateral defense relationship with the United States.

This policy had a number of entirely national requirements, which demanded that the Spanish army continue to provide forces to maintain the garrisons in its North African enclaves and the need to maintain security within the Basque areas of northwest Spain. However, with limitations placed on manpower levels and a restricted defense budget, these requirements have created considerable ongoing problems for the Spanish armed forces.

While the Spanish army attempts to meet the challenges of the twenty-first century by continuing a major restructuring program, it faces a difficult balancing act. While trying to create a truly flexible, all arms, and highly mobile rapid reaction force, they are also reducing manpower levels. The army must also maintain the capability to defend Spain's national integrity, play a growing part in NATO's peacekeeping role within Europe, and continue to support Spain's newfound military commitment to an international role through UN operations.

Flashpoints and deployments

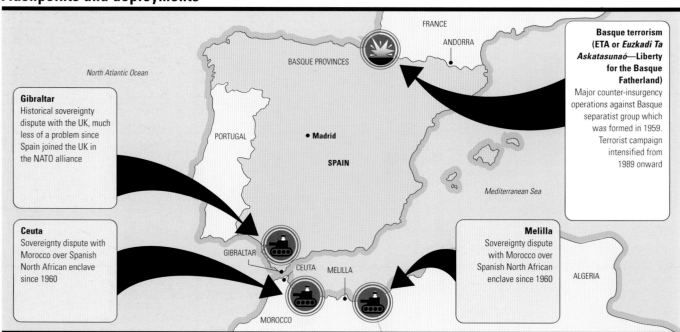

Basque terrorism (ETA or *Euzkadi Ta Askatasunaó*—Liberty for the Basque Fatherland)
Major counter-insurgency operations against Basque separatist group which was formed in 1959. Terrorist campaign intensified from 1989 onward

Gibraltar
Historical sovereignty dispute with the UK, much less of a problem since Spain joined the UK in the NATO alliance

Ceuta
Sovereignty dispute with Morocco over Spanish North African enclave since 1960

Melilla
Sovereignty dispute with Morocco over Spanish North African enclave since 1960

North Atlantic Ocean

FRANCE
ANDORRA
BASQUE PROVINCES
PORTUGAL
• Madrid
SPAIN
Mediterranean Sea
GIBRALTAR
CEUTA   MELILLA
MOROCCO
ALGERIA

Operations

The Spanish army's operational deployment is dictated by its commitments to NATO and especially to the Rapid Reaction Corps (or ARRC). In addition, it has a long-standing involvement in the enclaves of Ceuta and Melilla on the coast of North Africa, ongoing internal security problems of Basque terrorism by ETA in northwest Spain, and a need for a national crisis reaction force.

Retreat from Africa

One of Spain's longest running military operations was its involvement in North Africa. Morocco was granted its independence from France in 1956, after which Spain was forced out of its territories within that country, with the exception of the enclaves at Ceuta and Melilla. Although Spain also made attempts to hold on to the Spanish Sahara, the pro-independence Polisario Guerrillas finally forced the Spanish to consider granting independence. However, Morocco, who also laid claim to this territory, pre-empted this by threatening to "peacefully" invade with the Green March of 500,000 civilians. The Spanish army accepted the inevitable and left in October 1975, to be quickly replaced by Moroccan forces.

Th M48A5E main battle tank provided the backbone of Spain's armored units for many years. This design can be traced back through the M47 and M46 Patton tanks to the M26 Pershing introduced in 1945.

Spanish paratroopers from the rapid reaction force airborne brigade boarding a C-212 transport aircraft.

Current military deployments

FMA or *Fuerza de Maniobra* (Mobile Force) with Brunete Mechanized Infantry Division, headquarters at Madrid has
• Guadarrama Armored Infantry Brigade, headquarters at El Goloso
• Guzmán el Bueno Mechanized Infantry Brigade, headquarters at Córdoba
• Extremadura Mechanized Infantry Brigade, headquarters at Badajoz
FAR or *Fuerza de Accion Rapida* (Rapid Reaction Force) with
• Almogavares Parachute Brigade, headquarters at Alcalá de Henares
• Rey Alfonso Legion Infantry Brigade, headquarters at Almeria
• Galicia Airmobile Infantry Brigade, headquarters at Pontevedra
• Aragon Mountain Infantry Brigade, headquarters at Huesca
• Castillejos Armored Cavalry Brigade, headquarters at Zaragosa
Ceuta and Melilla garrisons
2 Armored cavalry, 2 Legions, and 2 Motorized infantry battalions
Balearic Islands garrison
1 Motorized infantry regiment and 3 Motorized infantry battalions
Canary Islands garrison
3 Motorized infantry regiments

Other deployments abroad

Spanish military personnel have been deployed abroad with NATO peacekeeping operations in Bosnia (SFOR-11, Standing Force) since 1995, and Yugoslavia (KFOR, Kosovo Force) since 1999.

🖤 **Weapons and units** / overview of an army

The present strength of the Spanish army is 100,000 including 4,000 women, with approximately 65,000 personnel available for combat duty. The army has made great strides in recent years, improving both the quality and variety of its weapons and equipment. The firepower of some Spanish units is now a match for many similar formations elsewhere in NATO. The production under license in Spain of some 220 German Leopard–2 main battle tanks will ensure that this process is further maintained.

Army units

The present organization has

1 mechanized infantry division
1 rapid reaction force
2 armored brigades
1 mountain infantry brigade
3 light infantry brigades (cadre only, therefore needing major reinforcement with reservists to become operational)
2 legion regiments
3 garrison commands
1 artillery brigade
1 air defense regiment

In addition there is

1 engineer brigade
1 army aviation brigade
1 air defense command
3 special operations battalions
1 coast artillery command
2 coast defense regiments

A Spanish mountain artillery unit equipped with Italian Oto Melara 105mm M56 pack howitzer.

MILAN Anti-Tank Missile

Country of origin	France
First entered service	1973 with French army
Wire-guided, range	440 yds–1.2 miles (400 m to 2 km)
Speed	430 mph (720 km/h)
Capable of penetrating	352mm of armor plating
Crew	2
Thousands built, in service with more than 41 armies	

Spain has some 108 Mistral manportable surface-to-air systems. These fire-and-forget missiles have high-technology infrared homing guidance, a speed of mach 2.5, and a range of 3 miles (5 km).

Average allocation Armor, artillery, and helicopters within each brigade

Mechanized Infantry Division	Rapid Action Force
🛩️ **150** M48/M60 main battle tanks	🛩️ **300** BMR-VEC armored reconnaissance
🛩️ **600** M113 and BMR600 armored personnel carriers	🛩️ **500** M113 and BMR600 armored personnel carriers
🛩️ **30** 155mm M109A1 self-propelled artillery	🛩️ **50** 105mm L118 towed artillery
🛩️ **30** TOW anti-tank missiles (on BMR armored carriers)	🛩️ **50** Milan anti-tank missiles (on BMR armored carriers)

KEY 🛩️ Airborne 🛩️ Armor 🛩️ Infantry 🛩️ Artillery 🛩️ Missiles

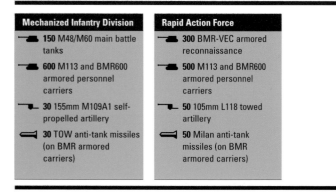

The Spanish armored corps received a huge boost in its capability with the transfer of 108 advanced German Leopard-2A4 main battle tanks.

Infantry small arms

9mm star automatic pistols

9mm Z45/62/70 sub-machine guns

9mm Z84 sub-machine guns

7.62mm CETME automatic rifles

7.62mm AMELI machine guns

7.62mm MG1A3 machine guns

12.7mm M2 HB heavy machine guns

Firepower   The cutting edge

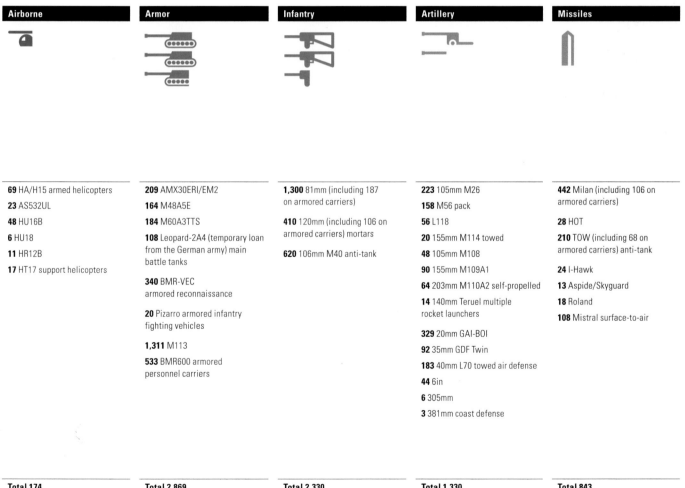

Airborne	Armor	Infantry	Artillery	Missiles
69 HA/H15 armed helicopters	**209** AMX30ERI/EM2	**1,300** 81mm (including 187 on armored carriers)	**223** 105mm M26	**442** Milan (including 106 on armored carriers)
23 AS532UL	**164** M48A5E		**158** M56 pack	
48 HU16B	**184** M60A3TTS	**410** 120mm (including 106 on armored carriers) mortars	**56** L118	**28** HOT
6 HU18	**108** Leopard-2A4 (temporary loan from the German army) main battle tanks	**620** 106mm M40 anti-tank	**20** 155mm M114 towed	**210** TOW (including 68 on armored carriers) anti-tank
11 HR12B			**48** 105mm M108	
17 HT17 support helicopters	**340** BMR-VEC armored reconnaissance		**90** 155mm M109A1	**24** I-Hawk
	20 Pizarro armored infantry fighting vehicles		**64** 203mm M110A2 self-propelled	**13** Aspide/Skyguard
	1,311 M113		**14** 140mm Teruel multiple rocket launchers	**18** Roland
	533 BMR600 armored personnel carriers		**329** 20mm GAI-BOI	**108** Mistral surface-to-air
			92 35mm GDF Twin	
			183 40mm L70 towed air defense	
			44 6in	
			6 305mm	
			3 381mm coast defense	
Total 174	**Total 2,869**	**Total 2,330**	**Total 1,330**	**Total 843**

Support Excellent Average Poor   = 1,000

◮ Fighting structure

Joining NATO in 1986 gave the Spanish army an excuse to modernize its command structure and thinking, and to re-equip and restructure its military formations, many of which had barely changed since the Civil War of 1936–39. The counter-insurgency role, particularly against the Basque terrorist group ETA, remains vitally important, and Spanish special forces are well organized and numerous. Spanish garrisons in the North African enclaves of Ceuta and Melilla provide reasons for retaining the Spanish Legion.

The commitment to NATO's Rapid Reaction Force allowed a major and long overdue restructuring of the Spanish army's main combat formations. Improving command and control, the provision of new armored vehicles, self-propelled artillery, missile systems, and the re-equipment of much of the infantry are continuing. Spain is creating a small yet very effective modern fighting force within a relatively short time.

Fighting Structure Overview

1 Mechanized infantry division ◮

The armored cavalry regiment has Leopard 2A4 and AMX30EM2 main battle tanks. The mechanized infantry brigades have BMR-VEC armored reconnaissance and M113 and BMR-600 armored personnel carriers. The artillery regiment operates 155mm M109A1 self-propelled guns and Milan, HOT, and TOW anti-tank guided weapons systems. They also have Roland and Mistral mobile surface-to-air missiles.

Air support is available from the army aviation regiment with HR15 HOT armed attack helicopters.

1 Rapid Reaction Force (FAR) ◮

This is a potent force, highly trained and well-equipped. The three Legion regiments, an effective elite infantry have BMR-600 and M113 armored personnel carriers and similar infantry support weapons to the mechanized infantry.

Airborne and airportable brigades: elite infantry units with support from the army's aviation regiment, operating large numbers of AS532UL, HU16B, and HU18 helicopters. These units have a considerable degree of mobility.

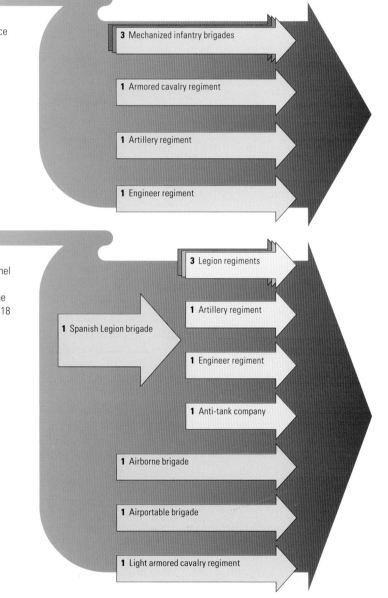

3 Mechanized infantry brigades

1 Armored cavalry regiment

1 Artillery regiment

1 Engineer regiment

3 Legion regiments

1 Artillery regiment

1 Spanish Legion brigade

1 Engineer regiment

1 Anti-tank company

1 Airborne brigade

1 Airportable brigade

1 Light armored cavalry regiment

Special forces

The Spanish army has a long tradition of special operations and elite forces. As far back as the Civil War of 1936–39, the Spanish Legion was able to provide long-range reconnaissance units for the Nationalist Army. The intervening years have seen the growth of domestic terrorism, and, as a result, the Spanish army currently has a number of special forces units, with the Spanish Legion providing the bulk of the special operations capability.

Bank siege

While not as well known as its British or U.S. counterparts, the Spanish GEO is a first-rate counter-terrorist unit. It proved its quality in May 1981, when 60 members of the GEO assaulted the Central Bank in Barcelona where 24 right-wing terrorists had taken more than 200 hostages. The operation was so skillfully handled that only one hostage was wounded. However, one terrorist was killed and ten were captured, while the others managed to escape among the large number of hostages who were involved.

BOEL (Special Operations Legion Battalion)

Based in Almeria, near Granada in southern Spain, this unit is trained and equipped to the Spanish Legion's highest standards operating in wartime in a long-range reconnaissance and patrol (LRRP) role. In addition, this unit has specialist intelligence gathering, mountain warfare, and sabotage and demolitions squads, and together with the 3rd and 4th Tercio (Legion regiment-sized units), is committed to the rapid reaction force.

The regular army provides a major counter-terrorist capability with:

Spanish special forces are prepared to use any form of weapon, from the highly advanced to the positively ancient; in fact, the traditional bow and arrow can be a highly effective silent killer.

GOE-11 (Grupo Operaciones Especiales)

Formed in 1978 and based just outside Madrid, this is an effective special forces formation, largely based on the British SAS. It is a highly trained unit that covers most of the techniques common to similar units, such as HALO (High Altitude Low Opening), airborne insertion, mountain and desert warfare, and survival techniques. In addition, combat swimming, combat shooting, marksmanship, hostage rescue, anti-hijacking, prisoner interrogation, prisoner-of-war rescue, and clandestine operations behind enemy lines play a part in their overall operational capability. The GOE has access to a wide range of domestic and foreign weapons, including Israeli 9mm miniUzi, German 9mm MP5 sub-machine guns, PSG1 sniper rifles, 5.56mm M16A1 automatic rifles, and those of standard army issue. A ready-action squad is kept on 30-minute alert at all times. This regular unit is further supported by the GOE-111 and 1V, which are both reserve units. They play a similar role to that of the British SAS 21st and 23rd Territorial Regiments to the Regular 22nd.

Special Intervention Unit

The Spanish army also has a much more secretive force, the Special Intervention Unit, which was created in February 1982. This came just two years after a Special Training Center was established in August 1980 for the selection of personnel for a then unnamed formation.

The Special Intervention Unit is company-sized, with all personnel parachute and commando trained with an emphasis on peak physical fitness. Personnel are capable of passing a series of rigorous and intensive training programs, and are proficient in all forms of special operations techniques, and armed and unarmed combat in all terrains and weather conditions. The soldiers of the Special Intervention Unit, in their black uniforms, have created an elite counter-terrorist force now known to have been responsible in 1997 for the rescue of terrorist-hostage Jose Antonio Ortega Lara, and for the destruction of ETA's Bizkaia commando unit.

Italy

Italy, like most NATO nations, has had to face a future without an obvious enemy since the end of the Cold War. But, with typical Italian pragmatism, considerable effort has been made to ensure an effective and meaningful role within an enlarged North Atlantic Treaty Organization. Initially, the Italian Defense Ministry had doubts about NATO's willingness to commit combat forces to peacekeeping operations within Europe. However, the Italians were soon to provide considerable forces for duties in Albania, Bosnia, and, later, in Kosovo.

Italy became the main front-line state in the Balkan conflicts throughout the 1990s, when Allied air strikes were largely staged out of Italian airfields. Its huge network of military bases and seaports provided the all-important logistical infrastructure for the planned land invasion, which became unnecessary, and, of course, for the eventual huge humanitarian military operation that took place after the forced Serbian withdrawal from Kosovo in 1999.

With Italy's position in the geostrategically important central Mediterranean, there grew an awareness that there was now an opportunity to re-establish its traditional influence in many of the potential areas of conflict. With the developing crisis in the Balkans, and the ever-present threat of conflict in the eastern Mediterranean, North Africa, and the Middle East, it became apparent to the Italian government and its armed forces that they could only benefit from the bolder approach that NATO was now taking.

As a result, the Italian army is now creating a force of highly mobile, quick-reaction units that are capable of deployment throughout Europe and the Mediterranean. These are the new, heavily armed and equipped brigades, which will provide Italy with a considerable military capability in the future.

Flashpoints and deployments

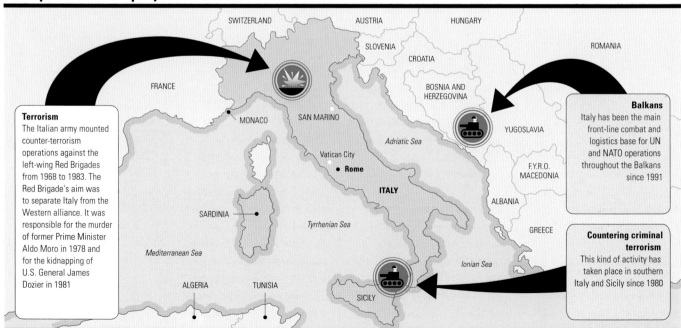

Terrorism
The Italian army mounted counter-terrorism operations against the left-wing Red Brigades from 1968 to 1983. The Red Brigade's aim was to separate Italy from the Western alliance. It was responsible for the murder of former Prime Minister Aldo Moro in 1978 and for the kidnapping of U.S. General James Dozier in 1981

Balkans
Italy has been the main front-line combat and logistics base for UN and NATO operations throughout the Balkans since 1991

Countering criminal terrorism
This kind of activity has taken place in southern Italy and Sicily since 1980

⊞ Operations

The Italian army has been restructured to take on the numerous tasks it now faces in the new post-Cold War Europe. It has commitments to maintain forces available to NATO, in particular with the ARRC (Allied Rapid Reaction Corps), to the United Nations and its peacekeeping operations, and to the new European Rapid Reaction Force. In addition, there is an on-going requirement for an anti-terrorist capability, highlighted during 1992–94, when both the Garibaldi and Friuli Brigades took part in an internal security operation named *Vespri Siciliani* against organized criminal terrorism in southern Italy.

Italian infantry with a mixture of Folgore anti-tank weapons and Beretta AR-70 automatic rifles.

Regular combat formations
The army's present operational deployment provides for a Projection Force (FOP) with a crisis reaction capability based on a headquarters in Milan in northern Italy, with
• the Garibaldi Mechanized Infantry Brigade, headquarters in Caserta
• the Folgore Parachute Infantry Brigade, headquarters in Livorno
• the Friuli Airmobile Mechanized Infantry Brigade, headquarters in Bologna
• the Serenissima Amphibious Infantry Brigade, headquarters in Venice

The Projection Force (FOP) forms the nucleus of the 3rd (It) Division, with its headquarters in Milan, which is operationally committed to NATO's own Rapid Reaction Force (ARRC). This force consists of the Garibaldi and Fruili Brigades. It also has the ability to add the Julia Mountain Brigade to give it an even greater flexibility.

Mountain brigades (*Alpini*)
Tasked for operations in the mountains of northern Italy, on the borders of Switzerland, Austria, and Croatia, and as

Peacekeeping in the Balkans

The *Incursori* (raiders) of the 9th Regiment *Col. Moschin* were the first Italian troops to serve in Bosnia. They arrived in August 1995, together with the Forward Operative Base unit and headquarters, to prepare the ground for the introduction of Italian armored and mechanized units as part of SFOR, which is NATO's peacekeeping force. Some 60 elite *Incursori,* with support from AB205 helicopters, have proven highly successful in operations to help maintain a ceasefire.

elite special infantry are the renowned *Alpini*. They are based near a headquarters in the northern city of Bolzano, and there are three main combat units
• the Taurinese Mountain Infantry Brigade, headquarters in Torino
• the Julia Mountain Infantry Brigade, headquarters in Udine
• the Tridentina Mountain Infantry Brigade, headquarters in Bressanune

Defense force commands
There are two divisional-sized defense force commands for operations within Italy and to provide reinforcement to NATO in wartime. These are
• the 1st FOD (Operational Defense Force), headquarters

in Vittorio Venetto, which covers northern Italy, with the Ariete Armored Brigade, headquarters in Pordenone, the Centaro Mechanized Infantry Brigade, headquarters in Novara, the P. del Friuli Armored Cavalry Regiment, headquarters in Gorizia
• the 2nd FOD, headquarters in San Giorgio a Cremano, in Naples, which covers southern Italy, as well as the islands of Sardinia and Sicily, has the Sassari Mechanized Infantry Brigade, headquarters in Sassari on Sardinia, the Gioia di Savoia Mechanized Infantry Brigade, headquarters in Rome, the Aosta Mechanized Infantry Brigade, headquarters in Messina on Sicily, and the Pinerolo Armored Regiment, headquarters in Bari.

Other deployments abroad
Italian forces are presently deployed around the world on peacekeeping duties. They have been with NATO in Bosnia since 1994, with a mechanized infantry brigade group (Standing Force or SFOR-11), and in Yugoslavia (Kosovo Force KFOR) since 1999, and with the United Nations in long-running commitments in Egypt (Military Observers), India/Pakistan (UNMOGIP), Iraq/Kuwait (UNIKOM), Lebanon (UNIFIL), and Western Sahara (MINURSO).

⬙ Weapons and units / overview of an army

The strength of the Italian army is 153,000, with some 80,000 personnel available to the combat units. The army is well supported by fine logistical and medical facilities and, thus, provides a well-equipped and highly potent fighting force.

Army units

The present structure has an operational command with three military regions and four divisional-sized units, with

2 armored brigades
5 mechanized infantry brigades
3 mountain infantry brigades
1 armored cavalry brigade
1 air mobile
1 airborne brigade
1 projection force
1 mountain force
2 defense forces
3 combat engineer regiments
4 aviation regiments
1 artillery brigade
1 air defense missile division

Ariete C-1 Main Battle Tank

Country of origin Italy

First entered service 1995 with Italian army

Main armament 120mm smoothbore gun (40 rounds)

Max. road speed 40 mph (67 km/h)

Max. range 325 miles (550 km)

Crew 4

Over 700 to be built

An Italian armored unit deployed in Kosovo as part of the NATO UFOR operation, equipped with wheeled Centaurs B1 tank destroyers.

U.S. Hawk surface-to-air towed missile system provides the backbone of the Italian army's air defense.

Average allocation   Armor, artillery, and helicopters within each brigade

Projection Force	Mountain Force	Defense Force
Mechanized brigade	**Amphibious brigade**	**Divisional defense force (1)**
🡒 **50** Leopard A1A5 main battle tanks	🡒 **100** VCC1/2 armored personnel carriers	🡒 **250** Leopard/Ariet/Centauro main battle tanks
🡒 **150** M113 armored personnel carriers	🡒 **15** LVTP-7 amphibious carriers	🡒 **250** M113 armored personnel carriers
🡒 **150** VCC1/2 armored personnel carriers	🡒 Airmobile and airborne brigades	🡒 **150** VCC1/2 armored personnel carriers
🡒 **24** 155mm M109 self-propelled artillery	🡒 Armored vehicles attached as required	🡒 **24** 155mm M109 self-propelled artillery

Divisional defense force (2)

🡒 **300** Leopard/Ariete/Centauro main battle tanks

🡒 **350** M113 armored personnel carriers

🡒 **200** VCC1/2 armored personnel carriers

🡒 **96** 155mm M109 self-propelled artillery

KEY 🡒 Airborne   🡒 Armor   🡒 Infantry   🡒 Artillery   🡒 Missiles

Firepower   The cutting edge

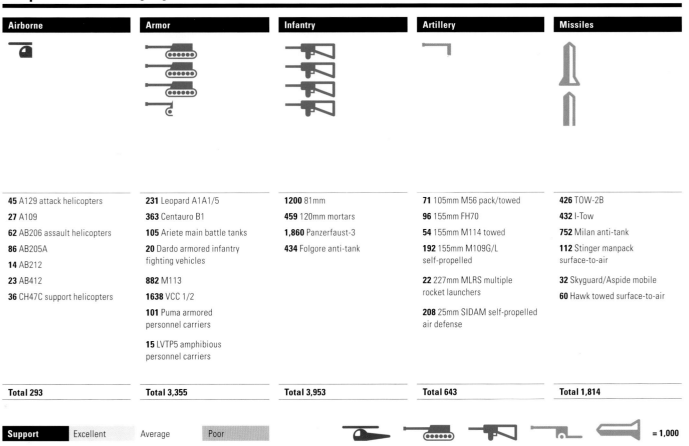

Airborne	Armor	Infantry	Artillery	Missiles
45 A129 attack helicopters	**231** Leopard A1A1/5	**1200** 81mm	**71** 105mm M56 pack/towed	**426** TOW-2B
27 A109	**363** Centauro B1	**459** 120mm mortars	**96** 155mm FH70	**432** I-Tow
62 AB206 assault helicopters	**105** Ariete main battle tanks	**1,860** Panzerfaust-3	**54** 155mm M114 towed	**752** Milan anti-tank
86 AB205A	**20** Dardo armored infantry fighting vehicles	**434** Folgore anti-tank	**192** 155mm M109G/L self-propelled	**112** Stinger manpack surface-to-air
14 AB212	**882** M113		**22** 227mm MLRS multiple rocket launchers	**32** Skyguard/Aspide mobile
23 AB412	**1638** VCC 1/2		**208** 25mm SIDAM self-propelled air defense	**60** Hawk towed surface-to-air
36 CH47C support helicopters	**101** Puma armored personnel carriers			
	15 LVTP5 amphibious personnel carriers			
Total 293	**Total 3,355**	**Total 3,953**	**Total 643**	**Total 1,814**

Support   Excellent   Average   Poor   = 1,000

Infantry small arms

9mm Beretta M92 automatic pistols

9mm M12 sub-machine guns

7.62mm BM59 automatic rifles

5.56mm AR70 assault rifles

5.56mm AR70/90 assault rifles

7.62mm MG42/59 machine guns

5.56mm M70/78 machine guns

7.62mm M73 machine guns

12.7mm M2 HB heavy machine guns

Alpine specialists

An unusual force operating within the Italian army is the Alpine Commando Unit—in particular, the *"Battaglione Alpini Sciatori Monte Cervino,"* or Monte Cervino Alpine Ski Battalion. This elite unit is made up of expert parachutists and skiers, who are specially trained to carry out high-risk special operations, such as reconnaissance, infiltration, heliborne insertion, and sabotage, often in adverse mountain conditions.

The elite Bersaglieri light infantry unit serving with NATO's IFOR operation in Bosnia, equipped with VCC-1/2 armored personnel carrier.

▲ Fighting structure

In the years since the end of the Cold War, Italy, in common with most Western European nations, has both downsized, and reorganized its traditional formations to take account of the rapidly changing demands now placed on its army. Italy has very successfully restructured its armored and mechanized units to create an effective, integrated mobile force capable of fulfilling its commitments to NATO and the new European Rapid Reaction Force. These formations are structured to have a high degree of flexibility, considerable firepower, impressive mobility, and—together with suitable logistical and air support—an ability to dominate all but the most difficult battlefield scenarios without NATO reinforcement. The Italian army also has a high percentage of elite troops in the form of light infantry, mountain (*Alpini*) troops, and special forces, all with a well-deserved reputation for being both tough and highly effective.

Fighting Structure Overview

Operational command headquarters

1 Projection force (division size) ▲

This divisional-sized formation has a mechanized brigade capable of rapid deployment, and is equipped with Leopard 1AS main battle tanks, M113 and VCC1/2 armored personnel carriers. There is also support from airmobile and airborne brigades, and an amphibious brigade with 15 US LVTP-7 assault vehicles. Artillery includes 155mm FH70 field guns, and a range of modern support weapons are in use, including 120mm mortars, TOW and Milan anti-tank guided weapons, and Stinger manportable surface-to-air missiles.

- 1 Mechanized brigade
- 1 Airmobile brigade
- 1 Airborne brigade
- 1 Amphibious brigade

1 Mountain force (division size) ▲

These units are equipped to the same standard as the rest of the Italian army, with the artillery having 105mm M56 pack howitzers capable of being broken down into more manageable loads. The aviation regiment provides close support with AB205 and CH47C helicopters.

- 3 Mountain brigades
- 1 Engineer regiment
- 1 Aviation regiment
- 1 Alpine airborne battalion

2 Divisional defense forces ▲ ▲

The armored brigades have Italian Ariete and Centauro BI main battle tanks, as well as German Leopard 1A5 main battle tanks, Dardo armored infantry fighting vehicles, and M113 and VCC1/2 armored personnel carriers. The artillery battalions within the armored and mechanized brigades have both 155mm towed FH70 artillery pieces, self-propelled M109G/L artillery pieces, TOW and Milan anti-tank guided weapons, and Skyguard and Aspide air defense systems. An aviation regiment provides further support with AB206 helicopters.

- 1 Armored brigade
- 1 Armored cavalry brigade
- 3 Mechanized brigades
- 1 Engineer regiment
- 1 Mechanized brigade
- 1 Engineer regiment
- 1 Armored brigade
- 1 Aviation regiment

Special forces

The Italian special forces form part of a tradition that stretches back to World War II, when Italian combat swimmers established a reputation for excellence. This was partly based on the daring raid made on the British Mediterranean fleet in Alexandria harbor in 1942, which resulted in the sinking of two battleships at their moorings. This reputation still survives today in the activities of the Navy's COMSUBIN (special forces).

The NOCS

The NOCS (special operations division of the anti-terrorism state police) are known as the *teste di cuoio,* or leatherheads, because of their distinctive headgear. They are a para-military force comprising only 50 men, which achieved lasting fame with the rescue of U.S. General, James Dozier from the terrorist Red Brigade in January 1982. The NOCS train at the Abbosanta special base in Sardinia, where they focus intensively on many special forces techniques, but with a considerable concentration on night operations and the use of sophisticated electronic surveillance equipment.

Folgore Parachute Brigade and the *Col. Moschin*

The main special forces unit is provided by the Folgore Parachute Brigade at Livorno, near Pisa. The Folgore forms part of the Italian army's Rapid Reaction Force, and within this it includes the 1st Carabinieri Parachute Regiment, but more importantly the 9th Para-Assault Regiment *Col. Moschin* (the name refers to a mountain peak). This unit was created for sabotage and intelligence operations during the Cold War, but proved to be so well organized and flexible that its responsibilities were extended to cover all aspects of special operations and counter-terrorism. The brigade is structured into the 1st Battalion *Incursori* (raiders), with two companies, the 110th and the 120th Incursori and one company of *Guastatori* (long-range reconnaissance and patrol, or LRRP), which, unlike the *Incursori,* is part of NATO's ACE Rapid Reaction Corps, or ARRC.

The training program for this regiment includes an initial eight-month period at the Pisa Parachute School, and it is a further year before the surviving volunteers, virtually all NCOs or officers, are considered fit to join the *Col. Moschin.* The training is specially designed to ensure that each soldier has the ability to operate in any environment. Its personnel are taught survival, evasion, and escape techniques, interrogation and counter-interrogation, free-fall parachuting (HALO and HAHO), heliborne insertion, mountain, desert and underwater warfare, combat shooting and sniping, unarmed combat, clandestine intelligence operations, hostage rescue, counter-terrorism, sabotage, and long-range patrol. In addition, the brigade can call upon a specialist squadron of the Italian Air Force from the 15th Wing, in the form of HH3F helicopters, or from the 46th Air Brigade, with G222 (U.S. C27 Spartan) fixed wing transports for special operations.

The weapons available to this unit include 9mm Beretta-92 automatic pistols, 9mm MP5 sub-machine guns, 5.56mm SCP70/90 para-automatic rifles, MSG90, SP86, and Barrett M82A1 sniper rifles, Beretta RS202 combat shotguns, 5.56mm Minimi machine guns, and even Milan anti-tank missiles.

The *Col. Moschin* regiment has taken part in counter-terrorist and special operations missions in the Alto-Adige in the 1960s, the hijacking of the ocean liner *Achille Lauro* in 1985, secret missions to Kurdistan and Ethiopia in 1991, Somalia in 1992–95, Rwanda in 1994, and Yemen in 1994. It was also deployed in Bosnia, Albania, and Kosovo in 1996–2000. This regiment provides the Italian army with one of the best trained, most effective, and most widely experienced special forces units found anywhere in the world today.

Rescue of a U.S. general

One of the best known operations carried out by the Italian Counter-Terrorist Unit was the successful rescue of the U.S. Brigadier General James Dozier in 1982. Dozier had been taken hostage by an Italian neo-Communist revolutionary group called the Red Brigade. A 12-man NOCS (Special Operations Division) combat unit under Captain Edoardo stormed the group's hideout and released Dozier in a well-planned and executed operation.

Italian special forces in one-piece suits, equipped with 9mm Beretta BM-12 sub-machine guns.

Greece

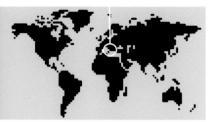

The Greek army regards itself as the guardian of the European tradition and intends to remain the defender of the gateway to the heartland of Europe. It sees its geostrategic position as being the main military force at the meeting point of three continents: Africa, Asia, and Europe.

Greece has a long-term commitment to, and interest in, the complicated affairs of its Balkan neighbors. Its long-standing enmity toward Turkey remains apparent through the numerous flashpoints and conflicts along their shared land border. The dispute over the island of Cyprus began immediately after the Turkish invasion of northern Cyprus in 1974, and the dispute over the more easterly Aegean Islands is ongoing today. This has been a factor in helping the Greeks create a highly trained and well-motivated combat force. The army is now largely deployed in preparation for any possible confrontation with Turkey, rather than the more conventional external threat once provided by the now defunct communist Warsaw Pact forces.

Based on the experiences of World War II and the 1948–49 civil war, the Greek army has a considerable capability in counter-insurgency and mountain warfare. These skills have been honed and expanded through a growing range of special

forces units. Highly trained in the arts of mountain warfare, amphibious assault, and counter-insurgency, these special forces would almost certainly be the first units to see combat in the event of any conflict with Turkey.

The Greek army has started to re-create ancient links with the Arab world—in particular, close military links with Egypt, driven by the need to counterbalance Turkey's friendship with Israel. There is also the wish to establish a new and more positive role for Greece in the Middle East.

The Greek army has a well-deserved reputation for being a fearsome fighting force. Within the constraints of a limited budget and the unwillingness of some NATO partners to risk being accused of starting an arms race in the Aegean, the Greek army has created a force capable of defending its national territory. In addition, it can also take a limited yet important military role within a vital geostrategic region.

Flashpoints and deployments

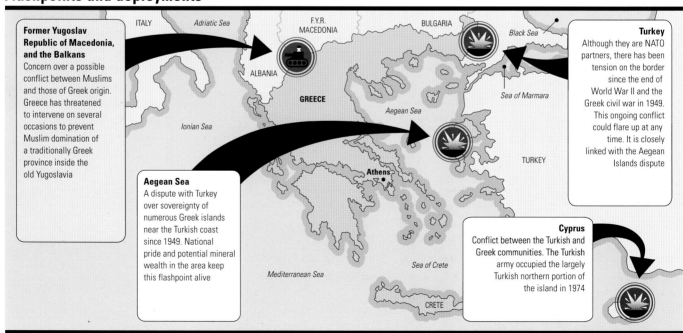

Former Yugoslav Republic of Macedonia, and the Balkans
Concern over a possible conflict between Muslims and those of Greek origin. Greece has threatened to intervene on several occasions to prevent Muslim domination of a traditionally Greek province inside the old Yugoslavia

Aegean Sea
A dispute with Turkey over sovereignty of numerous Greek islands near the Turkish coast since 1949. National pride and potential mineral wealth in the area keep this flashpoint alive

Turkey
Although they are NATO partners, there has been tension on the border since the end of World War II and the Greek civil war in 1949. This ongoing conflict could flare up at any time. It is closely linked with the Aegean Islands dispute

Cyprus
Conflict between the Turkish and Greek communities. The Turkish army occupied the largely Turkish northern portion of the island in 1974

Operations

The Greek army's operational deployment is governed strictly by the need to protect its national integrity from the potential threat posed by Turkey. Greece does commit forces to NATO's Allied Rapid Reaction Corps (ARRC) and to various United Nations peacekeeping roles, but since the end of the Cold War, only the threat of conflict with its neighbor requires the operational capability of the modern Greek army.

Civil war

Even before World War II had ended, EAM and ELAS Communist insurgents attempted to seize power in Greece. The resulting vicious civil war provided the Greek army with considerable experience in both street warfare and, in particular, mountain warfare operations under atrocious conditions. Armed and equipped by both the U.S. and UK, the Greek army eventually completely defeated the insurgents, and the war ended on October 16, 1949.

352 Leopard-1 main battle tanks equip the Greek armored brigades.

Mechanized units

The Greek army has an operational requirement to provide mechanized units to defend the land border with Turkey. Two infantry divisions and five mechanized infantry brigades, supported by four independent armored brigades, fulfill this role under the command of 1st Army Headquarters. The commitment to NATO is covered by B Army Corps, and includes the 2nd Mechanized Infantry Division based in Edessa and tasked for the Allied Rapid Reaction Corps (ARRC) since September 1992. Its 33rd Mechanized Infantry Brigade is based in Polikastro Kilkis, and the 34th Mechanized Infantry Brigade is based in Thessaloniki.

Inner Islands Command

The Inner Islands Command has one infantry division available, supported by a marine amphibious brigade, a commando regiment, and an airborne regiment. This command also covers the area of the disputed Aegean Islands close to the Turkish mainland. This command was also on operational alert during the *Imia-Kardak* incident in 1996, when disputes arose over the grounding of a Turkish freighter on one of the Imia Islands. Only U.S. diplomatic intervention prevented escalation into a full-scale crisis. This highlighted the risks of future conflict in this volatile area.

Other deployments abroad

The Greek army continues to plan military operations to counter Turkey's threat of military confrontation to seize a number of small Aegean Islands. The Turks could use this occupation as a bargaining lever in the wider arguments with Greece over the Aegean. In all probability the Greek army would find it very difficult to mount a successful amphibious or airborne operation to prevent such an attack, and would have even less chance of recapturing the islands later.

Greek operational planning does in fact have an alternative; they could open up a second front. The deployment of the powerful armored and mechanized forces of the 1st Army in the eastern provinces would give the Greek army a much better chance of spoiling any Turkish invasion.

💣 Weapons and units / overview of an army

The Greek army has a current strength of 110,000, with 2,700 women and some 65,000 personnel available for combat duty. The army is currently embarked on a program of rationalizing its formations to create smaller, better-equipped, more mobile combat units, but with enhanced firepower.

Over 600 Leonidas MK-1/2 armored personnel carriers have been built for the Greek army—who currently have some 300 of them in service—or for export to Cyprus and Macedonia.

Army units

The present organization has

3 military regions

    1 army command

    2 regional commands

5 corps headquarters

Under these are

    5 divisional headquarters

    5 infantry divisions

    5 independent armored brigades

    7 mechanized brigades

    5 infantry brigades

    1 army aviation brigade

    1 marine brigade

    4 reconnaissance regiments

    5 field artillery battalions

    10 air defense battalions

    2 surface-to-air battalions

Infantry small arms

9mm MPi69 automatic pistols

9mm M3A1 sub-machine guns

9mm SUMAK-9 sub-machine guns

7.62mm G3 automatic rifles

7.62mm FAL automatic rifles

7.62mm M1A1 carbines

5.56mm M16A1 automatic rifles

5.56mm Minimi machine guns

7.62mm MAG machine guns

7.62mm EHK-11 machine guns

12.7mm M2 HB heavy machine guns

Average allocation Armor, artillery, and helicopters within each brigade

5 Infantry Divisions

Infantry brigades

- **150** M113/Leonidas armored personnel carriers
- **10** M901/TOW anti-tank guided weapons, self-propelled

Armored battalion

- **50** M48/M60 main battle tanks
- **50** M113 armored personnel carriers

Artillery regiment

- **24** 105mm M101 towed
- **12** 155mm M114 towed

5 Independent Armored Brigades

Armored battalions

- **50** Leopard/M60 main battle tanks
- **50** BMP-1 armored infantry fighting vehicles
- **10** M901/TOW anti-tank guided weapons self-propelled

Mechanized infantry battalion

- **150** M113 armored personnel carriers
- **30** M901/TOW anti-tank guided weapons

Self-propelled artillery battalion

- **24** 155mm M109 self-propelled

The Greek army has two battalions of MIM23A Hawk surface-to-air missiles, which provide valuable air defense for the armored units stationed on the Turkish border.

KEY 🛩 Airborne   🚂 Armor   🔫 Infantry   🔧 Artillery   🏹 Missiles

Firepower   The cutting edge

Airborne	Armor	Infantry	Artillery	Missiles

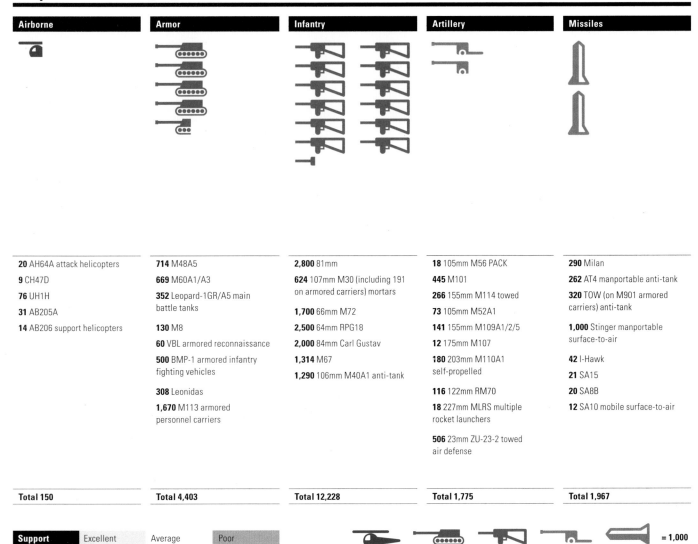

Airborne	Armor	Infantry	Artillery	Missiles
20 AH64A attack helicopters	**714** M48A5	**2,800** 81mm	**18** 105mm M56 PACK	**290** Milan
9 CH47D	**669** M60A1/A3	**624** 107mm M30 (including 191 on armored carriers) mortars	**445** M101	**262** AT4 manportable anti-tank
76 UH1H	**352** Leopard-1GR/A5 main battle tanks	**1,700** 66mm M72	**266** 155mm M114 towed	**320** TOW (on M901 armored carriers) anti-tank
31 AB205A	**130** M8	**2,500** 64mm RPG18	**73** 105mm M52A1	**1,000** Stinger manportable surface-to-air
14 AB206 support helicopters	**60** VBL armored reconnaissance	**2,000** 84mm Carl Gustav	**141** 155mm M109A1/2/5	**42** I-Hawk
	500 BMP-1 armored infantry fighting vehicles	**1,314** M67	**12** 175mm M107	**21** SA15
	308 Leonidas	**1,290** 106mm M40A1 anti-tank	**180** 203mm M110A1 self-propelled	**20** SA8B
	1,670 M113 armored personnel carriers		**116** 122mm RM70	**12** SA10 mobile surface-to-air
			18 227mm MLRS multiple rocket launchers	
			506 23mm ZU-23-2 towed air defense	
Total 150	**Total 4,403**	**Total 12,228**	**Total 1,775**	**Total 1,967**

Support	Excellent	Average	Poor		= 1,000

M109 Self-Propelled Gun

Country of origin U.S.

First entered service 1962 with U.S. army

Main armament 155mm Howitzer (36 rounds)

Max. road speed 35 mph (56 km/h)

Max. range 210 miles (350 km)

Crew 6

Over 4,000 built, in service with some 27 armies

◮ Fighting structure

The Greek army traditionally defends the routes to the East, and with a growing regional presence has a significant geostrategic position to maintain. But the current demands made on the army in terms of deployment are considerable. Its main combat units, including many armored and infantry formations, are largely structured and deployed to fight the conflict on its eastern borders. While its airmobile or amphibious forces are tasked to secure the sovereignty of the Aegean Islands off the Turkish coast, there are also commitments to NATO and other peacekeeping operations. The main combat units of the Greek army are yet to receive the massive reequipment or reorganization they require to fulfill their role effectively. However, recent government defense reviews make clear the intention to maintain an army to meet the nation's needs, and that priority will be given to restructuring and reequiping its fighting forces. Normal budgetary restrictions may have to be waived to achieve this aim.

The Greek army aviation units have 20 AH-64 attack helicopters armed with rapid-firing cannon and missiles. These offer a considerable anti-tank capability or support to special forces operations.

Fighting Structure Overview

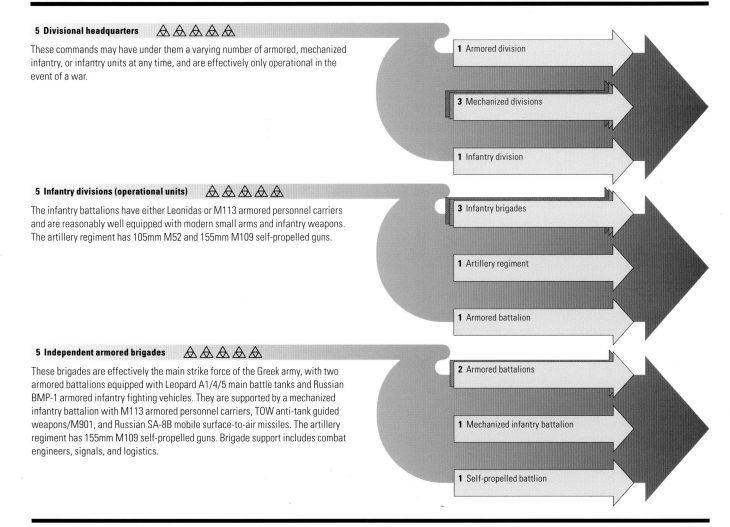

5 Divisional headquarters ◮◮◮◮◮

These commands may have under them a varying number of armored, mechanized infantry, or infantry units at any time, and are effectively only operational in the event of a war.

1 Armored division

3 Mechanized divisions

1 Infantry division

5 Infantry divisions (operational units) ◮◮◮◮◮

The infantry battalions have either Leonidas or M113 armored personnel carriers and are reasonably well equipped with modern small arms and infantry weapons. The artillery regiment has 105mm M52 and 155mm M109 self-propelled guns.

3 Infantry brigades

1 Artillery regiment

1 Armored battalion

5 Independent armored brigades ◮◮◮◮◮

These brigades are effectively the main strike force of the Greek army, with two armored battalions equipped with Leopard A1/4/5 main battle tanks and Russian BMP-1 armored infantry fighting vehicles. They are supported by a mechanized infantry battalion with M113 armored personnel carriers, TOW anti-tank guided weapons/M901, and Russian SA-8B mobile surface-to-air missiles. The artillery regiment has 155mm M109 self-propelled guns. Brigade support includes combat engineers, signals, and logistics.

2 Armored battalions

1 Mechanized infantry battalion

1 Self-propelled battlion

⚜ Special forces

The Greek army has built its modern reputation on the use of special or elite units in mountain warfare. During World War II, they provided the British Special Operations Executive (SOE) with many of their finest troops for sabotage operations behind German lines in Crete and the Greek mainland. Greek army personnel were also successful in defeating Communist forces in the Greek civil war of 1945–48. Today, this tradition is maintained by a number of special forces units.

ETA *(Ediko Tmima Alexiptotiston)*

The primary Greek army special forces unit is known as ETA *(Ediko Tmima Alexiptotiston)*, or "special airborne unit." It was formed in 1959 as a Long Range Reconnaissance Patrol (LRRP) and tasked for conducting operations similar to the British Special Air Service or the U.S. Delta Force. Among other techniques, it specializes in direct action raids, sabotage missions, and strategic reconnaissance. ETA uses a wide variety of NATO and commercial weapons, including M16 assault rifles, M203 40mm grenade launchers, and Belgian MINIMI 5.56mm light machine guns.

Training for ETA, as with most elite units, is rigorous and concentrates on physical strength and stamina. Because of the Greek terrain, there is particular emphasis on rock climbing and the rigors of mountain warfare. This is complemented by additional courses in parachuting, unconventional warfare, and combat swimming on the Greek navy's MYK (underwater warfare) course and at NATO's LRRP School in Germany.

This Greek special forces unit has gained a considerable reputation while on joint training exercises with other similar NATO units, apart from those of Turkey. They are considered to be an effective and hard fighting force under most circumstances. ETA personnel have also trained with the Egyptian Unit-777 counter-terrorist unit and are believed to be developing considerable experience operating in the Middle East.

This is a highly secretive unit, but it is known that they regularly carry out clandestine operations inside FYR Macedonia and other former Yugoslav republics. ETA's prime areas of operation, however, are the borders with Turkey, Cyprus, and the disputed islands of the eastern Aegean Sea.

13th Commando Regiment

Based in Athens, these well-trained and highly motivated units are tasked for a wide variety of missions. These include deep penetration raids in the event of an invasion, and making the occupation of any disputed Aegean Islands an extremely difficult option. The commandos use standard army-issue weapons and equipment.

Home-grown terrorism

The Greek terrorist organization "November-17" was formed in 1973. It was responsible for the murder of a number of high-ranking people, including CIA station chief Richard Welch in 1975, and British military attaché Brigadier Stephen Saunders in 2000. "November-17" itself was the main target of the Greek army's special forces unit, ETA, formed in 1959. This unit expanded into a full-scale counter-terrorist organization in the mid-1970s and by 1996–97 was eventually able to successfully hunt down and destroy much of the "November-17" group.

U.S. M109A5 155mm self-propelled Howitzers equip the artillery units of the armored brigades.

Other special forces

1st Commando Special Operations Regiment
Created in 1946 for specialist anti-Communist operations, now a primary counter-insurgency unit with

B Commando Macedonia
D Commando Macedonia
E Commando Thrace
C Commando (Amphibious Warfare) Athens
A Commando Thrace

Saudi Arabia

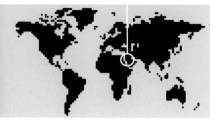

The Saudi Arabian army was built up in the 1960s on the back of burgeoning oil revenues; its first roles were to protect the country's vast oil fields from terrorism or outside intervention and maintain the integrity of its vast desert areas and long borders. With considerable help from Western nations, Saudi Arabia has created an effective, well-trained, motivated, and largely pro-Western army. Indeed, it was to prove a valuable partner in the 1991 Gulf campaign to push the Iraqi invasion forces out of Kuwait.

Today's Saudi Arabian army, built at considerable expense, consists of a well-balanced force of modern armored vehicles, mobile artillery, and attack helicopters that is sufficient for its present defense needs. The future, however, is less certain. If U.S. forces were to withdraw from the region, it is doubtful whether the Saudi army could continue to play an effective major military role in this vitally important geostrategic area.

However, the U.S. has made a considerable commitment to the security of the region, and as a result has suffered losses in attacks carried out by Osama Bin Laden's terrorists. These include incidents within Saudi Arabia as well as such outrages as the suicide attack on the warship *U.S.S. Cole* in the Yemeni seaport of Aden. The new U.S. administration appears to be determined to pursue confrontation with Iraq, to strengthen its ties with Saudi Arabia, and accept the likelihood of being drawn into further conflict. The Middle East is entering a period of complex and constantly shifting alliances, and Saudi Arabia is aware that its relationship with the U.S. must remain strong.

Saudi Arabia will probably find itself involved in coalitions and defense pacts to split (or at least balance) the threat of potential enemies in the area. This, in turn, raises a major question regarding the flexibility and cohesiveness of such a narrowly recruited force in an otherwise multi-cultural and multi-religious region.

Flashpoints and deployments

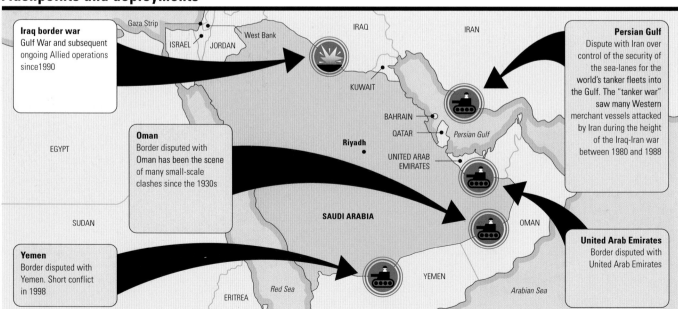

Iraq border war
Gulf War and subsequent ongoing Allied operations since 1990

Oman
Border disputed with Oman has been the scene of many small-scale clashes since the 1930s

Yemen
Border disputed with Yemen. Short conflict in 1998

Persian Gulf
Dispute with Iran over control of the security of the sea-lanes for the world's tanker fleets into the Gulf. The "tanker war" saw many Western merchant vessels attacked by Iran during the height of the Iraq-Iran war between 1980 and 1988

United Arab Emirates
Border disputed with United Arab Emirates

⚑ Operations

The Saudi Arabian army has a number of operational responsibilities that cause considerable strain to their fairly small army. These include traditional concerns over the long-disputed borders of the Arabian peninsula, the oil-rich areas of the eastern provinces, and the more pressing concerns of the threat from Iraq and the uncertainty of future relations with Iran. Saudi units on the southern border have fought numerous battles with Yemeni forces in recent years, and the threat of further conflict is considerable. The risk of damage to oil fields from external attack or sabotage by immigrant workers is a constant internal security headache. However, the driving force behind the Saudi army's present operational deployment is the possibility of a resumption of the Gulf conflict with Iraq, and concern about Iran's intentions over the security of the sea-lanes in the Arabian Gulf.

A Saudi Arabian armored unit in action in 1991 during the Gulf War with Iraq. They are equipped with French-built AMX-30 main battle tanks—seen here in "hull-down" position to reduce its target signature.

Current military deployments

The current Area Operational Commands are:

Eastern Command Headquarters at Dhanran
• 1 Mechanized infantry battalion

Northern Command Headquarters at Hafr al-Batin
• 14th Armored Brigade
• 8th Mechanized Infantry Brigade
• 20th Mechanized Infantry Brigade
• 1 Aviation battalion

Northwestern Command Headquarters at Tabuk
• 12th Armored Brigade
• 6th Mechanized Infantry Brigade
• 1 Airborne brigade

Southern Command Headquarters at Khamis Mushayt
Jizan sub-area
• 4th Armored Brigade
Najran sub-area
• 11th Mechanized Infantry Brigade
Sharurah Force Command
• 10th Mechanized Infantry Brigade

Border conflicts

Saudi Arabia's relations with its southern neighbor, Yemen, have been strained since 1934, when the Saudi leader, Abdul Aziz, sent an army to conquer the region. A short but bloody conflict ended with a cease-fire. Further clashes occurred again in 1994–95, but the most serious border conflict erupted in May 1998, when Yemeni forces seized the island of Duwaima in the Red Sea. Repeated attempts by the Saudis to eject the invaders failed, and, by July, 1998 Yemeni forces claimed to have the island fully under their control.

Western Command Headquarters at Jeddah
• 1 Mechanized infantry battalion
Operational deployment is likely to change considerably between 2001 and 2005, as the Saudi Arabian forces are to be restructured into two U.S.-style armored divisions.

The highly effective U.S. M163 Vulcan anti-aircraft gun, deployed by the Saudi air defense force in 1991, in support of the army units during the Gulf War.

⬙ Weapons and units / overview of an army

The Saudi Arabian army is 75,000 strong, with around 40,000 personnel available to the combat units. The Saudi army relies on having a major qualitative edge over the much larger armies of its Middle East neighbors. Vast sums have been spent on ensuring that the most modern and effective weapons are available in considerable numbers.

The National Guard

The para-military National Guard is also equipped with the most modern weaponry and is virtually a second army with a further 100,000 personnel, organized into three mechanized infantry brigades and five infantry brigades. Equipped with some 2,500 LAV-25, Commando and Piranha armored vehicles, 40 105mm and 30 155mm towed artillery and 111 TOW anti-tank missile launchers mounted on LAV-25 vehicles.

Army units

Current organization has

3 armored brigades
5 mechanized infantry brigades
1 airborne infantry brigade
1 Royal Guards mechanized regiment
8 artillery battalions
1 army aviation command

M2 Bradley Armored Infantry Fighting Vehicle

Country of origin	U.S.
First entered service	1981 with U.S. army
Main armament	25mm chain-gun and twin TOW AT missiles
Max. road speed	45 mph (75 km/h)
Max. range	300 miles (500 km)
Crew	3 + 7 infantrymen
Over 6,000 built, in service with 2 armies	

Average allocation Armor, artillery, and helicopters within each brigade

Armored Brigade
- **150** M1A2 Abrams/M60A3 main battle tanks
- **250** M2 Bradley and AMX10P armored infantry fighting vehicles
- **150** M113A3 armored personnel carriers
- **24** 155mm M109A2 self-propelled artillery
- **80** TOW-2 anti-tank missiles (on VCC1 armored carriers)
- **20** ASTROS-11 multiple rocket launchers
- **10** Crotale self-propelled surface-to-air missiles

Mechanized Brigade
- **50** M60A3 main battle tanks
- **450** AMX10P armored infantry fighting vehicles
- **450** M113A2/3 armored personnel carriers
- **24** 155mm M109 and GCT self-propelled artillery
- **10** Crotale self-propelled surface-to-air missiles

Airborne Brigade
- **120** M2 Bradley armored infantry fighting vehicles

KEY ➤ Airborne   ➤ Armor   ➤ Infantry   ➤ Artillery   ◁ Missiles

The upgraded Shahine mobile surface-to-air missile system, based on the French Crotale. It provides forward air defense for armored units of the Saudi army.

Infantry small arms

9mm Beretta M51 automatic pistols

7.62mm G3 automatic rifles

5.56mm AUG automatic rifles

5.56mm M16A1 automatic rifles

7.62mm M60 machine guns

12.7mm M2 HB heavy machine guns

One of the Saudi army's 315 MIA2 Abrams main battle tanks, seen here moving at speed across flat desert terrain that makes up much of Saudi Arabia's vulnerable northern border with Iraq.

Firepower   The cutting edge

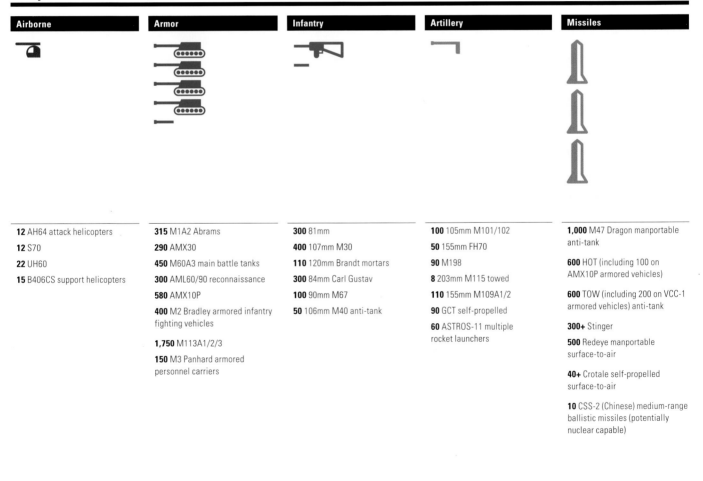

Airborne	Armor	Infantry	Artillery	Missiles
12 AH64 attack helicopters	**315** M1A2 Abrams	**300** 81mm	**100** 105mm M101/102	**1,000** M47 Dragon manportable anti-tank
12 S70	**290** AMX30	**400** 107mm M30	**50** 155mm FH70	
22 UH60	**450** M60A3 main battle tanks	**110** 120mm Brandt mortars	**90** M198	**600** HOT (including 100 on AMX10P armored vehicles)
15 B406CS support helicopters	**300** AML60/90 reconnaissance	**300** 84mm Carl Gustav	**8** 203mm M115 towed	
	580 AMX10P	**100** 90mm M67	**110** 155mm M109A1/2	**600** TOW (including 200 on VCC-1 armored vehicles) anti-tank
	400 M2 Bradley armored infantry fighting vehicles	**50** 106mm M40 anti-tank	**90** GCT self-propelled	
	1,750 M113A1/2/3		**60** ASTROS-11 multiple rocket launchers	**300+** Stinger
	150 M3 Panhard armored personnel carriers			**500** Redeye manportable surface-to-air
				40+ Crotale self-propelled surface-to-air
				10 CSS-2 (Chinese) medium-range ballistic missiles (potentially nuclear capable)
Total 61	**Total 4,235**	**Total 1,260**	**Total 508**	**Total 3,050+**

Support	Excellent	Average	Poor		= 1,000

◬ Fighting structure

The Saudi army has created a highly mobile, hard-hitting, armored, and mechanized force. Soldiers are well-trained and equipped with the best that oil money can buy, with everything from modern main battle tanks and self-propelled artillery to missile systems. Its fully integrated units operate comfortably alongside those of the United States and its other Western Allies along the desert borders with Kuwait and Iraq. To the south,

traditional border disputes, which sometimes result in conflict (as with the recent short border war with Yemen in 1999–2000), have led to the creation of light, highly mobile and self-contained units that are capable of operating in the hot, dry mountains and deserts of the United Arab Emirates, Oman, and Yemen.

Fighting Structure Overview

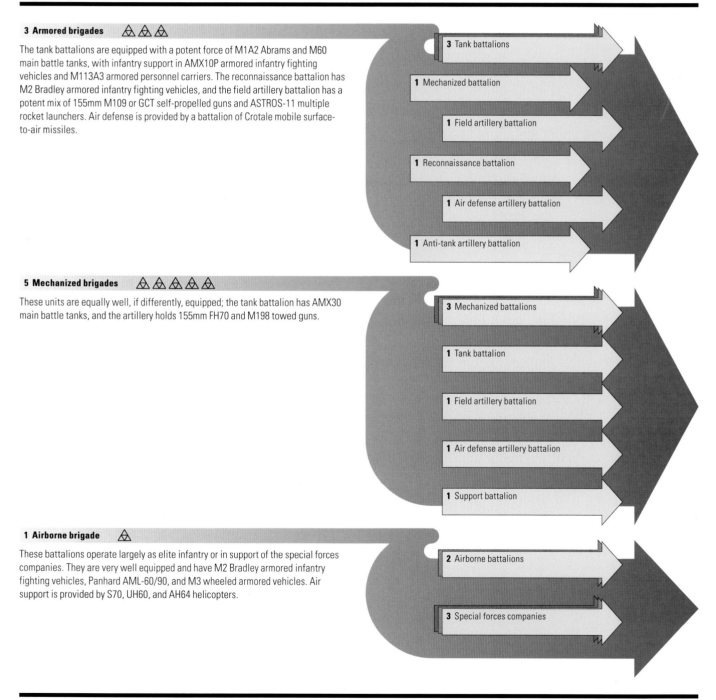

3 Armored brigades ◬ ◬ ◬

The tank battalions are equipped with a potent force of M1A2 Abrams and M60 main battle tanks, with infantry support in AMX10P armored infantry fighting vehicles and M113A3 armored personnel carriers. The reconnaissance battalion has M2 Bradley armored infantry fighting vehicles, and the field artillery battalion has a potent mix of 155mm M109 or GCT self-propelled guns and ASTROS-11 multiple rocket launchers. Air defense is provided by a battalion of Crotale mobile surface-to-air missiles.

- 3 Tank battalions
- 1 Mechanized battalion
- 1 Field artillery battalion
- 1 Reconnaissance battalion
- 1 Air defense artillery battalion
- 1 Anti-tank artillery battalion

5 Mechanized brigades ◬ ◬ ◬ ◬ ◬

These units are equally well, if differently, equipped; the tank battalion has AMX30 main battle tanks, and the artillery holds 155mm FH70 and M198 towed guns.

- 3 Mechanized battalions
- 1 Tank battalion
- 1 Field artillery battalion
- 1 Air defense artillery battalion
- 1 Support battalion

1 Airborne brigade ◬

These battalions operate largely as elite infantry or in support of the special forces companies. They are very well equipped and have M2 Bradley armored infantry fighting vehicles, Panhard AML-60/90, and M3 wheeled armored vehicles. Air support is provided by S70, UH60, and AH64 helicopters.

- 2 Airborne battalions
- 3 Special forces companies

Special forces

For years, the Saudi government has been conscious of the potential threat to its major oil fields in the east and along the Gulf coast. A particular problem is the large number of foreign workers, many of whom are Palestinian, who were brought in to run much of the country's industrial and commercial infrastructure. Therefore, it is not surprising that counter-terrorist and anti-sabotage operations are now receiving much more attention from the Saudi army.

Elite airborne soldiers parade in desert camouflage uniforms. They are armed with German 7.62mm G3 automatic rifles.

Special Security Force (SSF)

The Special Security Force was established in 1971 and gained its counter-terrorist and hostage rescue role in 1979. The SSF has some 3,500 personnel organized into eight battalions and independent company-sized units. The force receives regular training from the French GIGN and German GSG9.

Special Warfare Unit

The strongest special forces unit in Saudi Arabia is probably the 100-man Special Warfare Unit, formed entirely of volunteers from within the National Guard. They are armed with 5.56mm M16A1 automatic rifles, 9mm MP5 sub-machine guns, and M700 sniper rifles. They received special training from the French GIGN before launching the successful operation to retake the Great Mosque in Mecca, seized by radical Muslim terrorists in 1979.

Airborne Brigade

The Airborne Brigade controls an additional three dedicated special forces companies. These units are also made up of volunteers, who are fully trained parachutists. Their initial training period includes six months of basic fitness and combat skills, and then six months developing a range of advanced techniques

Religious revolt

The Saudi Special Security Force (SSF) faced an enormous test of its skill and confidence when, in 1979, it was required to retake the Great Mosque in Mecca from radical Islamic terrorists. The need to recapture this extremely important and holy building without major damage required a level of operational capability that would have taxed more famous special forces. The French GIGN gave specialist advice and equipment, and, along with elite units of the National Guard, the Mosque was successfully recaptured by the SSF without serious damage.

in all aspects of special operations. Parachute training includes HALO and HAHO, heliborne insertion, combat shooting, desert survival and warfare, close-quarter battle, hostage rescue, and long-range reconnaissance and patrol (or LRRP). Specialist explosives disposal training is also given to deal with potential sabotage within the petrochemical industry. These units regularly train with U.S. Delta Force and SEAL personnel, and are sent abroad for courses with the German GSG9 and French GIGN.

There is very close cooperation with the U.S. forces based in Saudi Arabia. Since the end of the Gulf War with Iraq, U.S. military bases have been the target of numerous terrorist

attacks by Osama Bin Laden and other groups, and prevention of further such outrages is high on the list of priorities for Saudi special forces. The threat of extremist Islamic terrorist activities spreading both to the migrant worker community and the indigenous population continues to be a grave concern to Saudi authorities, and to the security and special forces in particular.

The weapons available to these units are the pick of the world's arms, and a wide range has been purchased. The most popular are the 5.56mm M16A1 automatic rifles, Steyr AUG automatic rifles, and 9mm MP5 sub-machine guns, PSG-1 sniper rifles, and the M203 grenade launchers. A number

of specially converted UH60 helicopters are available for special forces use, and these have been of great value in operations along the disputed borders to the south with Yemen, Oman, and the United Arab Emirates, as well as along the northern border with Iraq.

Saudi Arabia has a need for more special forces units. During the next three years, a full brigade with an enhanced counter-terrorist capability is likely to be created.

Egypt

The Egyptian army suffered bitter failures in its wars with Israel in 1948, 1956, and 1967, and achieved only limited increases in morale and military proficiency during the War of Attrition with Israeli forces along the Suez Canal in 1968-70. Therefore, the highly successful opening attack by the Egyptian army in the 1973 Yom Kippur War came not a moment too soon. When a large force of tanks and infantry fought across the canal and penetrated Israeli defenses, it gave the Egyptian army a new level of belief in its abilities.

In the years following the Yom Kippur War, the Egyptian army has made huge changes in both the range and quality of its equipment. Under President Sadat, the Egyptian government took the decision to expel its Russian advisers, opting for modern Western military thinking instead of the dogma of a Soviet army still wedded to the tactics of World War II. As a result, the old Soviet T-55 and T-62 main battle tanks have gone, and Egypt's restructured armored units now train on state-of-the-art American M1 Abrams tanks, often alongside their U.S. army counterparts. The same can be said of much of the mechanized infantry, self-propelled artillery, and anti-aircraft units. The infrastructure, command, logistics, communications, and training of the present Egyptian armed forces have benefited

enormously from the new relationships forged with the United States, Western Europe, and, in particular, Greece.

The need to train and equip its forces for a war of maneuver against an enormously capable Israeli army still dominates the tactics and long-term strategy of the Egyptian army. The events in the West Bank and Gaza Strip have highlighted the underlying instability of the region, and demonstrated that peace agreements cannot be taken for granted. Egyptian public opinion wishes to see closer ties with other Arab nations, such as Syria and Iraq, and this could put intolerable pressure on the Egyptian government to once again take a more extreme Arab nationalist stance.

Flashpoints and deployments

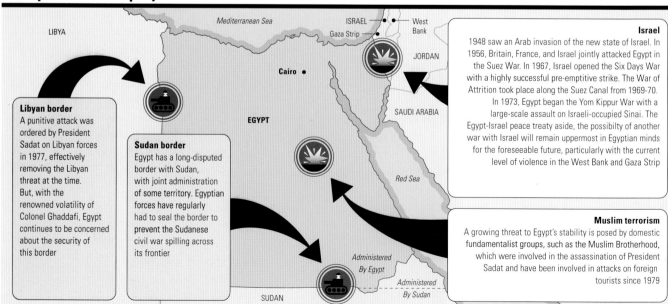

Libyan border
A punitive attack was ordered by President Sadat on Libyan forces in 1977, effectively removing the Libyan threat at the time. But, with the renowned volatility of Colonel Ghaddafi, Egypt continues to be concerned about the security of this border

Sudan border
Egypt has a long-disputed border with Sudan, with joint administration of some territory. Egyptian forces have regularly had to seal the border to prevent the Sudanese civil war spilling across its frontier

Israel
1948 saw an Arab invasion of the new state of Israel. In 1956, Britain, France, and Israel jointly attacked Egypt in the Suez War. In 1967, Israel opened the Six Days War with a highly successful pre-emptitive strike. The War of Attrition took place along the Suez Canal from 1969-70. In 1973, Egypt began the Yom Kippur War with a large-scale assault on Israeli-occupied Sinai. The Egypt-Israel peace treaty aside, the possibilty of another war with Israel will remain uppermost in Egyptian minds for the foreseeable future, particularly with the current level of violence in the West Bank and Gaza Strip

Muslim terrorism
A growing threat to Egypt's stability is posed by domestic fundamentalist groups, such as the Muslim Brotherhood, which were involved in the assassination of President Sadat and have been involved in attacks on foreign tourists since 1979

⚑ Operations

The Egyptian army's operational deployment is planned to prevent a repeat of the wars of 1948, 1956, and 1967. When Egyptian forces launched their surprise attack on the first day of the 1973 Yom Kippur War, their intention was to recover the territory lost in previous battles. The huge Egyptian army successfully crossed the Suez Canal and breached the sand barriers raised by the Israelis. Then, having isolated the forts built by the Israeli army along the Bar-Lev Line, they pushed a defensive line of infantry, heavily armed with anti-tank missiles, forward into the Sinai Desert.

Having succeeded brilliantly in the first part of this operation, the Egyptian forces then destroyed the initial piecemeal armored counterattacks hastily launched by the Israeli army. It was not until the Israeli army had defeated the more immediate Syrian threat on the Golan Heights that it had sufficient tanks available to reinforce its units in the south in order to launch a really effective counterattack. The Israelis finally punched a hole between two Egyptian armies and crossed the Suez Canal before a cease-fire could be agreed upon.

The main combat formations of the Egyptian army are tasked operationally to prevent a repeat of past Israeli triumphs and, with the highly uncertain future of this geostrategically important area, these units are very heavily equipped and increasingly well-trained.

An Egyptian armored unit in the Sinai Desert equipped with U.S. M60A3 main battle tanks armed with 105mm guns.

Field army deployments

Today, the Egyptian army deploys the 2nd Field Army between the Mediterranean Sea and Ismailia and the 3rd Field Army between Ismailia and the Red Sea. With some ten armored and mechanized infantry divisions between these two field armies, five are held between Cairo and the Suez Canal, while five are stationed forward and east of the canal, with a reinforced mechanized brigade in the Sinai Desert. This deployment is designed to ensure that any future conflict with Israel will be kept as far as possible from the Suez Canal and the Egyptian hinterland.

Other deployments

An additional reinforced mechanized division covers Cairo and the Nile Delta, while the Western Military Area, covering the desert west of Cairo, has another reinforced mechanized division facing the Libyan border. Beyond traditional military operations, the Egyptian army faces a growing internal threat from the Muslim Brotherhood, an Islamic terrorist organization responsible for numerous outrages, including the killing of foreign tourists. Many infantry battalions are now committed to supporting the special forces in counter-insurgency and anti-terrorist operations.

An Egyptian infantry unit deployed with the UN SFOR operation in Bosnia, with a Fahd wheeled armored personnel carrier.

Yemen intervention

In 1962, the Egyptian leader President Nasser sent an expeditionary force of around 65,000 troops to Yemen in support of the new socialist republican regime. However, Saudi Arabia supported the ousted royalist side and a bloody civil war developed. The Egyptian army was unable to defeat the royalists and after four years the highly relieved force was withdrawn, only to face the Israelis in the 1967 war and a catastrophic defeat.

Weapons and units / overview of an army

The Egyptian army is 320,000 strong, with some 220,000 personnel available for combat duty. The present structure of the army is heavily weighted toward armor, mechanized infantry, and self-propelled artillery. With any potential large-scale conflict being fought over the hot and dusty landscape of the Sinai and Negev Deserts, this weighting is likely to be further developed and enhanced in the future, particularly with the delivery of an additional 200 M1 Abrams main battle tanks by 2003.

However, recent Egyptian army reports have shown a growing concern about the overall readiness and combat capability of the main fighting formations, a matter of great concern in light of the present level of tension in the area.

Army units

The present organization has

4 military districts

2 army headquarters

    4 armored divisions

      8 mechanized infantry divisions

       1 Republican Guard armored division

4 independent armored brigades

4 independent mechanized infantry brigades

1 airmobile brigade

2 independent infantry brigades

1 parachute infantry brigade

6 commando groups

15 independent artillery brigades

2 surface-to-surface missile brigades

Average allocation Armor, artillery, and helicopters within each brigade

Armored Divisions

2 Armored brigades

- **93** M1A1 Abrams/M60A3 main battle tanks
- **123** M113 armored personnel carriers
- **30** BMR-600/YPR-765 armored infantry fighting vehicles
- **18** BRDM-2 reconnaissance
- **12** TOW/YPR-765 anti-tank self-propelled guided weapons-

Mechanized infantry brigade

- **40** M60A1/3 main battle tanks
- **140** M113 armored personnel carriers
- **12** TOW/YPR-765 anti-tank self-propelled guided weapons

Self-propelled artillery brigade

- **54** M109 155mm self-propelled
- **26** BM11/BM21 multiple launching rocket system

Air defense artillery and missile brigade

- **24** ZSU-23-4 SP anti-aircraft guns
- **12** SA-9/M54 Chaparral self-propelled surface-to-air missiles

Mechanized Infantry Divisions

2 Mechanized infantry brigades

- **40** M60A1/A3 main battle tanks
- **140** M113 armored personnel carriers
- **12** TOW/YPR-765 anti-tank self-propelled guided weapons

Armored brigade

- **93** M60A1/3 main battle tanks
- **123** M113 armored personnel carriers
- **30** BMR-600/YPR-765 AIFV
- **18** BRDM-2 reconnaissance
- **12** TOW/YPR-765 anti-tank self-propelled guided weapons

Artillery brigade

- **54** 130mm M46 towed
- **8** BM11/BM21 multiple launching rocket system

Air defense artillery brigade

- **30** ZSU-23-2 towed
- **20** 37mm M1939 towed

Infantry small arms

9mm Tokagypt automatic pistols

9mm Port Said sub-machine guns

9mm HK MP5 sub-machine guns

7.62mm AK47/AKM automatic rifles

5.56mm M16A1 automatic rifles

5.56mm AKS74 automatic rifles

7.62mm MAG machine guns

7.62mm RPK machine guns

7.62mm PK/PKM machine guns

12.7mm DSHK heavy machine guns

Many of Egypt's self-propelled artillery units are now equipped with the modern and highly effective U.S. M109 155mm guns.

An Egyptian infantryman on a desert training exercise armed with a Russian 7.62mm AK automatic rifle. By contrast he is equipped with U.S. pattern uniform and helmet.

KEY ⛴ Airborne   🛡 Armor   🔫 Infantry   🎯 Artillery   🚀 Missiles

Firepower   The cutting edge

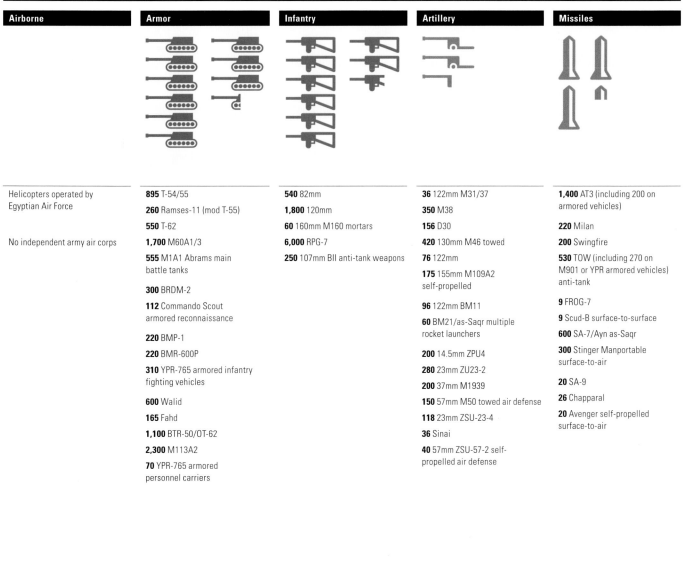

Airborne	Armor	Infantry	Artillery	Missiles

Helicopters operated by Egyptian Air Force	**895** T-54/55	**540** 82mm	**36** 122mm M31/37	**1,400** AT3 (including 200 on armored vehicles)
	260 Ramses-11 (mod T-55)	**1,800** 120mm	**350** M38	
No independent army air corps	**550** T-62	**60** 160mm M160 mortars	**156** D30	**220** Milan
	1,700 M60A1/3	**6,000** RPG-7	**420** 130mm M46 towed	**200** Swingfire
	555 M1A1 Abrams main battle tanks	**250** 107mm BII anti-tank weapons	**76** 122mm	**530** TOW (including 270 on M901 or YPR armored vehicles) anti-tank
	300 BRDM-2		**175** 155mm M109A2 self-propelled	
	112 Commando Scout armored reconnaissance		**96** 122mm BM11	**9** FROG-7
	220 BMP-1		**60** BM21/as-Saqr multiple rocket launchers	**9** Scud-B surface-to-surface
	220 BMR-600P		**200** 14.5mm ZPU4	**600** SA-7/Ayn as-Saqr
	310 YPR-765 armored infantry fighting vehicles		**280** 23mm ZU23-2	**300** Stinger Manportable surface-to-air
	600 Walid		**200** 37mm M1939	**20** SA-9
	165 Fahd		**150** 57mm M50 towed air defense	**26** Chapparal
	1,100 BTR-50/OT-62		**118** 23mm ZSU-23-4	**20** Avenger self-propelled surface-to-air
	2,300 M113A2		**36** Sinai	
	70 YPR-765 armored personnel carriers		**40** 57mm ZSU-57-2 self-propelled air defense	

Total 0	Total 9,357	Total 8,650	Total 2,393	Total 3,334

Support	Excellent	Average	Poor						= 1,000

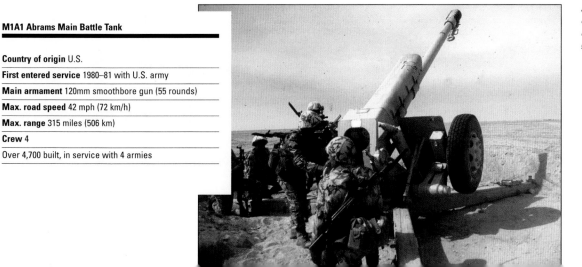

M1A1 Abrams Main Battle Tank

Country of origin U.S.	
First entered service 1980–81 with U.S. army	
Main armament 120mm smoothbore gun (55 rounds)	
Max. road speed 42 mph (72 km/h)	
Max. range 315 miles (506 km)	
Crew 4	
Over 4,700 built, in service with 4 armies	

An artillery battery equipped with a Russian D30 122mm quick-firing gun-howitzer.

◭ Fighting structure

The present Egyptian army has been restructured into effective, multiple-role combat units with much-enhanced mobility, command, and control. Its layered air defense of overlapping, mobile short-, medium-, and long-range surface-to-air missile systems, and the massive anti-tank missile and rocket launcher capability (that proved so valuable in the 1973 war against Israeli armored attacks) have been modernized.

Although renewed fighting with Israel seems unlikely in the near future, the armored and mechanized divisions (with considerable U.S. help) remain a formidable force for the future. However, with the steady growth of Islamic terrorism over the last twenty years, the Egyptian security forces now face a much different problem. The need to fight internal terrorism will necessitate a further restructuring, with the creation of large numbers of highly trained, specialist counter-insurgency units within the Egyptian army as it struggles to come to grips with an elusive and dedicated internal enemy.

An Egyptian anti-tank missile crew in the Sinai Desert equipped with U.S.-made TOW system.

Fighting Structure Overview

4 Armored divisions ◭◭◭◭

The armored brigades are equipped with an impressive mix of U.S. M1A1 Abrams and M60A1/3 main battle tanks and YPR-765 (with 25mm gun) armored reconnaissance vehicles, while the mechanized infantry brigades have U.S. M113 armored personnel carriers and BMR-600P armored reconnaissance vehicles. The modern Egyptian infantryman is exceptionally well-equipped with small arms, support weapons, anti-tank, and anti-aircraft missiles. The self-propelled artillery brigade has U.S. 155 M109 guns. The air defense brigade has an effective mix of ZSU-23-4 self-propelled anti-aircraft guns and M54 Chaparral surface-to-air missiles. It has considerable divisional support, including a combat engineer brigade with armored bridging and mine-clearing vehicles.

2 Armored brigades

1 Mechanized infantry brigade

1 Self-propelled artillery brigade

1 Air defense artillery and missile brigade

1 Combat engineer regiment

8 Mechanized infantry divisions ◭◭◭◭◭◭◭◭

The equipment of these divisions is largely the same as that of the armored divisions, with the exception of the armored brigade that has only M60A1 main battle tanks and the artillery brigade that still has some towed artillery, usually 130mm M46 long-range guns. These will be replaced in due course by additional U.S. M109 guns.

2 Mechanized infantry brigades

1 Armored brigade

1 Artillery brigade

1 Air defense artillery regiment

1 Combat engineer regiment

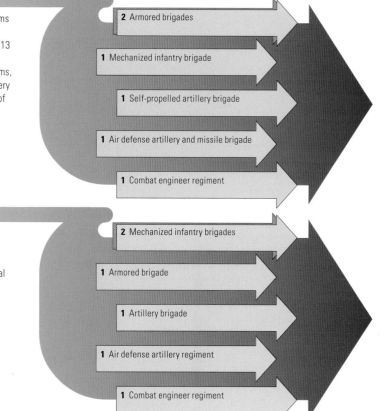

🎖 Special forces

Egypt has a number of special forces units, including the special operations troops of the Ministry of Interior's Central Security Force. This unit carries out VIP protection and SWAT (Special Weapons and Tactics) missions, and is often used to secure a perimeter around a terrorist incident prior to the arrival of Unit-777.

Unit-777

The Egyptian army formed Unit-777, or *Al-Saiqa* (thunderbolt), in 1978 following a dramatic growth in Islamic terrorism. Initial training was straightforward, using commando techniques, and from 1981, more advanced training was provided by the U.S. Despite this, Unit-777 suffered from a lack of experience, weapons, and support in its early days. This contributed to a number of bungled operations, the most public of which was the disastrously mishandled attempt at a hostage rescue operation at Nicosia Airport on November 23, 1985.

Today, Unit-777 is a 320-strong counter-terrorist organization. Its capability, weapons, and command have been significantly improved. The unit comes under the direct operational control of the Egyptian army's commando command. Training includes many traditional special forces techniques, including marksmanship, combat shooting, static-line airborne operations, and parachuting, although not the more advanced parachute skills. Advanced training is given in desert warfare skills and survival. Unit-777 has established connections, and trains regularly with Germany's GSG-9, French GIGN, and the U.S. Delta Force. Weapons include a wide range of Russian and Western small arms, from AKS and M16 assault rifles to Israeli UZI and German MP5 sub-machine guns.

The Egyptian army's Unit-777 is primarily tasked with the suppression of the Muslim Brotherhood, and while it is usually described as a domestic-oriented unit, it has conducted both overseas and cross-border operations, and is responsible for the regular protection of Egyptian embassies throughout the world. Whether Unit-777 is up to the task of defeating the growth of Islamic terrorism is questionable, and more work and some restructuring may be needed before Egypt has a genuine special forces or counter-terrorist unit of quality.

Unit-333

Unit-333 is a specialized hostage-rescue force (HRF) based in southern Cairo, and consists of 120 personnel. It has been part of state security since 1984, and is responsible for all such activities in Egypt.

The potent U.S.-made AH-64 Apache attack helicopter is now operated by the Egyptian air force.

Forgetting the basics

The reputation of Egypt's special forces was severely dented in March 1978 when 54 members of the Saiqa (lightning) Commandos assaulted a grounded Cypriot Airlines DC-8 carrying 15 hostages. As a result of a bungled operation and misunderstandings with the local security forces, a fire fight developed with the Greek Cypriot National Guard in which 15 Egyptians died. Luckily for the Saiqa commander, General Shukry, none of the hostages was killed.

This Egyptian infantryman's 7.62mm AK assault rifle is equipped with a telescopic sight.

Iran

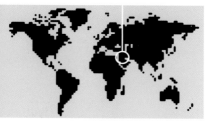

The modern Iranian Islamic army has been slowly rebuilt since the overthrow of the Shah in 1979. Its forces were tested in the bloody years of the 1980–88 Iran–Iraq war and proved their valor, fighting ability, and loyalty to the new Iran. However, the Islamic army is still struggling to regain its prerevolutionary strength.

Iran's rebuilding program has introduced a degree of modernization into the army, and has succeeded in partly re-equipping the land forces for the future in an increasingly unstable Middle East. However, beset with the problems of obtaining spare parts for the wide variety of old weapons from a multitude of sources would alone be sufficient to hamstring any force already struggling under the financial restraints imposed by a failing economy, international isolation, and the suffocating influence of religious dogma.

In addition, the Iranian army has to face considerable geostrategic problems. There is an ongoing, bitter feud over a disputed border with Iraq, and there has been no improvement in the strained relationships with the U.S. and Europe that have existed since the removal of the Shah. There is also a Kurdish insurgency that is fiercely anti-Iranian, anti-Iraqi, and anti-Turkish, and that is being fought in a vast triangle of land. This is an area of ever-changing and conflicting alliances and external involvements, including that of the U.S. Central Intelligence Agency (CIA), which supports the Kurdish groups who are fighting both the Iranian and Iraqi forces.

Iran is now in desperate need of either a fast-track diplomatic solution to its problems, or, the military capability to be able to deal with them effectively. With this in mind, Iran, while continuing to receive large quantities of arms from China, is also attempting to establish an improved relationship with Russia in order to acquire the modern weapons.

The Iranian army faces a troubled future, and, at present and in the short term, remains a force with just sufficient capability to defend its national borders and maintain internal stability. The army is as yet unable to pose any real military threat to its Arab neighbors in the Gulf in pursuit of the Iranian leadership's openly expressed wish to spread the Islamic Revolution throughout the Middle East.

Flashpoints and deployments

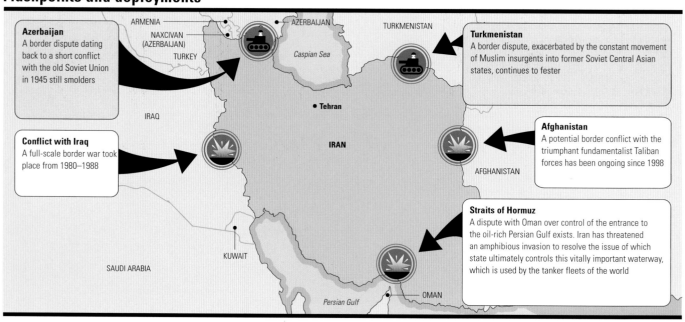

Azerbaijan
A border dispute dating back to a short conflict with the old Soviet Union in 1945 still smolders

Conflict with Iraq
A full-scale border war took place from 1980–1988

Turkmenistan
A border dispute, exacerbated by the constant movement of Muslim insurgents into former Soviet Central Asian states, continues to fester

Afghanistan
A potential border conflict with the triumphant fundamentalist Taliban forces has been ongoing since 1998

Straits of Hormuz
A dispute with Oman over control of the entrance to the oil-rich Persian Gulf exists. Iran has threatened an amphibious invasion to resolve the issue of which state ultimately controls this vitally important waterway, which is used by the tanker fleets of the world

Operations

The Iranian army has been heavily deployed along the Iraqi border since the start of the Islamic Revolution in 1979. At one time, some 80 percent of its major combat units were stationed there. The ever-present threat of a resumption of the conflict requires that a very large proportion of the Iranian army remain operational in the Western Operations Sector facing the Iraqi border. Its headquarters, in Kermanshah, is only 124 miles from Baghdad. An elite shock infantry force is provided by the 16th and 81st Armored Divisions, supported by the 84th Mechanized Infantry Division, as well as the 23rd Commando Division, with two additional independent commando brigades.

Missile assault

In early 2001 the Iranian Islamic army launched massive rocket attacks on camps occupied by Iranian opposition groups inside Iraq. In one attack alone some 60 modified Scud SRBM (Short Range Ballistic Missiles) were fired, believed to be only 10 percent of their Scud arsenal. Tension continues to increase along the border between Iran and Iraq and a resumption of the 1980–88 war between the two nations can no longer be ruled out.

Soldiers from an elite infantry unit during a victory parade in Tehran. They are armed with 7.62mm G3 automatic rifles.

Recent operations by the Iranian army have been conducted against determined and well-armed opponents along vast frontiers in desert conditions and great heat in the south and west, as well as in the freezing mountain borders of the north. While equipment, weapons, transport, and helicopters are not yet sufficient to create the mobile, flexible combat force so badly needed, the Iranian army continues to provide a tough and reliable fighting force for whatever operations it is called upon to carry out.

Revolutionary Guard Corps (IRGC)
In addition to the army, there is the Iranian Revolutionary Guard Corps (IRGC or *Pasdaran*). This corps has two armored, one mechanized infantry, one motorized infantry, and 23 infantry divisions deployed alongside the regular army in a parallel operational structure.

Southern Operations Sector
The Southern Operations Sector contains another armored division, the 81st, and one commando brigade.

This Sector faces the southern Iraqi border and the northern Gulf Coast, and has its headquarters in Dezful, only 118 miles (190 km) from the Iraqi city of Basra.

Northern Operations Sector
Operations against Kurdish separatist insurgents in Iranian Kurdistan, and the overall security of the borders with Turkey and Azerbaijan, are the responsibility of the Northern Operations Sector, with its headquarters in Reyaiyeh. The forces under its control include the 28th Mechanized Infantry Division, the 64th Infantry Division,

and several independent infantry and commando brigades.

Other border deployments
The breakdown of relations with the Taliban since their takeover of Afghanistan has severely complicated the operational deployment of the Iranian forces. Limited operations have been conducted along the Afghan border in recent years, resulting in several clashes with Taliban forces. Iran now deploys the 88th Armored Division and two full infantry divisions, the 30th and 77th, in this once peaceful region. However, operations in any of these sectors can only be

supported by the one mobile reaction force available, the Airborne Forces Group, with the 29th Airmobile Commando Division and the 55th Airborne Division, effectively an elite infantry unit.

Other deployments abroad
The only Iranian military presence known to be serving abroad are some 50 personnel training the Sudanese army and 350 Revolutionary Guards serving with the Hezbollah terrorist movement in Lebanon.

Weapons and units / overview of an army

The current strength of the Iranian army is 325,000, with some 240,000 personnel available for combat duty. The present army and Revolutionary Guard combat units, many of which are under strength, are further hindered by a lack of modern equipment and training, and are still nowhere near having a genuine war fighting capability.

Army units

The present organization has

4 corps headquarters

4 armored divisions

6 infantry divisions

1 commando division

1 special forces division

1 airborne brigade

5 artillery groups

The Revolutionary Guard has a further 100,000 personnel organized into

2 armored divisions

2 mechanized divisions

23 infantry divisions

Iran produces a modified version of the Russian-designed SS-1 short-range ballistic missile. It is seen here on its MAZ-543 TEL-transporter and launch vehicle.

Average allocation Armor, artillery, and helicopters within each brigade

Armored Divisions

Armored brigades
- **72** M60/Chieftain/T72/Type-59 main battle tanks
- **30** BMP-1/2 armored infantry fighting vehicles

Mechanized infantry brigades
- **120** M113/BTR50/BTR60 armored personnel carriers

Artillery battalions
- **40** M109 155mm self-propelled
- **15** M107/M110 175mm/203mm self-propelled
- **50** 130mm M46 towed

Infantry Divisions

Infantry brigades
No armored vehicles

Artillery battalions
- **30** 130mm M46 towed
- **10** Type-63 MRLS

Commando Division

Assault brigades
No armored vehicles

Special forces division
No permanently attached heavy weapons

Special forces brigades
- **30** Scorpion light tanks
- **10** Cascavel reconnaissance

Airborne brigade
No permanently attached heavy weapons

Airborne battlions
- Attached mechanized battalion
No armored vehicles

Infantry small arms

9mm M1911 automatic pistols

9mm Uzi sub-machine guns

9mm M3A1 sub-machine guns

7.62mm AK47/Type-56 automatic rifles

7.62mm G3 automatic rifles

7.62mm RPK machine guns

7.62mm MG1A1 machine guns

12.7mm M2 HB heavy machine guns

KEY 🛩 Airborne 🚙 Armor ⌐ Infantry 🔫 Artillery ◁ Missiles

Firepower   The cutting edge

Airborne	Armor	Infantry	Artillery	Missiles

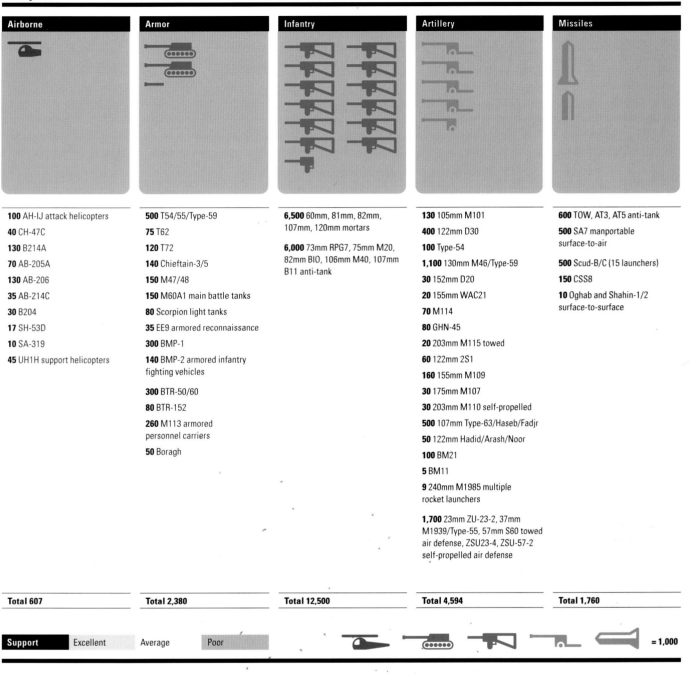

Airborne

100 AH-IJ attack helicopters
40 CH-47C
130 B214A
70 AB-205A
130 AB-206
35 AB-214C
30 B204
17 SH-53D
10 SA-319
45 UH1H support helicopters

Armor

500 T54/55/Type-59
75 T62
120 T72
140 Chieftain-3/5
150 M47/48
150 M60A1 main battle tanks
80 Scorpion light tanks
35 EE9 armored reconnaissance
300 BMP-1
140 BMP-2 armored infantry fighting vehicles
300 BTR-50/60
80 BTR-152
260 M113 armored personnel carriers
50 Boragh

Infantry

6,500 60mm, 81mm, 82mm, 107mm, 120mm mortars

6,000 73mm RPG7, 75mm M20, 82mm BIO, 106mm M40, 107mm B11 anti-tank

Artillery

130 105mm M101
400 122mm D30
100 Type-54
1,100 130mm M46/Type-59
30 152mm D20
20 155mm WAC21
70 M114
80 GHN-45
20 203mm M115 towed
60 122mm 2S1
160 155mm M109
30 175mm M107
30 203mm M110 self-propelled
500 107mm Type-63/Haseb/Fadjr
50 122mm Hadid/Arash/Noor
100 BM21
5 BM11
9 240mm M1985 multiple rocket launchers

1,700 23mm ZU-23-2, 37mm M1939/Type-55, 57mm S60 towed air defense, ZSU23-4, ZSU-57-2 self-propelled air defense

Missiles

600 TOW, AT3, AT5 anti-tank
500 SA7 manportable surface-to-air
500 Scud-B/C (15 launchers)
150 CSS8
10 Oghab and Shahin-1/2 surface-to-surface

Total 607   **Total 2,380**   **Total 12,500**   **Total 4,594**   **Total 1,760**

Support	Excellent	Average	Poor		= 1,000

The GHN-45 155mm gun-howitzer is an extremely powerful artillery weapon. It is in service with both Iran and Iraq, and has—with the use of specially enhanced ammunition —a range of up to 39km (24 miles).

BMP-2 Armored Infantry Fighting Vehicle

Country of origin	Russia
First entered service	1980–81 with Russian army
Main armament	30mm cannon & 4 AT5 AT missiles
Max. road speed	39 mph (65km/h)
Max. range	360 miles (580km)
Crew	2+ 8 infantrymen

Thousands built, in service with at least 18 armies

◬ Fighting structure

The Iranian army, though strong in manpower terms, is still constrained by the years of war with Iraq (which saw the destruction of the old imperial forces), under-investment in new equipment, and an unwillingness to address the problems of the modern battlefield. However, there are now signs that the Iranian army is addressing these issues with some success.

A major restructuring of its main combat units deployed on the Iraq border is underway to try to create effective mobile armored divisions with mechanized infantry support and self-propelled artillery. Specialist mountain warfare and counter-insurgency units are now receiving new equipment and enhanced training for their roles on the Afghan border and the conflict with Kurdish guerrillas. Moreover, units deployed along the length of the Persian Gulf regularly carry out amphibious warfare training and those on the Straits of Hormuz are known to be equipped with an array of Chinese-supplied coast defense and anti-ship missiles.

Fighting Structure Overview

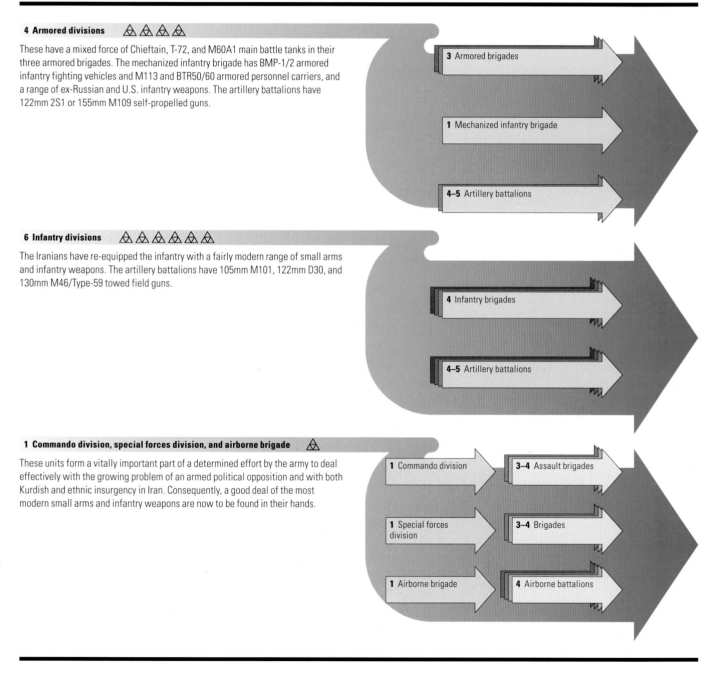

4 Armored divisions ◬ ◬ ◬ ◬

These have a mixed force of Chieftain, T-72, and M60A1 main battle tanks in their three armored brigades. The mechanized infantry brigade has BMP-1/2 armored infantry fighting vehicles and M113 and BTR50/60 armored personnel carriers, and a range of ex-Russian and U.S. infantry weapons. The artillery battalions have 122mm 2S1 or 155mm M109 self-propelled guns.

3 Armored brigades

1 Mechanized infantry brigade

4–5 Artillery battalions

6 Infantry divisions ◬ ◬ ◬ ◬ ◬ ◬

The Iranians have re-equipped the infantry with a fairly modern range of small arms and infantry weapons. The artillery battalions have 105mm M101, 122mm D30, and 130mm M46/Type-59 towed field guns.

4 Infantry brigades

4–5 Artillery battalions

1 Commando division, special forces division, and airborne brigade ◬

These units form a vitally important part of a determined effort by the army to deal effectively with the growing problem of an armed political opposition and with both Kurdish and ethnic insurgency in Iran. Consequently, a good deal of the most modern small arms and infantry weapons are now to be found in their hands.

1 Commando division   **3–4** Assault brigades

1 Special forces division   **3–4** Brigades

1 Airborne brigade   **4** Airborne battalions

🎖 Special forces

An overview of the Iranian special forces capability would see units that are equipped with a wide range of modern Western and Russian small arms, explosives, and communications. Training has traditionally concentrated on marksmanship, fitness, unarmed combat, combat swimming, and reliability. Many of the more technical and expensive aspects of special forces training that are accepted as a necessary part of an elite service, such as HALO (High Altitude Low Opening) parachute training are barely addressed. Iran simply does not have the infrastructure or finances to produce a true special forces capability at the present time. The current special forces, while tough, motivated, reliable, and with a considerable ability to conduct clandestine operations, lack the true special operations skills necessary to be considered an elite fighting force.

Special Operations Command

The Iranian Special Operations Command includes a full special forces division, with at least three light infantry brigades; in addition, the 23rd Commando Division has raised special forces units trained in mountain warfare, particularly along the border with Afghanistan.

Other special forces units

The 29th Airmobile Commando Division and the 55th Airborne Division are now usually deployed as elite infantry in support of counter-insurgency operations. Finally, there are four commando brigades and a number of special forces brigades. While there is an impressive list of units, most are not trained beyond the standard of good commando or elite infantry units.

Revolutionary Guards Corps

Within the Revolutionary Guards Corps *(Pasdaran Inqilab)* is a range of units, including one special forces division and five independent brigades, whose tasks go well beyond the normal range of special operations. These include maintaining Islamic purity, assassination, and the training, arming, and control of Islamic terrorist groups both within the Middle East and increasingly throughout the world. *Pasdaran* trained special forces personnel are attached to the main Iranian intelligence services, and often operate within Europe and the United States on clandestine intelligence-gathering and subversive missions.

Threat to oil supply

The 23rd Commando Division of the Iranian army's Special Operations Command includes a number of specialist assault and sabotage units whose main tasks are to destroy the oil platforms and giant tankers that crowd the narrow waters of the Arabian Gulf and the vital Straits of Hormuz. Other units would attempt an amphibious assault to occupy the southern coast of the straits in order to bring the waterway firmly under Iranian control.

Pasdaran, *Revolutionary Guards special forces unit, armed with Chinese Type-56 (AK47) assault rifles.*

Iraq

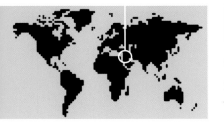

Iraq had one of the largest armies in the world in 1990, but by the end of the Gulf War in 1991, Iraq found its remaining forces in disarray. They were beset on all sides by enemies—the Turks in the north, Iranians to the east and south, Saudis, Kuwaitis, the U.S.-led Western Allies to the south and west, and Israel.

Even now only Jordan and (increasingly) Syria are considered military allies. There was also internal unrest within Iraq itself, with rebellion by Kurdish independence groups in the north and by the oppressed minority Shi'ite Muslim sect in the south.

It is against this background that President Saddam Hussein launched the rebuilding of the most loyal of the Republican Guard divisions, and then re-equipping the shattered Iraqi army. And despite United Nations embargoes, the shortfall in oil revenues, and the well-earned status as an international pariah state, the Iraqi armed forces have been rebuilt.

The Republican Guard was first restored to near full strength by stripping army units of their finest remaining weapons. They were then given the first consignments of illegally obtained arms, mainly smuggled in from Russia and Ukraine, usually via the Turkish border that was supposedly being closely monitored by the U.S. and the United Nations. These additional weapons

allowed the Republican Guards to quickly and brutally suppress the Shi'ite rebellion in and around the southern city of Basra in 1991–92 and within the no-fly zone (imposed by the Western Allies to directly protect the Shi'ite community). Saddam Hussein was then able to play one group of Kurds off against the other, and with limited but timely intervention by Republican Guard units, ensured the success of his strategy to re-establish Iraqi authority throughout Kurdish territory. These operations, conducted almost entirely by the elite guards and special forces units, also gave the shattered Iraqi army the valuable time it needed to rebuild and restore its forces into some semblance of military effectiveness.

The present Iraqi army has thus regained a measure of combat respectability. It is slowly gaining strength and better equipment, and is absorbing the lessons of the Gulf War.

Flashpoints and deployments

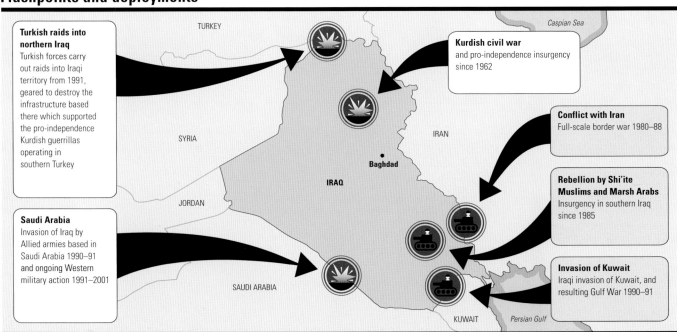

Turkish raids into northern Iraq
Turkish forces carry out raids into Iraqi territory from 1991, geared to destroy the infrastructure based there which supported the pro-independence Kurdish guerrillas operating in southern Turkey

Saudi Arabia
Invasion of Iraq by Allied armies based in Saudi Arabia 1990–91 and ongoing Western military action 1991–2001

Kurdish civil war
and pro-independence insurgency since 1962

Conflict with Iran
Full-scale border war 1980–88

Rebellion by Shi'ite Muslims and Marsh Arabs
Insurgency in southern Iraq since 1985

Invasion of Kuwait
Iraqi invasion of Kuwait, and resulting Gulf War 1990–91

TURKEY
Caspian Sea
SYRIA
IRAN
Baghdad
IRAQ
JORDAN
SAUDI ARABIA
KUWAIT
Persian Gulf

⚑ Operations

The Iraqi army has been on operational duty for most of the past 25 years, either dealing with internal Kurdish or Shi'ite insurgencies or with external conflicts with Iran, or the U.S.-led Gulf War Allies. In fact, the present army continues to face the same threats and problems, and its operational deployments strongly reflect this.

Chinese Type-59/69 main battle tank from a front line armored unit operating in flat desert in southern Iraq.

Main deployments

Apart from its obvious role in helping to ensure the survival of its commander-in-chief Saddam Hussein and his successor(s), the army is also heavily committed in the two sectors covering the Kurdish provinces.

The divisions deployed in these areas are:

1st Corps, headquarters in Kirkuk in northeastern Kurdistan, with the
• 5th Mechanized Division, and the 2nd, 8th, and 38th Infantry Divisions.

The 5th Corps, headquarters in Mosul in northwestern Kurdistan, with the
• 1st Mechanized Division and the 4th, 7th, and 16th Infantry Divisions.

These divisions are supported by the Republican Guards Northern Corps, covering the Kurdish areas with the 2nd "Al-Medinah" Armored Division, 17th "Adnam" Mechanized Division, and the 5th "Baghdad" Motorized Division.

Deployments to the south

The operational deployment of Iraqi forces in the south is greatly complicated by a three-fold threat—the Shi'ite rebellion, the threat of war with Iran, and the continuing confrontation with Saudi Arabia and the Western Allies over Kuwait. Three corps cover this area:

The 2nd Corps at Diwaniyah with the
• 3rd Armored Division, and 15th and 34th Infantry Divisions.

The 3rd Corps at Al-Naserria with the
• 6th Armored Division, 51st Mechanized Infantry, and 11th Infantry Divisions.

The 4th Corps at Al-Amara with the
• 10th Armored Division, and the 14th and 18th Infantry Divisions.

Again support comes from the Republican Guard Southern Corps with the "Al-Nedaa" Armored Division, the 1st "Hammurabi" Mechanized and 6th "Nebuchanezzer" Motorized Infantry Divisions.

The Iraqi army has made a considerable effort to rebuild after the Gulf War. However, while the main combat units have been restructured and redeployed, they still remain operationally limited by a lack of mobility, modern weapons,

and secure communications and command. Operationally, the Iraqi army can still secure the nation against successful insurrection, and deal with any potential threat from Iran, but it would not have much of a war-fighting capability against the Western Allies.

Iraq may rattle its sabers occasionally, and indeed did so in February 2001. The Iraqi 10th Armored Division and the Republican Guard *"Al-Nedaa"* Armored Division were deployed in western Iraq, ready to cross the Syrian border to support the Syrian army in the event of an Israeli attack (at this time, this

was a scenario considered likely by both the Syrian president and the Iraqi government). Iraq may also build up its forces on its southern border and create a sufficient threat to tie down the Allied forces in the Gulf. However, although this may draw Western attention away from developments elsewhere in the Middle East, it is highly unlikely that Iraqi tanks will be seen rolling across the Kuwait border in the near future.

A captured Iraqi 2SI 122mm self-propelled gun. Built in Russia, these effective weapons added greatly to the artillery's mobility in supporting armored operations.

Decisive battle

The Battle of Al Faw took place during the latter part of the Iraq-Iran war of 1980–88. This was the first part of the Iraqi army's final major offensive that was to end the war in a stalemate. Iraq used a two-corps force of the Republican Guards and the 7th Army Corps, massing 200,000 troops with huge artillery and attack helicopter support. This force, together with the widespread use of chemical weapons, finally broke the Iranian defenders who fled the battlefield leaving some 10,000 casualties behind.

🏴 Weapons and units / overview of an army

The current strength of the Iraqi army is 375,000, with about 280,000 personnel available for front-line duty. The Iraqi army has made a great effort to rebuild its combat formations following their decimation in the Gulf War. They have managed to acquire or build a relatively large amount of new equipment, but nowhere near enough to return the army to its pre-1991 firepower. However, Iraq is also still pursuing its long-term aim of developing a substantial ballistic missile capability, armed with chemical warfare or eventually nuclear warheads, despite UN sanctions.

Army units

The present organization has

7 corps under which are	
3 armored divisions	
3 mechanized divisions	
11 infantry divisions	
6 Republican Guard divisions	
7 Commando brigades	
2 Special forces brigades	

Captured Russian-built T72 main battle tanks armed with smoothbore 125mm guns. They proved surprisingly vulnerable to allied anti-tank operations in the Gulf War of 1991.

Average allocation Armor, artillery, and helicopters within each brigade

Armored Divisions

2 Armored brigades
- **150** T-55/T-62/Type59 main battle tanks
- **50** BTR60/152 OT62/64
- **20** BRDM/Sagger anti-tank guided weapons, self-propelled

Mechanized infantry brigade
- **100** BTR50/152, OT62/64 or M113 armored personnel carriers
- **50** BRDM-2 /AML90 reconnaissance

Artillery battalions
- **24** 122mm D30/74 or 130mm M46 towed
- **10** multiple launching rocket systems

Mechanized Infantry Divisions

Mechanized brigades
- **100** BTR50/152 OT62/64 or M113 armored personnel carriers
- **50** BRDM-2, AML60/90 or Cascavel reconnaissance

Armored brigade
- **50** T-55/T-62/Type-59 main battle tanks or M113 armored personnel carriers

4 Artillery battalions
- **24** 122mm D30/74 or 130mm M46 towed
- **10** multiple launching rocket systems

Infantry Divisions

3 Infantry brigades
- No armored vehicles

Tank battalion
- **30** T-55 main battle tanks

4 Artillery battalions
- **24** 122mm D30/74, 130mm M46, and 155mm G5/M114 towed
- **10** multiple rocket launching systems

Republican Guard Armored Division

3 Armored brigades
- **80** T-72 main battle tanks
- **30** BMP2 armored infantry fighting vehicles
- **50** BTR60/MTLB armored personnel carriers
- **10** VCTH/HOT anti-tank guided weapons, self-propelled

Mechanized brigade
- **150** BMP1/2 armored infantry fighting vehicles
- **100** BTR60/MTLB armored personnel carriers

3 Self-propelled artillery battalions
- **15** 122mm 2S1, 152mm 2S5, and 155mm M109 self-propelled
- **15** multiple rocket launching systems

Air defense brigade
- **30** ZSU-23-4 SP AA guns
- **10** SA-13 SP SAM launchers

Attack helicopter regiment
- **40** BO105/HOT, Mi-24, and SA3I6 helicopter gunships

Infantry small arms

9mm APS automatic pistols
9mm PM automatic pistols
7.62mm SKS carbines
7.62mm AK/AKMS automatic rifles
5.45mm AK74 automatic rifles
7.62mm RPK machine guns
5.45mm RPK74 machine guns
7.62mm PK/PKM machine guns
12.7mm DSHK heavy machine guns

KEY 🪂 Airborne   🔫 Armor   🔫 Infantry   🔫 Artillery   ◁ Missiles

Firepower   The cutting edge

Airborne	Armor	Infantry	Artillery	Missiles

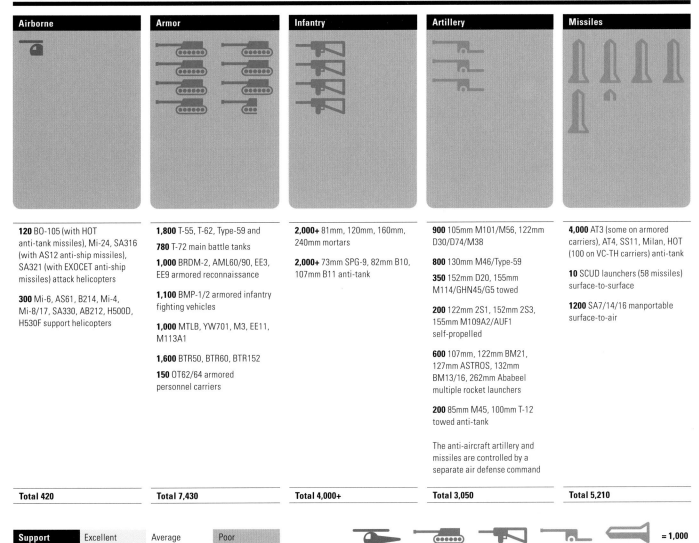

120 BO-105 (with HOT anti-tank missiles), Mi-24, SA316 (with AS12 anti-ship missiles), SA321 (with EXOCET anti-ship missiles) attack helicopters

300 Mi-6, AS61, B214, Mi-4, Mi-8/17, SA330, AB212, H500D, H530F support helicopters

1,800 T-55, T-62, Type-59 and
780 T-72 main battle tanks
1,000 BRDM-2, AML60/90, EE3, EE9 armored reconnaissance
1,100 BMP-1/2 armored infantry fighting vehicles
1,000 MTLB, YW701, M3, EE11, M113A1
1,600 BTR50, BTR60, BTR152
150 OT62/64 armored personnel carriers

2,000+ 81mm, 120mm, 160mm, 240mm mortars

2,000+ 73mm SPG-9, 82mm B10, 107mm B11 anti-tank

900 105mm M101/M56, 122mm D30/D74/M38
800 130mm M46/Type-59
350 152mm D20, 155mm M114/GHN45/G5 towed
200 122mm 2S1, 152mm 2S3, 155mm M109A2/AUF1 self-propelled
600 107mm, 122mm BM21, 127mm ASTROS, 132mm BM13/16, 262mm Ababeel multiple rocket launchers
200 85mm M45, 100mm T-12 towed anti-tank

The anti-aircraft artillery and missiles are controlled by a separate air defense command

4,000 AT3 (some on armored carriers), AT4, SS11, Milan, HOT (100 on VC-TH carriers) anti-tank

10 SCUD launchers (58 missiles) surface-to-surface

1200 SA7/14/16 manportable surface-to-air

Total 420 | **Total 7,430** | **Total 4,000+** | **Total 3,050** | **Total 5,210**

| Support | Excellent | Average | Poor | | | | | | = 1,000 |

The Austrian GHN.45 155mm gun-Howitzer has seen considerable service with the Iraqi army. It has proved accurate and reliable in combat.

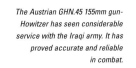

Mi-24 'HIND-D' Armed Helicopter

Country of origin	Russia
First entered service	1976 with Russian army
Main armament	30mm cannon & 12 AT-6 AT missiles
Max. speed	200 mph (335 km/h)
Max. range	570 miles (917 km) w/ external tanks
Crew	2+ up to 8 airborne troops

Thousands built, in service with at least 34 armies

◭ Fighting structure

After having so many of its armored units devastated in a matter of hours by Allied forces in 1991, Iraq has struggled to adapt its forces for the modern battlefield. However, as result of sanctions imposed by the West, it proved extremely difficult at first for Iraqi forces to replace or repair any major equipment.

More recently, however, Iraq has seen increasing success in rearming its major units. This is largely because many original infantry divisons have now been disbanded, and the emphasis has been placed on upgrading a growing number of armored, mechanized, and artillery units. Restructuring them fully into a modern integrated fighting force, however, is still quite a way off, although the Republican Guard is known to be back to full strength.

Fighting Structure Overview

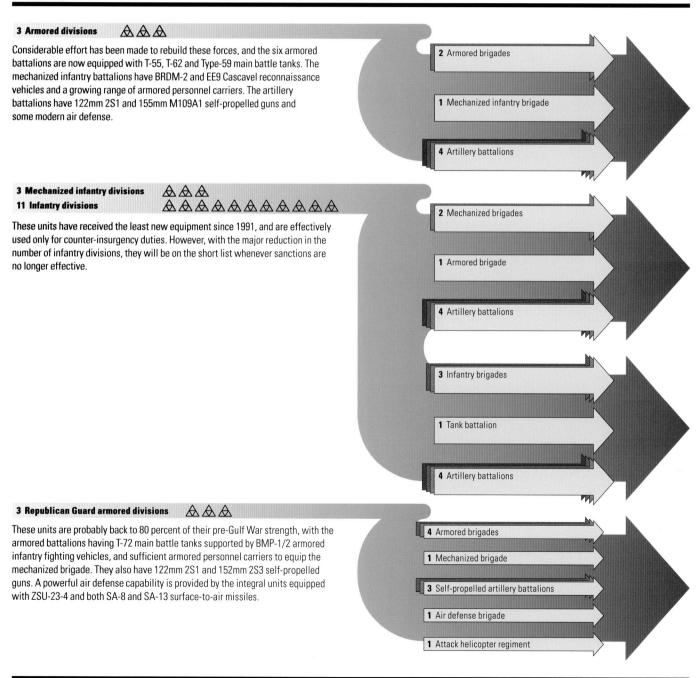

3 Armored divisions ◬ ◬ ◬

Considerable effort has been made to rebuild these forces, and the six armored battalions are now equipped with T-55, T-62 and Type-59 main battle tanks. The mechanized infantry battalions have BRDM-2 and EE9 Cascavel reconnaissance vehicles and a growing range of armored personnel carriers. The artillery battalions have 122mm 2S1 and 155mm M109A1 self-propelled guns and some modern air defense.

- 2 Armored brigades
- 1 Mechanized infantry brigade
- 4 Artillery battalions

3 Mechanized infantry divisions ◬ ◬ ◬
11 Infantry divisions ◬ ◬ ◬ ◬ ◬ ◬ ◬ ◬ ◬ ◬ ◬

These units have received the least new equipment since 1991, and are effectively used only for counter-insurgency duties. However, with the major reduction in the number of infantry divisions, they will be on the short list whenever sanctions are no longer effective.

- 2 Mechanized brigades
- 1 Armored brigade
- 4 Artillery battalions

- 3 Infantry brigades
- 1 Tank battalion
- 4 Artillery battalions

3 Republican Guard armored divisions ◬ ◬ ◬

These units are probably back to 80 percent of their pre-Gulf War strength, with the armored battalions having T-72 main battle tanks supported by BMP-1/2 armored infantry fighting vehicles, and sufficient armored personnel carriers to equip the mechanized brigade. They also have 122mm 2S1 and 152mm 2S3 self-propelled guns. A powerful air defense capability is provided by the integral units equipped with ZSU-23-4 and both SA-8 and SA-13 surface-to-air missiles.

- 4 Armored brigades
- 1 Mechanized brigade
- 3 Self-propelled artillery battalions
- 1 Air defense brigade
- 1 Attack helicopter regiment

⚜ Special forces

The Iraqi special forces, having gained a considerable reputation during the 1980–88 war with Iran, made a surprisingly poor showing in the 1991 Gulf War. A major reorganization of these forces took place during the late 1990s to address the perceived weaknesses. Greater emphasis has been placed on physical fitness, mental toughness, and motivation, with the help of a small number of Russian ex-*Spetsnaz* Special Forces officers. The problems caused by United Nations sanctions have been partly overcome by the widespread black market smuggling of new weapons, communications, and other specialist equipment from Russia and Ukraine.

Under the control of the Office of the Presidential Palace, with headquarters in Baghdad, are a number of reliable special forces with just one major mission, the protection of Saddam Hussein. These units include the Green Berets or 33rd Special Forces Brigade, and the Special Republican Guard Motorized Infantry Brigade—both are rapid reaction units. Also part of the presidential garrison is the Special Forces Brigade, or Unit-999, which is a general security, motorized infantry brigade.

The main task for the Iraqi special forces, apart from protecting the President, is the suppression of insurgency and civil unrest. In the Kurdish areas of northern Iraq, special forces battalions with the 7th Adan Republican Guard Mechanized Infantry Division, along with an entire special forces brigade within the Alabad Motorized Infantry Division are deployed for clandestine penetration of Kurdish-held areas. Here they carry out acts of assassination, sabotage, intelligence-gathering, and psychological warfare. These units also keep close surveillance of the Turkish and Iranian border areas.

It is worth noting that Iraqi special forces have a wider range of duties than is normally found within similar elite formations. They are responsible for airborne and air assault operations, counter-insurgency, suppressing riots, and unconventional warfare. They carry out limited special operations within Iraq and overseas, deep penetration raids, long-range reconnaissance, and ambushes deep behind enemy lines. There are also specially trained detachments for dedicated counter-terrorist and hostage rescue operations, as well as for presidential and VIP protection.

Iraqi special forces are still constrained by a shortage of high-mobility helicopter support and a lack of overall logistical support for critical operations. Considerable efforts have been made to improve overall standards and overcome sanctions, and these forces are once again becoming an effective and reliable prop for Saddam Hussein's regime. However, they remain with a severely limited ability to operate outside national boundaries.

Covert operations

The Special Forces Brigade belonging to the 7th Adan Republican Guards Mechanized Division has a number of highly specialized units tasked for deep penetration into Kurdish territory. Similar to the concept of the NATO LRRP (Long Range Reconnaissance Patrol), these units contain both Kurdish and Turkish speaking personnel. Regular special cross-border operations have been carried out into Turkey in order to keep close surveillance on Kurdish fighters and NATO operations from Turkish airbases.

Iraqi MIi-8/17 armed helicopter in camouflage mode. It has proved useful for special forces operations, particularly against the Kurdish guerillas.

Israel

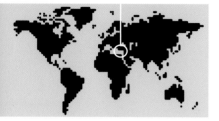

The Israeli army has been the effective regional superpower in the Middle East since its outstandingly successful armored blitzkrieg against Egypt, Jordan, and Syria in the Six Day War of 1967. With the exception of some severe initial defeats inflicted by Egypt in the early days of the 1973 war in the Sinai, and the near defeat at the hands of the Syrians on the Golan Heights, the Israeli army has largely remained a dominant force ever since.

However, the Israeli army does have some serious problems to resolve. These have been largely caused by the long, bloody, and ultimately disastrous campaign in Lebanon, which has had a steady, corrosive effect on the army. The invasion of Lebanon in 1982 eventually led Israeli forces to the outskirts of the capital, Beirut, and the large-scale destruction of much of the city. The campaign had been designed to defeat *Fatah*, the Palestinian guerrilla organization, and to prevent further shelling of the towns and settlements in northern Israel. This and similar operations were to result in the occupation of much of the southern half of Lebanon, with regular clashes with Arab guerrillas and Syrian forces in the Bekaa Valley area further to the east, and the militarization of the whole of Lebanon for a generation. It was also to turn into Israel's own Vietnam, and proved to be a huge drain on the small nation's finances and its army's manpower. The campaign was to end some 18 years later, with the rather ignominious and hurried withdrawal of Israeli forces and their allies, the South Lebanese army, from their heavily defended positions in Lebanon in the year 2000.

Flashpoints and deployments

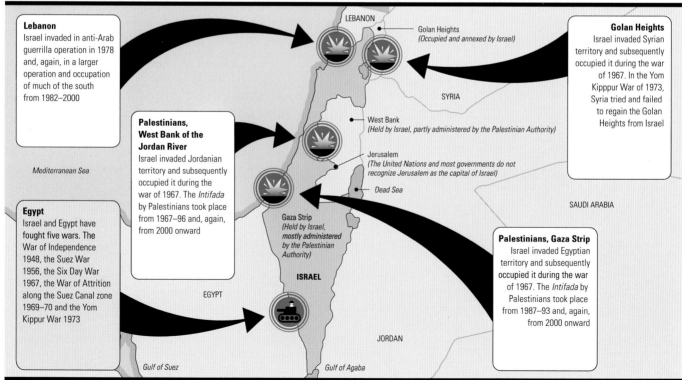

Lebanon
Israel invaded in anti-Arab guerrilla operation in 1978 and, again, in a larger operation and occupation of much of the south from 1982–2000

Golan Heights
Israel invaded Syrian territory and subsequently occupied it during the war of 1967. In the Yom Kipppur War of 1973, Syria tried and failed to regain the Golan Heights from Israel

Golan Heights
(Occupied and annexed by Israel)

LEBANON

SYRIA

West Bank
(Held by Israel, partly administered by the Palestinian Authority)

Jerusalem
(The United Nations and most governments do not recognize Jerusalem as the capital of Israel)

Dead Sea

SAUDI ARABIA

Palestinians, West Bank of the Jordan River
Israel invaded Jordanian territory and subsequently occupied it during the war of 1967. The *Intifada* by Palestinians took place from 1967–96 and, again, from 2000 onward

Mediterranean Sea

Gaza Strip
(Held by Israel, mostly administered by the Palestinian Authority)

Egypt
Israel and Egypt have fought five wars. The War of Independence 1948, the Suez War 1956, the Six Day War 1967, the War of Attrition along the Suez Canal zone 1969–70 and the Yom Kippur War 1973

Palestinians, Gaza Strip
Israel invaded Egyptian territory and subsequently occupied it during the war of 1967. The *Intifada* by Palestinians took place from 1987–93 and, again, from 2000 onward

ISRAEL

EGYPT

JORDAN

Gulf of Suez

Gulf of Aqaba

Live or die

When trying to understand Israel and the deployments of its army it is as well to remember its "Defense Strategy." This is that Israel cannot lose a single war! If war breaks out, then Israel must defeat the enemy quickly and decisively. Since it lacks strategic depth, Israel must prevent any enemy from entering its territory, and must try to quickly transfer the battle to enemy territory. The Israeli Defense Forces and the nation itself will live or die by that policy.

U.S.-built M60A1 main battle tanks deploy for combat with an Israeli armored brigade based on the Golan Heights in northern Israel.

This debacle has to be viewed alongside the Palestinian *Intifada*, or uprising, in the territories of the West Bank of the Jordan River and the Gaza Strip, which were occupied by the Israeli army in the 1967 war. The *Intifada* began in December 1987, when an Israeli truck drove into, and killed, four Palestinians. The violence spread and grew to a point that was to shock most ordinary Israelis. It was finally brought to an end by the Oslo Agreement signed between Israel and the Palestinians in September 1993. The agreement brought a temporary end to the conflict and established the new Palestinian Authority, which was to provide a limited degree of self-rule on the West Bank and in the Gaza Strip. The resumption of fighting and the obvious seriousness of the new *Intifada* in the Israeli occupied areas in September 2000 has quickly led to a growing disillusionment with the chances of ever achieving a peaceful solution, and also with the military alternative, long looked upon as the quick fix for so many of Israel's problems.

A reaction of anti-militarism has grown among many young Israelis, along with higher levels of draft dodging, a shocking symptom of a national malaise to many older Israelis. The additional awareness that Arab armies are growing in self-belief and combat effectiveness has created an atmosphere of uncertainty in Israel and the belief that any future war will not be the pushover of previous encounters.

However, even taking all these factors into account, the Israeli army still largely remains a cohesive, well-trained, and highly motivated force capable of ultimately dominating any potential Middle Eastern battlefield. Its powerful armored corps, a strike force still unmatched by any possible opponent, will continue, with the addition of elite infantry, mobile artillery, and attack helicopters, to be the deciding factor in any future Israeli victory.

Operations

The Israeli army's operational deployment is largely governed by the narrow strip of territory it has to defend, which at its narrowest is only about 12 miles wide. There is no room to be able to defend in depth, no room for fortifications, and therefore no ability to buy time to allow the international community to come to Israel's aid, or arrange a cease-fire, before the country is overrun. Thus, the Israeli army has to carry the fighting outside its own borders in order to survive. This driving need has created a force that is on constant alert, capable of bringing its reserve formations up to strength and into the front line within hours. Without a doubt, the Israeli army is truly the nation's shield.

The raid on Entebbe

Although it was not the first successful action against terrorists, the Israeli military raid on the Ugandan airport at Entebbe has become famous. An Air France jet with 254 passengers on board was hijacked on June 27, 1976. Although 151 were released, the remaining 103 hostages were in real danger. Israel staged a daring long-range operation to rescue them. Troops from the Golani and 35th Parachute Brigades flew the vast distance in C130 aircraft, successfully eliminated the terrorists and their Ugandan army supporters, destroyed 11 Ugandan MiG fighters, and with minimal casualties rescued the remaining hostages.

Israeli infantry on combat patrol in an occupied West Bank village, armed with an Israeli-made Galil automatic rifle and a U.S. M203 40mm grenade launcher.

An Israeli combat patrol from infantry brigade based in northern Israel, equipped with U.S. 5.56mm M16AI

Defending the Golan Heights

The Israeli army is naturally very sensitive about its current deployment of units, but it can be said with a degree of certainty that most regular brigades are deployed bearing in mind the threat of a Syrian armored thrust across the Golan Heights.

The elite 500th Armored Brigade is based at Bkhot Army Base in central Israel. The most famous of all Israeli armored units, the elite 7th Armored Brigade is actually based on the Golan Heights, where, in the 1973 Yom Kippur War, it largely saved Israel from total defeat in the early hours of the first day by holding back an attack by over 800 Syrian tanks.

Regular combat formations

There are four regular infantry brigades, with both the elite Golani Brigade and the Givaty Brigade based in northern Israel and tasked for operations on the Golan Heights. The Nahal Brigade is held in reserve in central Israel and, finally, there is the T'zanhanim Parachute Infantry Brigade, which acts as a strategic reserve unit, ready to deploy to any front in a crisis.

Defending the Gaza Strip and the West Bank

As part of the growing need for units trained to deal with insurgency problems caused by the Palestinian *Intifada*, the Israeli army now has two operational, divisional-sized commands covering the occupied territories of the Gaza Strip and the West Bank. In order to provide these commands with an effective military capability, five new mechanized infantry battalions were formed in the mid-1990s: Harouv, Shimshon, Rimon, Ducifhat, and Nachshon. While all are capable of carrying out counter-insurgency operations, they are not true special forces units, and are therefore conventionally trained as mechanized infantry units as well.

Other deployments

Israel's army will continue to be deployed to conduct mainly armored warfare operations in the north against Syria, but it maintains the outstanding ability to switch large forces south very quickly in the event of a renewed conflict with Egypt. Because the elite infantry and parachute units, supported by armored forces and attack helicopters, are constantly on alert for operations into Lebanon or elsewhere, the Israeli army is very much a lion that now always sleeps with one eye open!

Daring to succeed

During the so-called War of Attrition from 1969–1970, the Israelis made a number of daring raids deep into Egyptian territory. The most audacious of these occurred in December 1969, when a group of elite commandos and engineers landed on the Egyptian coast and attacked a radar site near Ras Gharib. Here they captured a new Soviet P-12 radar, dismantled it and returned safely to Israel in one of the intelligence coups of the decade.

The Israeli-built Merkava-2 main battle tank, with its highly effective 120mm gun, forms the backbone of the tank corps.

Weapons and units / overview of an army

The Israeli army is 130,000 strong, but can mobilize a further 400,000 trained reserves within a matter of days, virtually all of whom are available for combat duties. The army has a well-earned reputation for being able to make the best use of not only indigenous production, but also imported and captured weaponry, often improving the equipment to suit Israel's own specialist needs. Israel is also understood to have around 100 nuclear warheads, and, together with 20 U.S. Lance short-range missiles, now has a growing number of Jericho-1/2 medium-range ballistic missiles.

Army units

The present organization has

3 territorial and **1** home front commands, organized into

    3 operational corps with a total of

        3 armored divisions

        2 divisional headquarters controlling anti-*Intifada* units in Gaza and the West Bank

    3 regional infantry division headquarters controlling border defense units

    4 mechanized infantry brigades including

        1 parachute-trained

    3 artillery battalions with multiple launching rocket systems

These units can be reinforced by

8 full armored divisions

1 air-mobile mechanized division

10 regional infantry brigades, each tasked to defend a sector of Israel's border

An Israeli tank unit deploys its heavily protected U.S. M60A3 battle tanks in the Neqev Desert.

Average allocation Armor, artillery, and helicopters within each brigade

Armored Division

Regular

- **350** Merkava or M60A3 main battle tanks
- **450** M113A1/2 armored personnel carriers
- **72** 155mm M109 self-propelled artillery
- **24** 227mm MLRS/160mm LAR160 mulitiple rocket launchers

Reserve

- **350** Merkava/M60/M48/ Centurion main battle tanks
- **350** M113 armored personnel carriers
- **72** 155mm M109/L33 self-propelled artillery

Airmobile Divisions

Armored vehicles attached when required

COIN Divisions (COunter INsurgency)

The constituent brigades each have:

- **150** M48/Ti-67/T62 main battle tanks
- **200** BTR50, PUMA, M113 armored personnel carriers and M3 armored half-tracks

As these divisions are used in an anti-Intifada role, in most cases the heavier armor is not deployed.

Infantry small arms

9mm Beretta 951 automatic pistols

9mm UZI/mini UZI sub-machine guns

5.56mm M16A1 automatic rifles

5.56mm GALIL automatic rifles

7.62mm FAL automatic rifles

7.62mm AK47/AKM automatic rifles

7.62mm FALO heavy automatic rifles

7.62mm MAG machine guns

7.62mm PK machine guns

12.7mm M2 HB heavy machine guns

KEY ⬟ Airborne ⬟ Armor ⬟ Infantry ⬟ Artillery ⬟ Missiles

Firepower   The cutting edge

Airborne	Armor	Infantry	Artillery	Missiles

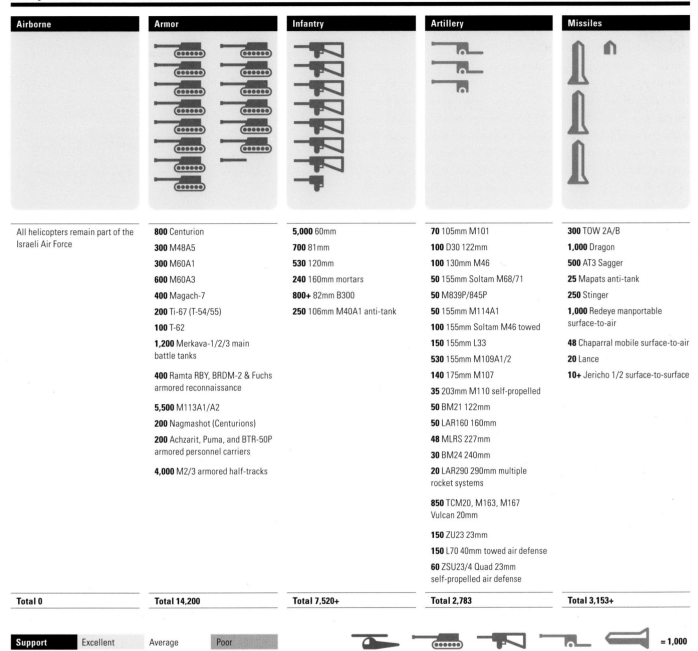

Airborne	Armor	Infantry	Artillery	Missiles
All helicopters remain part of the Israeli Air Force	**800** Centurion	**5,000** 60mm	**70** 105mm M101	**300** TOW 2A/B
	300 M48A5	**700** 81mm	**100** D30 122mm	**1,000** Dragon
	300 M60A1	**530** 120mm	**100** 130mm M46	**500** AT3 Sagger
	600 M60A3	**240** 160mm mortars	**50** 155mm Soltam M68/71	**25** Mapats anti-tank
	400 Magach-7	**800+** 82mm B300	**50** M839P/845P	**250** Stinger
	200 Ti-67 (T-54/55)	**250** 106mm M40A1 anti-tank	**50** 155mm M114A1	**1,000** Redeye manportable surface-to-air
	100 T-62		**100** 155mm Soltam M46 towed	**48** Chaparral mobile surface-to-air
	1,200 Merkava-1/2/3 main battle tanks		**150** 155mm L33	**20** Lance
	400 Ramta RBY, BRDM-2 & Fuchs armored reconnaissance		**530** 155mm M109A1/2	**10+** Jericho 1/2 surface-to-surface
	5,500 M113A1/A2		**140** 175mm M107	
	200 Nagmashot (Centurions)		**35** 203mm M110 self-propelled	
	200 Achzarit, Puma, and BTR-50P armored personnel carriers		**50** BM21 122mm	
	4,000 M2/3 armored half-tracks		**50** LAR160 160mm	
			48 MLRS 227mm	
			30 BM24 240mm	
			20 LAR290 290mm multiple rocket systems	
			850 TCM20, M163, M167 Vulcan 20mm	
			150 ZU23 23mm	
			150 L70 40mm towed air defense	
			60 ZSU23/4 Quad 23mm self-propelled air defense	
Total 0	**Total 14,200**	**Total 7,520+**	**Total 2,783**	**Total 3,153+**

Support	Excellent	Average	Poor

= 1,000

Merkava Mk-3/4 Main Battle Tank

Country of origin Israel	
First entered service 1980 with Israeli army	
Main armament 105mm M68 gun (85 rounds)	
Max. road speed 29 mph (46 km/h)	
Max. range 240 miles (400 km)	
Crew 4	
More than 1,200 built so far	

Israeli-built Merkava main battle tanks were specifically designed with extra thick frontal armor and a very large ammunition capability for its 120mm main gun.

▲ Fighting structure

No army has been so frequently battle-tested, or has had to absorb so many hard-learned lessons into the very fabric of the organization, training, and equipment of its major units, than that of Israel. The threat posed to Israel, with so little land to defend in depth, has created an army constantly poised to fight its battles on its neighbor's territory. A number of armored brigades (and Israel has a higher percentage of tank units than any other army) are in constant readiness. While yet more units, with tanks and artillery already positioned, require less than 48 hours' notice for well-trained reservists to turn them into fully operational combat units.

Israel has a very special army, with an often original approach to tactics, unit structures, and equipment. While the armed forces face the problem of a growing unwillingness among the country's youth to accept military service, Israel continues to maintain one of the world's most effective fighting forces.

A column of Centurion main battle tanks from an Israeli reserve armored brigade moves quickly toward its front-line combat position.

Armored fist

Israel's armored formations have a unique organization. With the exception of a limited number of full-time units, most are made up of a nucleus of regulars and the remainder are businessmen, teachers, lawyers, gardeners, mailmen, and a vast range of other civilians. The armored vehicles, superbly maintained, are pre-positioned in front-line bases and can be operational within a matter of hours.

The Israeli-built MAR-290 multiple rocket launching system has four 15.5 mile (25km)-range, 290mm projectiles mounted on a converted Centurion tank chassis.

Fighting Structure Overview

3 Armored divisions (Combat ready divisions)

The Israeli army's armored divisions are probably some of the most effective combat units in the world today. Its armored brigades are equipped with Israel's own Merkava—1/2/3 main battle tank—and the artillery brigade with 155mm M109A1/2 self-propelled guns. A third armored brigade and a mechanized infantry brigade (which are added on mobilization) create an immensely powerful and self-sufficient formation, capable of lightning responses and fearsome firepower.

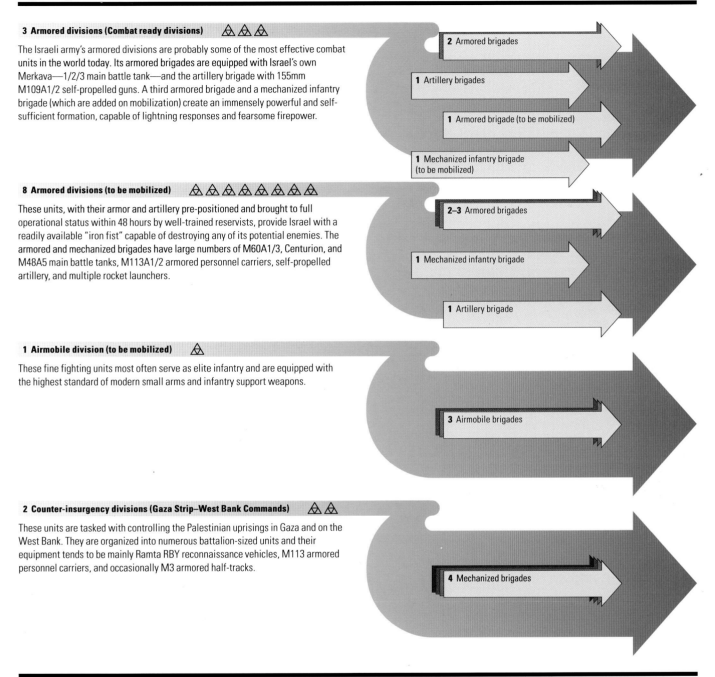

2 Armored brigades

1 Artillery brigades

1 Armored brigade (to be mobilized)

1 Mechanized infantry brigade (to be mobilized)

8 Armored divisions (to be mobilized)

These units, with their armor and artillery pre-positioned and brought to full operational status within 48 hours by well-trained reservists, provide Israel with a readily available "iron fist" capable of destroying any of its potential enemies. The armored and mechanized brigades have large numbers of M60A1/3, Centurion, and M48A5 main battle tanks, M113A1/2 armored personnel carriers, self-propelled artillery, and multiple rocket launchers.

2–3 Armored brigades

1 Mechanized infantry brigade

1 Artillery brigade

1 Airmobile division (to be mobilized)

These fine fighting units most often serve as elite infantry and are equipped with the highest standard of modern small arms and infantry support weapons.

3 Airmobile brigades

2 Counter-insurgency divisions (Gaza Strip–West Bank Commands)

These units are tasked with controlling the Palestinian uprisings in Gaza and on the West Bank. They are organized into numerous battalion-sized units and their equipment tends to be mainly Ramta RBY reconnaissance vehicles, M113 armored personnel carriers, and occasionally M3 armored half-tracks.

4 Mechanized brigades

The devastating firepower of the new AH-64D Apache Longbow helicopter gunships provide important extra anti tank capability.

Building the foundations

Probably the most famous unit in the Israeli army is the Golani Brigade. Formed on February 28, 1948, it was based in the valleys of Lower Galilee. It was made up of members of the Jewish Home Defense Organization *(Haganah)*, local settlers, and a number of ex-soldiers. New immigrants to Israel flocked to help, and many joined the Golani. Equipped with a few civilian trucks, old Czech rifles, and worn out Sten-guns, the fiercely determined volunteers first stopped, then defeated, the combined forces of Iraq, Syria, and Lebanon, and helped ensure the survival of the new state of Israel.

🎖 Special forces

The Israelis have long had an interest in unconventional warfare, have gained a reputation second to none since 1949 for their efficiency in it, and today have a wide range of special forces available.

Palsar units

The Israeli army has highly specialist Palsar, or long-range reconnaissance and patrol groups (LRRP), attached to each of the regular infantry brigades as the Sayeret Golany Palsar-95, Sayeret Givaty Palsar-435, Sayeret Nahal Palsar-374, the T'zanhanim (parachute) Palsar, and similar units attached to the regular armored brigades, the Palsar-7 and 500. These units carry out clandestine reconnaissance patrols deep behind enemy lines, and ensure that the parent brigade has the best possible information at all times about any potential threat.

Field intelligence and military intelligence (AMAN)

The Field Intelligence Corps and Military Intelligence, or AMAN, have a further range of dedicated units, such as Unit Yachmam for intelligence and target acquisition, Unit T'zasam for special reconnaissance duties in Palestinian areas, and Unit-504, which handles human clandestine intelligence resources. In addition there is Sayeret Duvedevan, a secretive unit based on the Israeli-Egyptian border. It is a *mistaravim*, or "becoming an Arab," force for deep-cover, clandestine operations inside Egypt, and its personnel are experts at merging successfully with the local population.

It is the realistic quality of training, such as the use of difficult low-visibility conditions, that so often gives the Israeli front-line units such a decisive edge in actual combat.

Special forces, equipped with U.S. M16A1 automatic rifles, operating at night on the Golan Heights preparing to medivac a casualty.

Storming to success

Sayaret MATKAL, or Unit-269, is a highly effective counter-terrorist and special operations group under the direct command of the Chief of Israeli Intelligence. It carried out the very first successful assault on a hijacked airliner in May 1972. A Sabena 707 and its 100 passengers and crew were forced to fly to Israel by four members of the Palestinian "Black September" terrorist organization. Sayaret MATKAL assaulted the airliner, killing two terrorists and arresting the others. All but one of the hostages was released alive and safe.

Sayeret MATKAL

The main counter-terrorist force is the Sayeret MATKAL. Formed in 1958, and absorbing the operational experience gained by the original Israeli special operations force, Unit-101, it adopted an SAS-style structure. In 1974, MATKAL and other special forces units started to acquire genuine counter-terrorist training provided by the British SAS and the U.S. SEAL and Delta units. By 1980, it had a high degree of both operational experience and capability.

In 1985, the Israelis established a discreet special forces base at Miktan Adam with a Special Training Installation (Maha-7208) and the Counter-terrorism Warfare School (Unit-707). This now included hostage-rescue, close-quarter battle, combat shooting, and other specialist facilities. Training, which is remarkably tough, even by normal special forces standards, includes combat swimming, explosives, sniping, specialist parachuting HALO (High Altitude Low Opening), cold weather and desert warfare techniques, heliborne insertion, and sabotage. Weapons used include U.S. M16A1 automatic rifles and its CAR-15 carbine version, 9mm Mini-Uzi, 9mm P226 automatic pistols, Remington 870 combat shotguns, and sniper rifles (including Mauser SR82, U.S. M24 7.62mm and the long-range .5 Barrett M82A1). In addition, they also have available a wide range of captured, or specially brought-in, small arms for under-cover operations.

This highly capable force, the Sayeret MATKAL, which is tasked for operations outside Israel, along with its civilian counterpart, Unit Yamam, a GSG-9-style counter-terrorist unit tasked for domestic operations, is required to provide two action-ready units at all times for counter-terrorist operations anywhere in the world.

A well-equipped special forces soldier, armed with a folding stock 5.56mm assault rifle and a hand-held 40mm grenade launcher, takes aim during a house-clearing anti-terrorist operation.

Deadly tactics

One of the tactics employed by the Israelis to combat terrorist activities by members of Hezbollah and Hamas within Israel is a deliberate policy of assassination. Leading Palestinians who are believed to be militants are targeted by deep cover special operations personnel. They are either shot by marksmen, blown up by "booby trap" devices, or ambushed, often by rocket-firing helicopters destroying a marked car and killing the occupants. These covert units are mainly drawn from the Israeli commandos and Sayaret MATKAL.

Syria

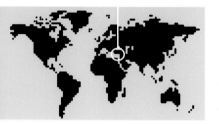

The Syrian army was established in 1920 by France and was known as the 1st Levantine Force. Its officers came entirely from the French army, and it maintained effective security in Syria until April 1946, when the French and British occupying forces finally left Syria for good.

An indigenous Syrian army was then established, but it took many years to transform itself from basically an infantry force, with a few cast-off French armored vehicles in the 1948 conflict with the newly established state of Israel, to a more diversified force under Soviet training. It also suffered the devastation of the loss of the Golan Heights, as well as the comprehensive defeat by the Israeli "blitzkrieg" of the 1967 Six Day War. Finally, a huge armored force was created, which proved capable of nearly breaking through the Israeli defense line on the Golan Heights in the early hours of the 1973 war. Eventually defeated, but in no sense humiliated, the Syrians immediately set about a major rebuilding program.

Today, the Syrian army is a large, well-trained, reliable and motivated force. It is well-armed, but continues to hold a high percentage of obsolete weapons. Syria has to fight off demands for the final withdrawal of its forces in Lebanon, particularly now that Israel no longer controls the south of that country. However, with the change of government in Israel in 2001, and the increase in regional tension, including renewed Israeli attacks on Syrian positions, withdrawal is unlikely in the near future. The Syrian army is highly skilled in assault and the breaching of defenses, obviously an important consideration in any future conflict to regain the Golan Heights from Israel.

The death of President Hafez Assad, a respected and powerful leader, in June 2000 has left Syria temporarily lacking its usual influence in the Middle East. This situation is compounded by uncertainty about future arms supply and the potential of a renewed conflict with Israel, all of which has clouded Syrian army planning in recent years. But under President Putin, Russia's new and more aggressive attitude to the massive resupply of Syria's arsenal, and the growing alliance with Iraq, another of Russia's client states, the Syrian army can look forward with greater confidence to retaining its powerful role in the Middle East.

Flashpoints and deployments

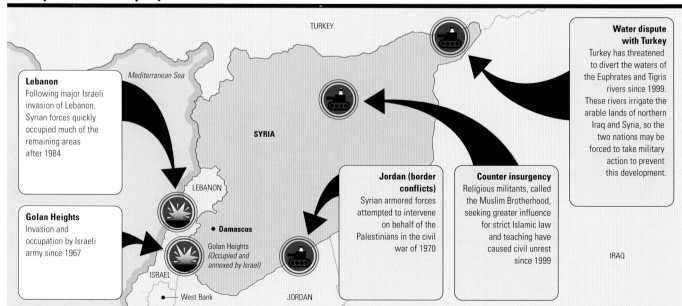

Lebanon
Following major Israeli invasion of Lebanon, Syrian forces quickly occupied much of the remaining areas after 1984

Golan Heights
Invasion and occupation by Israeli army since 1967

Jordan (border conflicts)
Syrian armored forces attempted to intervene on behalf of the Palestinians in the civil war of 1970

Counter insurgency
Religious militants, called the Muslim Brotherhood, seeking greater influence for strict Islamic law and teaching have caused civil unrest since 1999

Water dispute with Turkey
Turkey has threatened to divert the waters of the Euphrates and Tigris rivers since 1999. These rivers irrigate the arable lands of northern Iraq and Syria, so the two nations may be forced to take military action to prevent this development.

TURKEY

Mediterranean Sea

SYRIA

LEBANON

• Damascus

Golan Heights
(Occupied and annexed by Israel)

ISRAEL

• West Bank

JORDAN

IRAQ

⊞ Operations

The Syrian army has had considerable operational experience over the last 40 years, ranging from major counter-insurgency campaigns to a string of honorable defeats at the hands of the Israeli armed forces. The capture by Israel of the Golan Heights during the Six Day War in 1967, the failed Syrian attempt to recapture that same territory in the Yom Kippur War of 1973, and the numerous hard-fought battles with the Israeli forces to control parts of Lebanon have all been part of the Syrian army's experience. Syria also deployed a mechanized infantry division to support the Western Allies in Saudi Arabia during the Gulf conflict with Iraq in 1991, where it acquitted itself well alongside the other Arab forces.

In addition, the Syrian army had a brief but bitter border conflict with the Jordanian army in September 1970, when Syria attempted to help the Palestinians during their uprising. Syrian forces have also been deployed to put down large-scale revolts in some of the northern cities, such as that in Hama in February 1982, when an uprising by the Muslim Brotherhood was put down with considerable loss of life.

A Syrian elite infantry soldier, probably serving in eastern Lebanon.

Current deployment of operational units

The present deployment is strongly dictated by potential operations against Israel and the ongoing occupation of large parts of Lebanon.
1 corps headquarters covers the capital city of Damascus and the front line along the Golan Heights and has
• 5 armored divisions
• 2 mechanized infantry divisions
• 1 Republican Guard armored division
• 1 special forces division
• 2 independent anti-tank brigades
• 4 independent special forces regiments
1 corps headquarters covers

Lebanon and the coast up to the northern city of Aleppo and has
• 2 armored divisions
• 1 mechanized division (based in the Bekaa Valley, Lebanon)
• 2 independent special forces regiments
• 1 coastal defense missile brigade
1 corps headquarters covers the interior and the long desert borders with Jordan, Iraq, and Turkey and has

• 4 independent infantry brigades
• 1 independent armored regiment
• 4 independent special forces regiments
• 1 border guard brigade

Bitter legacy

In February 1982, a revolt by a fanatical religious group, the Muslim Brotherhood, broke out in the city of Hama. Officials of the ruling Ba'ath Party and the security forces were murdered, government buildings were seized or destroyed, and appeals for a national insurrection were broadcast from mosques. The Syrian army's response was devastating. Tanks and artillery soon ringed the city and, with armed helicopter support, Syrian elite infantry and commandos stormed Hama. The army did not halt the operation until half the city had been leveled and up to 25,000 of its inhabitants killed.

Syrian infantrymen in typical combat gear. Though defeated on numerous occasions by the superior Israeli forces, the Syrians have proved to be formidable soldiers and have earned the respect of their Israeli opponents.

Weapons and units / overview of an army

The Syrian army has a strength of 225,000, with some 160,000 personnel available to the main combat units. A traditionally strong, well-equipped, and well-organized fighting force, the Syrian army now suffers from a lack of modern weapons capable of challenging Israel's regional military supremacy. Attempts to modernize and enhance Syria's firepower have so far met with little success.

Army units

The present organization has

3 corps headquarters
> **7** armored divisions
> **3** mechanized infantry divisions
> **1** Republican Guard division
> **1** special forces division
> **4** independent infantry brigades
> **1** border guard brigade

There are also 2 independent artillery brigades

2 independent anti-tank brigades
1 independent tank regiment
10 independent special forces regiments
3 surface-to-surface missile brigades
1 coast defense missile brigade

Average allocation Armor, artillery, and helicopters within each brigade

Armored Division	Mechanized Division	Republican Guard Division
300 T62/T72 main battle tanks	**200** T55/T62/T72 main battle tanks	**350** T62/T72 main battle tanks
300 BMP armored infantry fighting vehicles	**250** BMP armored infantry fighting vehicles	**350** BMP-2/3 armored infantry fighting vehicles
300 BTR50/BTR60/BTR70 armored personnel carriers	**250** BTR151/BTR60 armored personnel carriers	**350** BTR60/BTR70 armored personnel carriers
50 BRDM armored reconnaissance	**50** BRDM armored reconnaissance	**50** BRDM-2 armored reconnaissance
30 122mm 2S1 self-propelled artillery	**30** 122mm 2S1 self-propelled artillery	**30** 122mm 2S1 and 20 152mm 2S3 self-propelled artillery
30 23mm ZSU-23-4 self-propelled air defense	**30** 23mm ZSU-23-4 self-propelled air defense	**50** 23mm ZSU-23-4 self-propelled air defense
20 122mm BM21 multiple rocket launchers	**20** 122mm BM21 multiple rocket launchers	**30** 122mm BM21 multiple rocket launchers

KEY Airborne   Armor   Infantry   Artillery   Missiles

T72 Main Battle Tank

Country of origin Russia
First entered service 1971 with Russian army
Main armament 125mm smoothbore gun (39 rounds)
Max. road speed 36 mph (60 km/h)
Max. range 540 miles (870 km)
Crew 3
Thousands built, in service with over 28 armies

Infantry small arms

9mm PM/APS automatic pistols
7.62mm AK/AKM/AKMS automatic rifles
5.45mm AK74/AKS74 automatic rifles
7.62mm RPK machine guns
5.45mm RPK74 machine guns
7.62mm PK/PKM machine guns
12.7mm DSHK heavy machine guns

The main Syrian armored units are equipped with over 1,700 T72 and T72M main battle tanks, armed with 125mm high-velocity guns. Some T72M1 tanks with additional armor are now believed to be entering service.

Firepower   The cutting edge

Airborne	Armor	Infantry	Artillery	Missiles

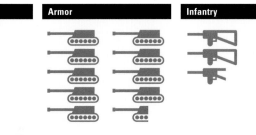  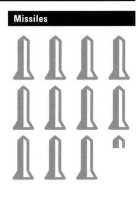

All helicopters are under Syrian Air Force control	**1,000** T54/55/MV	**400** 82mm	**100** 122mm M31/37 (in static defensive positions)	**1,500** AT3
	1,000 T62M/K	**350** 120mm mortars		**200** AT4
	1,700 T72/72M main battle tanks	**2,000** RPG-7/18/22 anti-tank	**150** M38	**200** AT5
	1,000 more T54/55 tanks are in static defensive positions		**500** D30	**200** AT7
			800 130mm M46	**2,000** AT10
	950 BRDM-2 armored reconnaissance		**20** 152mm D20	**300** AT14
			50 M1937	**200** Milan anti-tank
	2,400 BMP-1/2/3 armored infantry fighting vehicles		**20** 180mm S23 towed	**2,500** AT-3/BRDM (mounted on armored carriers)
			400 122mm 2S1	
	1,600 BTR50/60/70/80/151 armored personnel carriers		**50** 152mm 2S3 self-propelled	**4,000** SA7 manportable surface-to-air
			200 Type-63 107mm	
			280 BM21 122mm multiple rocket launchers	**20** SA9
				35 SA13 self-propelled surface-to-air
			100 160mm M160	
			10 240mm M240 towed mortars	**18** FROG-7
			650 23mm ZSU23-2	**22** SS21
			300 37mm M39	**26** SCUD-B/C self-propelled surface-to-surface
			675 57mm S60	
			30 100mm KS19 towed air defense	**6** SSC1B
			400 23mm ZSU23-4	**6** SSC3 coast defense missiles
			10 57mm ZSU57-2 self-propelled air defense	

Total 0	**Total 9,650**	**Total 2,750**	**Total 4,745**	**Total 11,233**

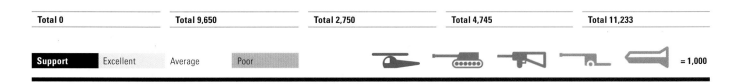

Support	Excellent	Average	Poor		= 1,000

◬ Fighting structure

Once the strongest Arab land force in the Middle East, the Syrian army has recently embarked on a major restructuring program of all its main combat units. Armored and mechanized divisions are to receive tank upgrades, or new vehicles, more self-propelled artillery, improved air defense, and increased numbers of mechanized infantry battalions. Syria intends to create an integrated and responsive mechanized force capable of not only securing its long borders with Turkey, Iraq, and Jordan, but also of maintaining its presence as an occupying army in Lebanon. It will have the task of supporting, where necessary,

the counter-insurgency and special forces actions to maintain control in such rebellious areas as Hama, but most importantly, to keep pressure on the Israelis over the occupation of the Golan Heights. However, it is unlikely that any present or future restructuring or re-equipping of the Syrian army would be sufficient for it to take on, or defeat, the Israeli army.

Fighting Structure Overview

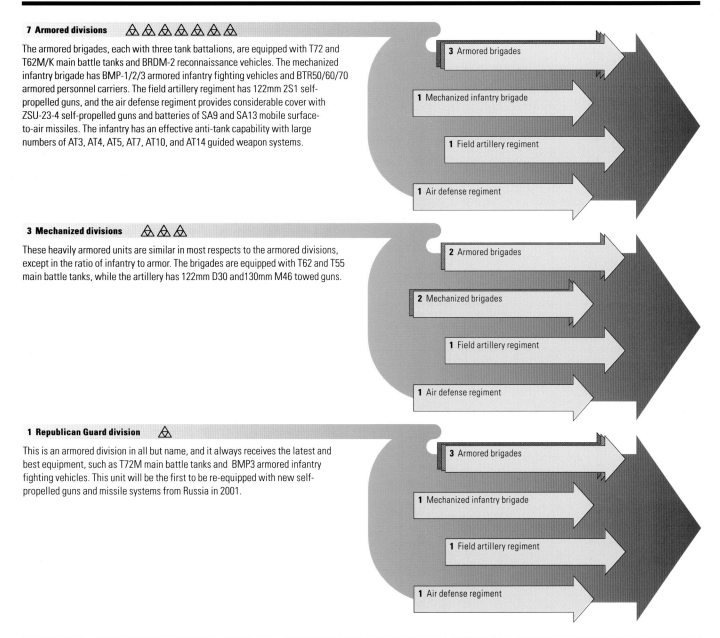

7 Armored divisions ◬ ◬ ◬ ◬ ◬ ◬ ◬

The armored brigades, each with three tank battalions, are equipped with T72 and T62M/K main battle tanks and BRDM-2 reconnaissance vehicles. The mechanized infantry brigade has BMP-1/2/3 armored infantry fighting vehicles and BTR50/60/70 armored personnel carriers. The field artillery regiment has 122mm 2S1 self-propelled guns, and the air defense regiment provides considerable cover with ZSU-23-4 self-propelled guns and batteries of SA9 and SA13 mobile surface-to-air missiles. The infantry has an effective anti-tank capability with large numbers of AT3, AT4, AT5, AT7, AT10, and AT14 guided weapon systems.

- **3** Armored brigades
- **1** Mechanized infantry brigade
- **1** Field artillery regiment
- **1** Air defense regiment

3 Mechanized divisions ◬ ◬ ◬

These heavily armored units are similar in most respects to the armored divisions, except in the ratio of infantry to armor. The brigades are equipped with T62 and T55 main battle tanks, while the artillery has 122mm D30 and 130mm M46 towed guns.

- **2** Armored brigades
- **2** Mechanized brigades
- **1** Field artillery regiment
- **1** Air defense regiment

1 Republican Guard division ◬

This is an armored division in all but name, and it always receives the latest and best equipment, such as T72M main battle tanks and BMP3 armored infantry fighting vehicles. This unit will be the first to be re-equipped with new self-propelled guns and missile systems from Russia in 2001.

- **3** Armored brigades
- **1** Mechanized infantry brigade
- **1** Field artillery regiment
- **1** Air defense regiment

Special forces

The first attempt to create a viable special forces capability took place in 1958, when the 1st Parachute Battalion was raised. Interest in such units increased over the years until in the opening moves of the 1973 Yom Kippur War with Israel, a daring helicopter-borne raid by the Syrian 82nd Para-Commando (special forces) Battalion successfully captured the Israeli observation site on Mount Hermon overlooking the approaches to the Golan Heights. Syrian special forces had come of age.

Syria will continue to make considerable use of special forces in any future military operations. Indeed, this is one of the areas that has seen the new strategic alliance between Syria and Iraq begin to take shape, with the two nations beginning to share both training and intelligence.

Special forces command
Today the Syrian army has a special forces command with headquarters in Damascus that now controls a large number of units including the 14th Special Forces Division. This unit is based just outside Damascus with three regiments largely tasked to ensure the integrity of the country, both in peacetime and in any future conflict with Israel. Trained as both elite infantry and as commandos for special operations, these troops are heavily armed and have access to heavy armored vehicles and modern missiles.

In a more traditional role are 10 special forces regiments, which are commando trained. A number are permanently based in Lebanon, where they have had some limited success against Israeli forces in the Bekaa Valley. Other tasks include protection of Syria's long borders and the suppression of civil unrest throughout the country, and developing the skills necessary to successfully storm the strongly held Israeli positions

A Syrian special forces commando in full nuclear, biological, and chemical (NBC) warfare kit and armed with an AKM assault rifle.

on the Golan Heights in any future conflict.

Counter-terrorist unit
The counter-terrorist capability is provided by one of the special forces regiments, known as *Al Saiqa* ("lightning"). This unit is trained in a whole range of special operations techniques, including combat shooting, hostage rescue, anti-hijacking, intelligence gathering, clandestine operations, and long-range reconnaissance and patrol. In addition, *Al Saiqa* has trained in recent years with the *Spetsnaz* in Russia and is also believed to have a small

number of ex-East Germans and non-Israeli Jews attached to its operations section. It is known to have operated with some success within Lebanon, Jordan, the Palestinian areas on the West Bank of the Jordan River and, on a few occasions, within Israel itself. It has the pick of standard issue arms from the Syrian army, and has access to foreign weapons often acquired on the black market. So it is not unusual to see U.S. 5.56mm M16A1 automatic rifles, Israeli 9mm UZI, Italian 9mm Beretta BM12, and German MP5K silenced sub-machine guns used for clandestine operations.

Russia

oday the Russian army is a mere shadow of its former Soviet size and power. In 1991, it was 1,400,000 strong. By 2001, it had diminished to 350,000, and its influence and role in Russian society had been similarly reduced. Throughout the 1990s, the army's morale and military performance reached shockingly low levels, with mass desertions and a growing number of military disasters against insurgents in different areas of Russia. President Putin, however, is determined to restore the army's combat capability as quickly as possible.

Long-term under-investment in modern equipment and high technology, particularly computers, was painfully exposed during the Gulf War in 1991, when the Western Allies quickly eliminated Iraq's much vaunted Russian-style air defense systems. The Allies also had no problem dealing with Iraq's range of missile and radar systems or their Soviet-equipped armored forces in the Gulf.

The realization of just how far the Soviet Union had fallen behind the United States was a major reason for the final collapse of the Communist Party in 1991 and the military coalition that had for so long dominated the old Soviet Union. Even the Soviet army had to finally accept what economic reformers already knew: that the money needed to catch up with the West was simply not available, nor would it be in the foreseeable future.

During the presidency of Boris Yeltsin (the first president of the new Russian Federation), the rebuilding of the army was hampered because of two major factors; first, Russia's inability

The advanced T90 main battle tank shows of its speed and agility during demonstrations in front of international arms buyers.

New for old

Following the collapse of the Communist regime, the once powerful and proud Red Army was split between the 15 newly independent nations. Would they all develop into truly national forces, as has happened with Ukraine, or would they slowly unify under Russian control? The answer appears to be essentially the latter. A majority of the former Soviet republics have now either integrated their military commands with Russia or have accepted Russian forces garrisoned on their territory. The second is true particularly in Central Asia.

Flashpoints and deployments

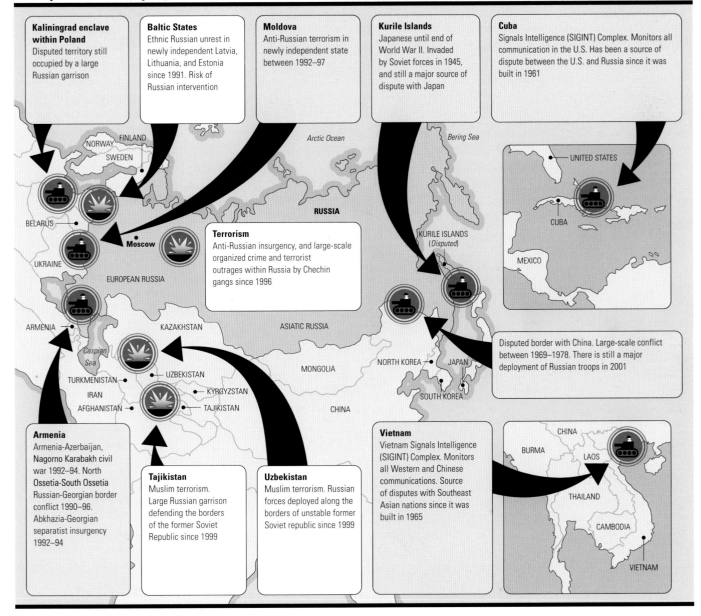

Kaliningrad enclave within Poland
Disputed territory still occupied by a large Russian garrison

Baltic States
Ethnic Russian unrest in newly independent Latvia, Lithuania, and Estonia since 1991. Risk of Russian intervention

Moldova
Anti-Russian terrorism in newly independent state between 1992–97

Kurile Islands
Japanese until end of World War II. Invaded by Soviet forces in 1945, and still a major source of dispute with Japan

Cuba
Signals Intelligence (SIGINT) Complex. Monitors all communication in the U.S. Has been a source of dispute between the U.S. and Russia since it was built in 1961

Terrorism
Anti-Russian insurgency, and large-scale organized crime and terrorist outrages within Russia by Chechin gangs since 1996

Disputed border with China. Large-scale conflict between 1969–1978. There is still a major deployment of Russian troops in 2001

Armenia
Armenia-Azerbaijan, Nagorno Karabakh civil war 1992–94. North Ossetia-South Ossetia Russian-Georgian border conflict 1990–96. Abkhazia-Georgian separatist insurgency 1992–94

Tajikistan
Muslim terrorism. Large Russian garrison defending the borders of the former Soviet Republic since 1999

Uzbekistan
Muslim terrorism. Russian forces deployed along the borders of unstable former Soviet republic since 1999

Vietnam
Vietnam Signals Intelligence (SIGINT) Complex. Monitors all Western and Chinese communications. Source of disputes with Southeast Asian nations since it was built in 1965

to defeat the Chechin and other ethnic insurgencies mainly in southern Russia and the central Asian former Soviet republics; and second, the lack of resources available to properly pay, feed, clothe, or house its army. For a once proud military force steeped in the glorious victories of the civil war and World War II, this was hard to accept. During the 1990s, many experienced officers resigned for better paying civilian positions or took early retirement.

The collapse of much of the military ultimately undermined President Yeltsin's authority. His successor, Vladimir Putin has quickly sought to restore the president's important standing within the armed forces, and has ordered a substantial rehabilitation of the Russian army. He is currently in the process of realigning the army to provide a faster, more responsive and flexible force better suited for Russia's new military challenges.

The army is still beset with anti-Russian insurgencies, terrorism, and numerous peacekeeping commitments in former Soviet republics such as Tajikistan and Georgia. It lacks the influence it once enjoyed as a world superpower, and is unsure of its long-term relationships with China and the West. However, the army is currently undergoing a huge rebuilding program. It is dumping vast amounts of obsolete weaponry and rearming its main combat units with the intention of once again becoming the deciding influence on Russia's future.

⚑ Operations

The Russian army has found it hard to come to terms with the fundamental changes of the last ten years. It is no longer the great superpower confronting NATO in central Europe, but instead Russia faces a multitude of rebellions, insurgencies, and criminal terrorism. The performance of the Russian army is further complicated by the fact that most combat units are operating at 50 per-cent or less of their full strength.

Today, the much smaller army is struggling to cope with problems in many areas, including Chechnya, Georgia, Moldova, and Tajikistan. The range of geographic and climatic difficulties faced by the Russian army is the most extreme of any nation, encompassing all of the following: the cold shores of the Baltic Sea in Europe, the arctic tundras of Siberia, the Pacific Ocean opposite Japan, the frozen wastelands across the North Pole on the island of Novaya Zemlya, and the arid deserts along the borders of Iran, where Russian border guards still patrol on camels.

Chechnyan nightmare

Russian forces moved back into Chechnya in December 1994 to prevent its secession. The Chechin people had not willingly accepted Russian control since imperial expansion into the area in the 19th century, and in 1920, after the Russian Revolution, Chechnya's brief independence was brutally suppressed by the Red Army. The recent conflict cost tens of thousands of lives, and ended only in an uneasy cease-fire in 1996. However, Russian forces renewed their offensive in 1999, and fighting in the area continues.

Current military deployments
The Kaliningrad Operational Strategic Group (Russian enclave on the Baltic Coast) has
- 2 motor rifle divisions
- 1 armored brigade
- 1 surface-to-surface missile brigade
- 1 air defense missile regiment
- 1 attack helicopter regiment

The Leningrad Military District with headquarters in St. Petersburg has
- 1 airborne division
- 2 independent motor rifle brigades
- 1 surface-to-surface missile brigade
- 1 special forces brigade
- 4 air defense missile brigades

The Moscow Military District with headquarters in Moscow has
- 1 army HQ, 1 corps HQ with
- 2 armored divisions
- 2 motor rifle divisions
- 2 airborne divisions
- 1 artillery division
- 1 independent motor rifle brigade
- 3 surface-to-surface missile brigades
- 1 special forces brigade
- 4 air defense missile brigades
- 2 attack helicopter regiments

The Volga Military District/ Ural Military District with headquarters in Samara has
- 1 armored division
- 2 motor rifle divisions
- 1 airborne brigade
- 1 surface-to-surface missile brigade
- 1 air defense missile brigade
- 1 special forces brigade

The North Caucasus Military District with headquarters in Rostov-on-Don has
- 1 army HQ
- 1 corps HQ
- 2 motor rifle divisions
- 1 airborne division
- 3 motor rifle division
- 3 airborne brigades
- 1 special forces brigade
- 1 surface-to-surface missile
- 4 air defense missile brigades
- 2 attack helicopter regiments

The Siberian Military Districts with headquarters at Novosibirsk has
- 2 corps HQ
- 3 armored divisions
- 2 motor rifle divisions
- 3 motor rifle brigades
- 2 special forces brigades
- 2 surface-to-surface missile brigades
- 2 air defense missile brigades

The latest BTR-80 armored personnel carrier, with its greater mobility and side doors, is a considerable improvement over earlier models such as the widely used BTR-60.

Russian return

In May 1992, insurgents seized power from the Tajik Supreme Soviet, and a civil war began, which was to see both Russian and Uzbeki forces become jointly involved. Following the defeat of the opposition Muslim forces, Tajikistan's new government negotiated the return of a Russian garrison. The Russian 201st Motorized Infantry Division is now the principal fighting force in Tajikistan, and helps to prop up the authoritarian regime controlling a mineral-rich nation at the crossroads of Asia.

A close-up view of the weapons fit of the 2S6M Tunguska Air Defense System, with 8 SA19 Grisom surface-to-air missiles and two 30mm 2A38M anti-aircraft guns.

The Far Eastern Military District with headquarters in Vladivostok has

- 2 army HQ
- 2 corps HQ
- 10 motor rifle divisions
- 1 motor rifle brigade
- 3 surface-to-surface missile brigades
- 5 air defense missile brigades
- 1 special forces brigade
- 2 attack helicopter regiments

Other deployments abroad

Forces deployed outside the Russian Federation include

- 1 motor rifle brigade in Armenia
- 3 motor rifle brigades in Georgia
- 1 motor rifle brigade in Moldova
- 1 motor rifle division based in Tajikistan

Russian military personnel are also serving in Cuba (since 1961), in Syria as advisers, and in Vietnam. They serve alongside NATO in Bosnia (SFOR-11) and Kosovo-Yugoslavia (KFOR), and in UN peacekeeping operations in Croatia (UNMOP), East Timor (UNTAET), Iraq/Kuwait (UNIKOM), Sierra Leone (UNAMSIL), and Western Sahara (MINURSO).

The advanced BMP-3 provides Russian mechanized units with a highly capable and powerful armored vehicle. It is armed with a 100mm gun which can fire AT10 laser-guided anti-tank missiles.

Weapons and units / overview of an army

The present Russian army is 350,000 strong, with approximately 240,000 personnel available for front-line service.

While severely reduced in size and far short of the strength required for the range of internal problems it currently faces, there has been a slow qualitative improvement in the Russian army. New armored vehicles including T90 and T95 main battle tanks, improved artillery and missiles systems, and command and control systems are all entering service. An infrastructure of engineers, signals, and logistics still exists and with the determination of President Putin firmly behind the Russian General Staff, the army should achieve a much enhanced degree of military effectiveness over the next five years.

T90 Main Battle Tank

Country of origin Russia

First entered service 1994 with Russian army

Main armament 125mm smoothbore gun (43 rounds)

Max. road speed 39 mph (65 km/h)

Max. range 380 miles (630 km)

Crew 3

Over 400 being built, in service with Russia, later India

The widely used BM21 multiple rocket launching system with 40 x 122mm projectiles mounted on an all-terrain URAL-375D vehicle.

Army units

The present organization has

1 operational strategic group

7 regional military districts

6 army headquarters

3 corps headquarters

Combat units include

5 tank divisions

21 motor rifle divisions

4 airborne divisions

12 artillery divisions

18 independent artillery brigades

9 independent motor rifle brigades

3 airborne brigades

7 special forces brigades

15 surface-to-surface missile brigades (with nuclear capable SS21)

5 anti-tank brigades

3 anti-tank regiments

19 surface-to-air missile brigades (2 with SA4, 4 with SA11, 1 with SA12, and 12 with SA6, SA8, and SA15)

9 attack helicopter regiments

6 assault helicopter regiments

5 support helicopter regiments

Infantry small arms

9mm PM automatic pistols

9mm APS automatic pistols

5.45mm PSM automatic pistols

7.62mm AK47/AKM/AKMS automatic rifles

5.45mm AK74/AK74S automatic rifles

5.45mm AKSU-74 sub-machine guns

7.62mm SVD sniper rifles

9mm VAL silent sniper rifles

7.62mm RPK/RPKS machine guns

5.45mm RPK74/RPKS74 machine guns

7.62mm PK/PKS/PKB machine guns

12.7mm DSHK heavy machine guns

Average allocation Armor, artillery, and helicopters within each brigade

Armored Divisions

- **360** T64/T72/T80/T90 main battle tanks
- **150** BMP-2/3 armored infantry fighting vehicles
- **350** BTR70/80, BTR-D, and MTLB armored personnel carriers
- **120** 122mm 2S1 and 152mm 2S3/2S5/2S19 self-propelled artillery
- **40** 122mm BM21 and 220mm 9P140 multiple rocket launchers
- **72** SA6, SA8, SA11 and SA15 self-propelled surface-to-air missile systems

Motor Rifle Divisions

- **120** T64/T72 main battle tanks
- **120** BMP-1/2 armored infantry fighting vehicles
- **450** BTR60/70 and MTLB armored personnel carriers
- **120** 122mm 2S1 and 152mm 2S3 self-propelled artillery
- **72** SA8 and SA11 self-propelled surface-to-air missile systems

Airborne Divisions

- **240** BMD-1/2/3 airborne armored infantry fighting vehicles
- **90** 2S9 self-propelled gun-mortars

Artillery Divisions

- **280** 122mm D30 and 152mm D20/2A36/2A65 towed artillery
- **60** 122mm BM21 and 220mm 9P140 multiple rocket launchers
- **72** 100mm T12A towed anti-tank

KEY 🚚 Airborne 🚛 Armor ⌐ Infantry 🔫 Artillery ◁ Missiles

Firepower The cutting edge

Airborne	Armor	Infantry	Artillery	Missiles

900 M124

8 Ka-50 attack helicopters

140 Mi-24 armed reconnaissance helicopters

20 Mi-6

980 Mi-8/17

50 Mi-26 transport helicopters

1,800 BMD-1/2/3 airborne armored fighting vehicles

300 85mm ASU85 airborne self-propelled anti-tank

1,200 T55

2,200 T62

4,300 T64A/B

9,700 T72L/M

4,500 T80

120 T90 main battle tanks

150 PT76 light tanks

2,200 BRDM1/2 reconnaissance

12,200 BMP-1/2/3

700 BRM-1K armored infantry fighting vehicles

1,000 BTR50

5,200 BTR60/70/80

4,800 MTLB armored personnel carriers

6,000 82mm, 120mm

300 160mm M160 mortars

11,000 64mm RPG18, 73mm RPG7/16/22/26, 105mm RPG27/29 manportable anti-tank

2,000 73mm SPG9, 82mm bio anti-tank

1,200 122mm M30

3,050 D30

200 130mm M54

1,075 152mm D20

1,100 2A36

750 2A65

40 203mm B4M towed

1,725 122mm 2S1

1,600 152mm 2S3

700 2S5

550 2S19

130 203mm 2S7 self-propelled

850 120mm 2S9, 2B16, 2S23 self-propelled gun-mortars

526 100mm T12/12A towed anti-tank

1,800 120mm 2S12, PM38

430 240mm 2S4 self-propelled and towed mortars

1,750 122mm BM21, 9P138

675 220mm 9P140

106 300mm 9A52 multiple rocket launchers

6,000 23mm ZU23, 57mm S60, 100mm KS19, 130mm KS30 towed air defense

1,050 23mm ZSU23-4, 30mm 2S6, ZSU57-2 self-propelled air defense

---

8,000+ AT3, AT4, AT5, AT6, AT7, AT9, AT10 anti-tank

100 SA4 (twin)

400 SA6 (triple)

400 SA8 (2 x triple)

200 SA9 (2 x twin)

250 SA11 (quad)

100 SA12 (single)

350 SA13 (2 x twin)

150 SA15 (quad)

100 SA19 (2S6M) self-propelled surface-to-air (2 x quad and twin 30mm guns)

9,000+ SA7, SA14, SA16, SA18 manportable surface-to-air

200 SS21 self-propelled surface-to-surface

Total 4,198

Total 48,270

Total 19,300

Total 25,307

Total 19,250+

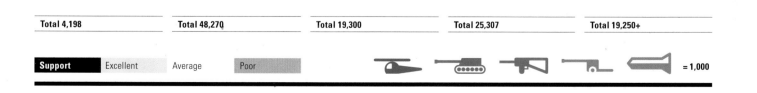

Support	Excellent	Average	Poor					= 1,000

◬ Fighting structure

A massive downsizing and break up of the old Soviet army occurred in the years following the end of Communist rule in 1991. In turn, the new Russian army has been humiliated by lightly armed rebels in Chechnya and elsewhere, entire units have virtually disintegrated, and scores of poorly maintained weapons have rusted into uselessness.

Since the organization of the main combat divisions had been designed for an attack against NATO, the entire structure of the army was in need of a complete overhaul. Its reliance on a massive tank and motorized infantry force, backed by huge artillery and multiple rocket launcher barrages, and the whole concept of a war fought under NBC (nuclear, biological, and chemical) conditions, had seriously distorted the balance of the Russian army.

Wholly unprepared for the situation it faced in the mid-1990s, a major restructuring of the Russian army is now well underway, although constrained as always by financial problems. There will be fewer armored and motorized divisions, each with more modern and well-maintained equipment. Greater emphasis will be placed on command and control, engineering, and logistic backup to create an integrated unit structure. This will encourage greater self-sufficiency and a quicker response to developing combat situations. The long-term aim of this restructuring is to produce a leaner, more professional, and combat-ready army.

When a guard is not a guard

The Russian army, like the old Soviet army, has a large number of units bearing the title *guards*. This is often taken to mean a particularly reliable fighting formation. However, this is not always the case. The title can be given to a unit for having carried out a particular operation well or for being politically loyal to the Communist Party. The finest combat units and elite formations can be called guards, but most often simply carry a numerical designation.

The fearsome firepower of the 2S6M highly mobile, forward air defense system includes eight advanced SA19 surface-to-air missiles. The 2S6M provides an enhanced capability for Russian armored units against attack helicopters and tank-busters.

The T80, now the mainstay of Russian armored units, is a considerable improvement over the earlier T72 used by Iraq in the Gulf War of 1991. Armor protection, survivability, and fire control are among those areas that have been upgraded.

Fighting Structure Overview

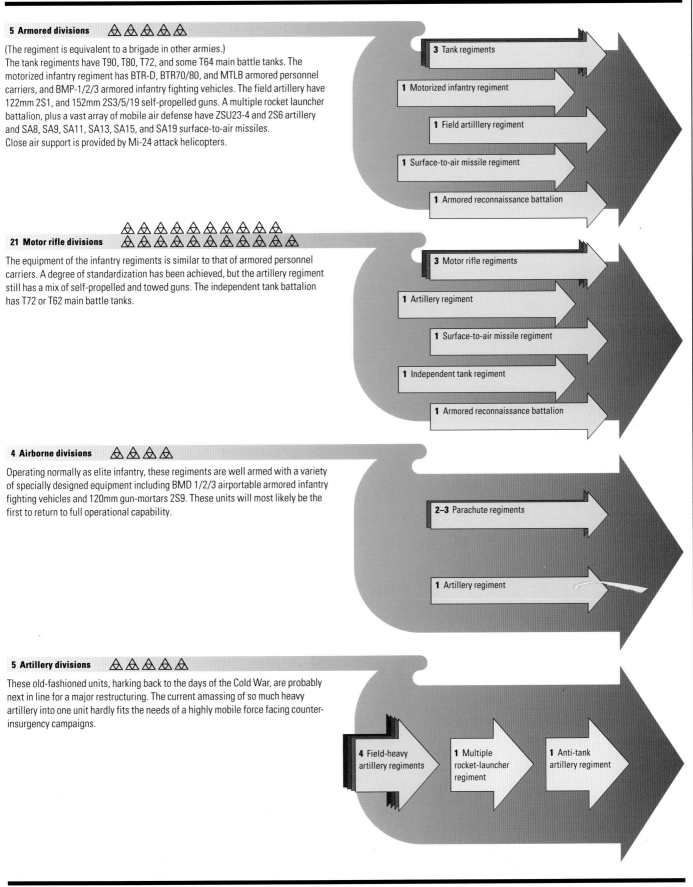

5 Armored divisions

(The regiment is equivalent to a brigade in other armies.)
The tank regiments have T90, T80, T72, and some T64 main battle tanks. The motorized infantry regiment has BTR-D, BTR70/80, and MTLB armored personnel carriers, and BMP-1/2/3 armored infantry fighting vehicles. The field artillery have 122mm 2S1, and 152mm 2S3/5/19 self-propelled guns. A multiple rocket launcher battalion, plus a vast array of mobile air defense have ZSU23-4 and 2S6 artillery and SA8, SA9, SA11, SA13, SA15, and SA19 surface-to-air missiles. Close air support is provided by Mi-24 attack helicopters.

3 Tank regiments

1 Motorized infantry regiment

1 Field artilllery regiment

1 Surface-to-air missile regiment

1 Armored reconnaissance battalion

21 Motor rifle divisions

The equipment of the infantry regiments is similar to that of armored personnel carriers. A degree of standardization has been achieved, but the artillery regiment still has a mix of self-propelled and towed guns. The independent tank battalion has T72 or T62 main battle tanks.

3 Motor rifle regiments

1 Artillery regiment

1 Surface-to-air missile regiment

1 Independent tank regiment

1 Armored reconnaissance battalion

4 Airborne divisions

Operating normally as elite infantry, these regiments are well armed with a variety of specially designed equipment including BMD 1/2/3 airportable armored infantry fighting vehicles and 120mm gun-mortars 2S9. These units will most likely be the first to return to full operational capability.

2–3 Parachute regiments

1 Artillery regiment

5 Artillery divisions

These old-fashioned units, harking back to the days of the Cold War, are probably next in line for a major restructuring. The current amassing of so much heavy artillery into one unit hardly fits the needs of a highly mobile force facing counter-insurgency campaigns.

4 Field-heavy artillery regiments

1 Multiple rocket-launcher regiment

1 Anti-tank artillery regiment

Special forces

The exact role of special forces was often unclear within the old Soviet army, and deep suspicion was cast upon any unit that developed an ethos or traditions that did not fit within the norms of the political officer whose main role was to ensure unswerving loyalty to the Communist Party. The *Spetsnaz* units created in World War II were not true special forces. They were simply politically trustworthy units that worked closely with the large special operations departments of the Intelligence services; Cheka, OGPU, and the NKVD, all forerunners of the KGB. It was not until the 1980s that the first, true Western-style special forces were established.

The airborne special forces use this versatile BMD-3 armored infantry fighting vehicle to give added mobility and enhanced firepower to their operations.

SMERCH reformed

One of the least well known of Russia's special forces is the *Vympel,* or Pennant Group. Its creation was specially agreed in 1974 at a closed session of the Ministerial Council of the USSR. As part of the KGB, its future tasks were to include the wartime assassination of any enemy's senior political and military officials. Following the collapse of Communism, control of the unit was transferred to the Interior Ministry (MVD), but it has since returned to the KGB's direct successor, the FSB. Its role now includes VIP protection and hostage rescue, in addition to re-creating the World War II Smerch, or death-to-spies-and-enemies organization made famous in the James Bond movies.

Russian special forces are particularly well-armed with large numbers of the potent SA18 Grouse manportable system to provide instant air defense.

Spetsnaz brigades

Today's Spetsnaz (*Spetsialnoje Naznachenie*) are organized into seven brigades attached to the regional military districts. Within individual units there are *Razvedchiki* (para-commandos) attached at divisional level, each made up of a company of long-range reconnaissance and patrol (LRRP) and a company for airborne operations. *Rejdoviki* (guard) units are found at brigade level, and 11-man *Vysotniki* (elite special forces) units are trained to a far higher standard, and attached at battalion level in the 103rd, 104th, and 105th airborne divisions.

Spetsnaz brigades are quite small, each no more than 1,500 strong with three small battalions, a headquarters, communications, intelligence, and support companies. Training has been increased in both range and techniques since the collapse of the Communist regime, and today includes weapons handling, familiarity with domestic and foreign arms, marksmanship, physical fitness (with an emphasis on endurance), tracking, patrolling, and camouflage and surveillance techniques. In addition, there is training in survival and warfare in desert, mountain, and arctic conditions, unarmed combat, sabotage and explosives, prisoner interrogation and prisoner-of-war rescue, language training, parachuting techniques including HAHO (High Altitude High Opening) and HALO (High Altitude Low Opening), heliborne-insertion, combat swimming, and counter-insurgency operations.

A wide range of domestic and foreign weapons, explosives, and communications equipment is now available to these units. These include 5.45mm AKS-74 automatic rifles, 5.45mm PRI automatic pistols, and such specialist weapons as the NR2, a combined combat knife with a blade that incorporates a short 7.62mm barrel that can be fired by clipping the scabbard and knife together.

Operational control of the *Spetsnaz* units has remained with the GRU (Military Intelligence) since its formation in World War II. The one exception to this was the 8th *Spetsnaz* Brigade, created in 1996 by the MVD (Interior Ministry) specifically for service in Chechnya. The other seven brigades continue to be closely involved in an intelligence support role and special operations.

Al'fa (Special Group A)

A more dedicated counter-terrorist and hostage rescue force is provided by *Al'fa,* or Special Group A. This was originally set up in 1974 by the (then) KGB's seventh directorate and was inspired by the British SAS and the U.S. Delta Force. It was this force that attacked the Dar-ul-aman Palace in Kabul and murdered the Afghan President Hafizullah Amin and his family on December 27, 1979 at the start of the Soviet invasion.

The *Al'fa* group is currently controlled by the FSB (Federal Security Service), which replaced the KGB in 1992 and maintains headquarters and one operational group in Moscow and three groups in St. Petersburg, Murmansk, and Vladivostok. It is the closest thing the Russians have in technical ability and organization to specialist counter-terrorist groups currently operated by major Western nations.

The Afghan war

Full-scale Soviet involvement in the Afghan conflict began on December 27, 1979, when airborne forces landed at Kabul Airport in response to repeated demands by President Amin to intervene on his behalf. Unfortunately for Amin, a Russian general with an *Al'fa* special action group drove straight to the presidential palace, entered and shot the President and his family dead. Wanting no witnesses, the Russian troops then murdered everyone else in the building, including the Russian general himself, "accidentally" killed by his own men.

The renowned Mil Mi-24 Hind-D armored and heavily armed attack helicopter is used to both insert and give close fire-support to Spetsnaz *units during special forces operations.*

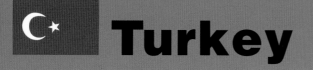

Turkey

For many years Turkey, with the Soviet Union to the east and Bulgaria to the west, was at the forefront of U.S. plans to provide a bulwark for NATO against the Warsaw Pact. Turkish forces controlled the vital naval access through the Dardenelle Straits to and from the Black Sea, making Turkey a prime target for a Soviet land invasion to seize these strategic waterways and thereby allow the powerful Black Sea Fleet free access to the Mediterranean.

However, Turkey's military role has been severely complicated by its dispute with Greece, a fellow NATO member, over the control of the Aegean islands. This situation, in conjunction with the ongoing problem of Cyprus, particularly following the invasion of the island by Turkish forces in 1974, continues to cloud relations with Greece and affects Turkey's overall acceptance by other European nations.

Since the collapse of Communism, Turkey has been searching for new roles to play and has sought to increase its influence within the Middle East. Its growing partnership with Israel is a considerable risk, but the Turkish government is highly suspicious of the more militant Islamic states. Also, Turkey views the combination of common enemies and a close relationship with the U.S. as major attractions of an alliance with Israel. Indeed, this alliance is part of Turkey's overall plan to achieve long-term acceptance by its Western neighbors, and to gain a secure place within the European Union.

However, to achieve and maintain the influence from this newfound military role, Turkey will need to rebuild, restructure, and rearm its army in a way far beyond its current economic ability. Therefore a continuing reliance on U.S. patronage and the growth of new and unexpected alliances in the Middle East are the best hope for the future of this financially weak nation.

Flashpoints and deployments

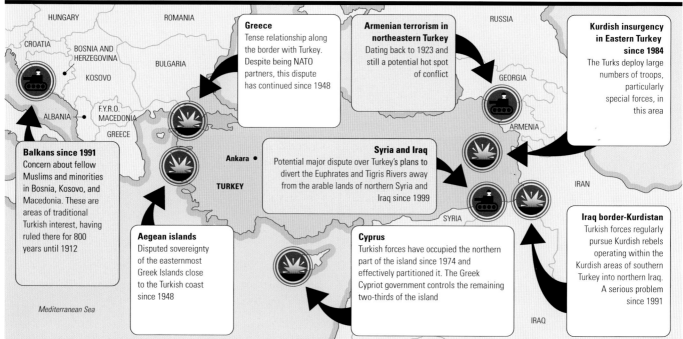

Greece
Tense relationship along the border with Turkey. Despite being NATO partners, this dispute has continued since 1948

Armenian terrorism in northeastern Turkey
Dating back to 1923 and still a potential hot spot of conflict

Kurdish insurgency in Eastern Turkey since 1984
The Turks deploy large numbers of troops, particularly special forces, in this area

Balkans since 1991
Concern about fellow Muslims and minorities in Bosnia, Kosovo, and Macedonia. These are areas of traditional Turkish interest, having ruled there for 800 years until 1912

Syria and Iraq
Potential major dispute over Turkey's plans to divert the Euphrates and Tigris Rivers away from the arable lands of northern Syria and Iraq since 1999

Aegean islands
Disputed sovereignty of the easternmost Greek Islands close to the Turkish coast since 1948

Cyprus
Turkish forces have occupied the northern part of the island since 1974 and effectively partitioned it. The Greek Cypriot government controls the remaining two-thirds of the island

Iraq border-Kurdistan
Turkish forces regularly pursue Kurdish rebels operating within the Kurdish areas of southern Turkey into northern Iraq. A serious problem since 1991

⚑ Operations

A Turkish armored battalion serving with the NATO peacekeeping force in Bosnia. This unit has M60 main battle tanks with 105mm guns.

The Turkish army was deployed in the front-line of NATO's southern flank for some 50 years. It faced a combination of Soviet forces on its eastern borders, and the combined threat of the Warsaw Pact armies of Bulgaria and Romania on its European borders in the west.

While these threats no longer exist, the operational problems facing the Turkish army are still considerable. In addition to NATO commitments, Turkey has a number of other problems. These include a need to prepare for the possible confrontation with Greece over the most easterly Aegean islands, to upkeep its garrison in the northern part of Cyprus, a serious water resource dispute with both Syria and Iraq, and a large-scale insurgency problem of 12 million Kurds seeking independence. The latter campaign began in earnest in 1984, and has resulted in a considerable deployment of forces for operations in the difficult terrain along the borders of southeast Turkey, and has included on a number of occasions the pursuit of rebels into the Kurdish areas of northern Iraq.

Current operational deployments
Army headquarters based in Istanbul and covering European Turkey and the Aegean
• 2 corps headquarters
• 8 independent armored brigades
• 4 independent mechanized infantry brigades
• 1 commando brigade
• 1 border defense regiment

Army headquarters based in Iskenderun and covering the Mediterranean coast, Southern Turkey, and Cyprus
• 3 corps headquarters (including 1 in northern Cyprus)
• 1 infantry division
• 2 independent armored brigades
• 5 independent mechanized infantry brigades
• 3 independent infantry brigades
• 1 commando brigade

Army headquarters based in Ankara and covering northern and central Turkey
• 1 corps headquarters
• 1 mechanized infantry division (this unit is earmarked for NATO's Rapid Reaction Corps or ARRC)
• 1 independent armored brigade
• 3 independent mechanized infantry brigades
• 2 independent infantry brigades
• 1 Presidential Guard regimental group

Army headquarters based in and covering the eastern and southeastern areas of Turkey and the Kurdish campaign
• 3 corps headquarters
• 3 independent armored brigades
• 5 independent mechanized infantry brigades
• 4 independent infantry brigades
• 2 commando brigades
• 4 border defense regiments

Other deployments abroad
Turkish army personnel are currently serving abroad in NATO peacekeeping operations in Bosnia (SFOR-11, standing force) since 1996, Yugoslavia (KFOR, Kosovo Force) since 1999, and with the United Nations in East Timor (UNTAET) since 1999, Georgia (UNOMIG) since 1996, and Iraq/Kuwait (UNIKOM) since 1992.

Weapons and units / overview of an army

The present Turkish army strength is 498,000, with some 380,000 personnel available for combat duty. The Turkish army was for many years in the forefront of NATO's defensive posture in this region, positioned to hold its ground against an expected Warsaw Pact invasion until reinforcements could arrive from other Allied forces. This led to a heavily armed, rather immobile, and largely obsolete force which Turkey is now making strenuous efforts to modernize, even to the point of considering an Israeli program for up-grades on its fleet of M60 tanks along with other modern armored vehicles.

FIM-92 Stinger Surface-to-Air Missiles

Country of origin U.S.	
First entered service 1987 with U.S. army	
Advanced, manportable supersonic system	
Max. vertical range 1.9 miles (3.1 km)	
Max. range 4.8 miles (8 km)	
Crew 2	
Tens of thousands built, in service with over 20 armies	

Army units

The present organization has

4 army headquarters	
9 corps headquarters	
	14 independent armored brigades
	1 mechanized division
	1 mechanized infantry division (headquarters only, no combat units permanently attached)
	1 infantry division
	17 mechanized infantry brigades
	9 infantry brigades
	4 commando brigades
	1 infantry regiment
	5 border defense regiments
	26 border defense battalions
	1 Presidential Guard regiment

The Cobra lightly armored four-wheel drive vehicle performs reconnaissance duties for Turkish armored units.

The M52T modified self-propelled howitzer with a longer barreled 105mm weapon. Over 350 still serve with the Turkish artillery.

Average allocation Armor, artillery, and helicopters within each brigade

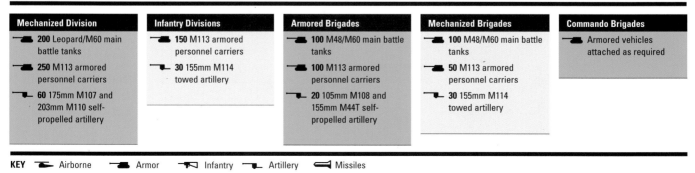

Mechanized Division	Infantry Divisions	Armored Brigades	Mechanized Brigades	Commando Brigades
200 Leopard/M60 main battle tanks	**150** M113 armored personnel carriers	**100** M48/M60 main battle tanks	**100** M48/M60 main battle tanks	Armored vehicles attached as required
250 M113 armored personnel carriers	**30** 155mm M114 towed artillery	**100** M113 armored personnel carriers	**50** M113 armored personnel carriers	
60 175mm M107 and 203mm M110 self-propelled artillery		**20** 105mm M108 and 155mm M44T self-propelled artillery	**30** 155mm M114 towed artillery	

KEY ⌐ Airborne ⌐ Armor ⌐ Infantry ⌐ Artillery ⌐ Missiles

Firepower   The cutting edge

Airborne	Armor	Infantry	Artillery	Missiles

37 AH1W/P attack helicopters

20 S70A

19 AS532UL

12 AB204

64 AB205A

20 AB206

28 H300C

94 UH1H support helicopters

Total 294

2,876 M48A5T1/2

932 M60A1/3

397 Leopard-1 main battle tanks

110 Akrep and Cobra armored reconnaissance

2,850 M113 armored personnel carriers

1,400 FMC/Nurol armored personnel carriers

Total 7,165

3,790 81mm

1,264 1097mm

757 120mm (including 180 on armored carriers) mortars

900 57mm M18

620 75mm

2,300 106mm M40A1 anti-tank

Total 9,631

---

600 105mm M101

517 155mm M114

162 203mm M115 towed

365 105mm M52T

26 M108T

222 155mm M44T

36 175mm M107

219 203mm M110A2 self-propelled

48 107mm

12 227mm MLRS multiple-rocket launchers

439 20mm GAI-DOI

120 35mm GDF

803 40mm L60/70

40 T1 towed air defense

262 40mm M42A1 self-propelled air defense

Total 3,871

---

180 Cobra

360 TOW (on armored carriers)

392 Milan anti-tank

500 Redeye

120 Stinger manportable surface-to-air

Total 1,552

Support	Excellent	Average	Poor	= 1,000

A Turkish armored infantry fighting vehicle with quick-firing cannon, mounted in a lightly armored turret.

Infantry small arms

7.65mm Kirrikale automatic pistols

9mm M3 sub-machine guns

7.62mm G3 automatic rifles

5.56mm M16A1 automatic rifles

7.62mm M60 machine guns

30 M1919 machine guns

12.7mm M2 HB heavy machine guns

◬ Fighting structure

The Turkish army has been attempting to restructure its main combat units to bring them closer in line with its NATO partners. It has achieved some success, although much of its organization remains firmly rooted in the Cold War period and its confrontation with Greece.

Turkey has a large number of old-fashioned tanks, self-propelled artillery, and quite inadequate numbers of armored personnel carriers and the more potent armored infantry fighting vehicles. It has purchased surplus weapons from a number of countries including the U.S. and Germany, but not nearly enough to facilitate a major restructuring of armored and mechanized formations into integrated, highly mobile fighting units.

The structure of the main infantry and armored units is out-of-date, lacking mobility and full integration into effective combined arms brigades. A major restructuring of the Turkish army is a necessity if it is not to fall seriously behind its potential enemies in this highly volatile region.

A M113 armored carrier forms the platform for the launch of a U.S. Stinger manpack surface-to-air missile.

Rapid reaction commitment

As part of Turkey's commitment to NATO, the 1st (TU) Mechanized Division, with its headquarters in Ankara, is one of the National Divisions available to Allied Command Europe—Rapid Reaction Corps or ARRC. This unit, one of the best equipped in the Turkish army, has an armored brigade and a mechanized infantry brigade, as well as considerable divisional self-propelled artillery and engineering support.

The ACV armored personnel carrier now supplements the M113 which has been in service for over 20 years, as the main infantry transporter.

Fighting Structure Overview

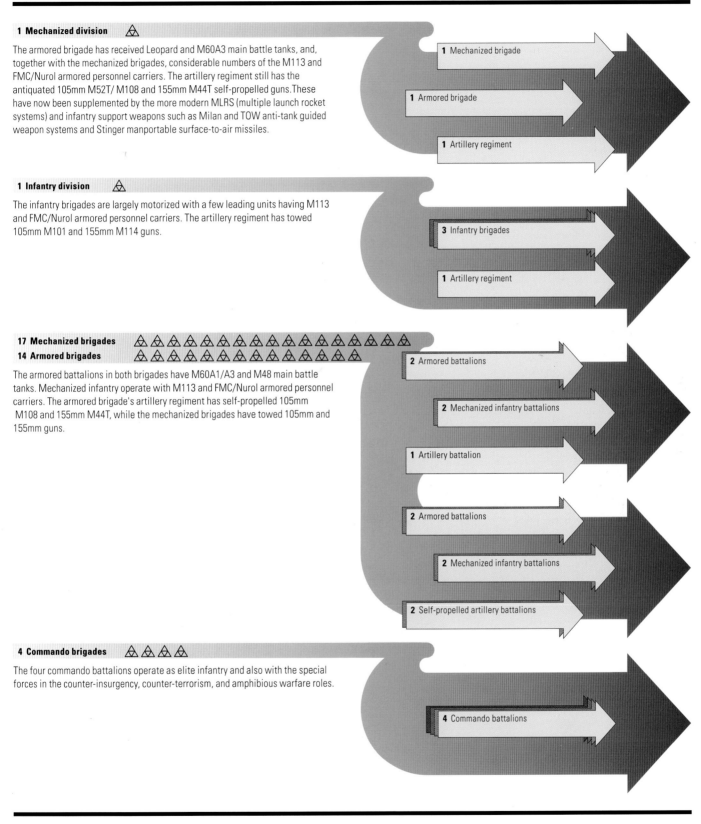

1 Mechanized division

The armored brigade has received Leopard and M60A3 main battle tanks, and, together with the mechanized brigades, considerable numbers of the M113 and FMC/Nurol armored personnel carriers. The artillery regiment still has the antiquated 105mm M52T/ M108 and 155mm M44T self-propelled guns. These have now been supplemented by the more modern MLRS (multiple launch rocket systems) and infantry support weapons such as Milan and TOW anti-tank guided weapon systems and Stinger manportable surface-to-air missiles.

1 Mechanized brigade

1 Armored brigade

1 Artillery regiment

1 Infantry division

The infantry brigades are largely motorized with a few leading units having M113 and FMC/Nurol armored personnel carriers. The artillery regiment has towed 105mm M101 and 155mm M114 guns.

3 Infantry brigades

1 Artillery regiment

17 Mechanized brigades
14 Armored brigades

The armored battalions in both brigades have M60A1/A3 and M48 main battle tanks. Mechanized infantry operate with M113 and FMC/Nurol armored personnel carriers. The armored brigade's artillery regiment has self-propelled 105mm M108 and 155mm M44T, while the mechanized brigades have towed 105mm and 155mm guns.

2 Armored battalions

2 Mechanized infantry battalions

1 Artillery battalion

2 Armored battalions

2 Mechanized infantry battalions

2 Self-propelled artillery battalions

4 Commando brigades

The four commando battalions operate as elite infantry and also with the special forces in the counter-insurgency, counter-terrorism, and amphibious warfare roles.

4 Commando battalions

🎖 Special forces

The Turkish army has a tradition of using special forces, dating back to the days of Kemal Ataturk in the 1920s, when elite units were used to devastating effect against the Greek army, and against insurgents of ethnic populations such as the Armenians. Today, Turkey has a considerable special operations capability for much the same reasons.

Warfare in the Aegean

The 3rd Amphibious Marine Commando Brigade is stationed in and around the Foca and Izmir areas on Turkey's Aegean coast. Attached to the 4th Army (the only major Turkish formation not committed to NATO), this highly trained unit would be deployed during any future conflict for special operations against the Greek offshore islands. Its many tasks include establishing beachheads, destroying airfields, communications sites, and ammunition dumps, and capturing heavily defended positions. Among its many specialist units are the combat frogmen of the SAT (*Su Alti Taaruz*) or underwater attack teams.

Special Warfare Operations Department

The Turkish army's Special Warfare Operations Department, with headquarters in Ankara, has under its command the
• 1st Commando Brigade, with headquarters in Kayseri, southeast of Ankara
• 2nd Commando Brigade, with headquarters in Bolu, northwest of Ankara
• 3rd Amphibious Marine Brigade, with headquarters in Foca/Izmir in western Turkey on the Aegean coast
• 4th Commando Brigade, with headquarters near Iskenderun, in southeast Turkey
    Each brigade has four battalions, with the 1st and 2nd Brigades deployed on counter-insurgency operations in southeastern Anatolia against the Kurds. Both brigades have also been involved in hot-pursuit operations in the Kurdish areas of northern Iraq. The 1st and 2nd Brigades have been reinforced on occasion by the 4th Brigade based in southern Turkey, but this unit's main task is to carry out special operations in northern Cyprus and along the Syrian border.

    The 3rd Brigade is tasked for amphibious operations in the eastern Aegean. In the event of a conflict with Greece it would attempt to seize the disputed offshore Aegean islands and probably attempt to sabotage communications, arms dumps, and airfields on the Greek mainland. The 3rd Brigade is also available to reinforce military operations in Cyprus.

    All of these units have a well-earned reputation for toughness and for being highly effective in combat against well-armed and determined insurgents. Training concentrates on assault commando techniques, and while heliborne insertion, combat shooting, mountain warfare, and unarmed combat play a major part in combat training, some of the more advanced techniques, such as the HALO (High Altitude and Low Opening) and HAHO (High Altitude and High Opening)

Turkish para-commandos waiting to embark on a UH-IH helicopter for a special forces mission.

skills are less well covered. Weapons in use include 5.56mm M16A1 automatic rifles, 9mm MP5 sub-machine guns, and PSG1 sniper rifles, and are among a wide range of standard army issue and specialist arms available.

OIKB (National Police Jandarma Commandos)

The main counter-terrorist unit is the OIKB (or National Police Jandarma Commandos), which is presently organized into three special forces companies. They are trained in anti-terrorist operations, hostage rescue, and anti-hijacking, as well as riot control. Members of this unit receive extensive training from selected army instructors at the Jandarma Security establishment at Foca, near Izmir. Operational control in peacetime is with the Ministry of Interior, but in wartime it passes to the Turkish army. Its personnel have seen regular action against such extremist groups as the left wing TPLA (or Turkish People's Liberation Army), Armenian rebels, and Kurdish insurgents.

Kurdish insurgency

Turkey's Special Warfare Operations Department regularly deploys one or two commando brigades in operations against Kurdish pro-independence guerrillas in southeastern Turkey.

Covert units operate intelligence-gathering missions on both sides of the border with Iraq, and long-range penetration patrols operate deep within northern Iraq. Turkey's special forces were also used to support U.S. CIA intelligence operations in support of anti-Saddam Hussein groups in Iraq.

Turkish special forces; the two soldiers left and right are equipped with 5.56mm M16A1 assault rifles, while the middle soldier carries a 7.62mm M60 machine gun.

India

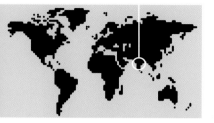

The modern Indian army was born during the 1948 partition of India and Pakistan. Although it has been severely tested throughout 50 years of bitter conflict, it still upholds its traditions of military excellence and loyalty to a democratically elected civilian government; it is the largest volunteer force in the world.

However, the Indian army faces the twenty-first century beset with internal unrest and the prospect of major conflicts, perhaps under nuclear conditions, with Pakistan and Communist China. This situation is further complicated by the extremes of both weather and geography throughout the subcontinent.

The wars with Pakistan in 1948, 1965, and 1971 continue to dominate the thinking of the Indian army's war planning staff. But the recent conflict in the high and inhospitable mountains of the Kargil in Kashmir has succeeded in highlighting many defects in both mountain and infantry units. The mechanization phase during the 1980s led to the dangerous neglect of small unit tactics and equipment, and steps are now underway to provide new close-support weapons, communications, and dedicated aviation units to rectify this weakness.

With these lessons in mind, and with an obvious need to match the increasing pace of arms procurement by both Pakistan and China, the Indian army has now embarked on a huge program of reorganization and rearmament to improve its war-fighting capability, and is purchasing state-of-the-art weapons from abroad on a large scale.

Potential flashpoints all along its vast northern and western borders, insurgency in Nagaland, Manipur, and Assam, and the ongoing problem of its troubled southern neighbor, Sri Lanka, place an increasing strain on both manpower and logistics. The Indian government, therefore, may find it very difficult to balance the needs of a modern army within its limited national budget.

India's fighting forces will need to remain highly motivated, confident, and well-armed to overcome the military threats of the new century and to maintain India's position as the pivotal power on the subcontinent.

Flashpoints and deployments

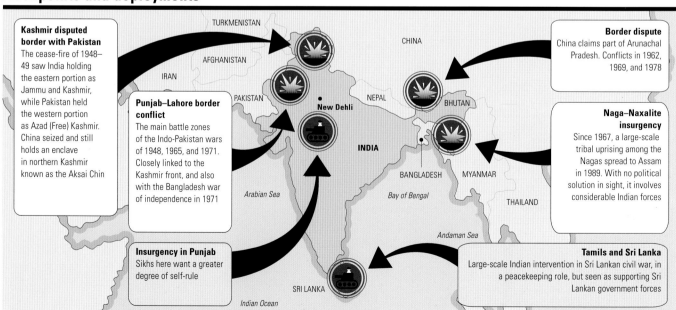

Kashmir disputed border with Pakistan
The cease-fire of 1948–49 saw India holding the eastern portion as Jammu and Kashmir, while Pakistan held the western portion as Azad (Free) Kashmir. China seized and still holds an enclave in northern Kashmir known as the Aksai Chin

Punjab–Lahore border conflict
The main battle zones of the Indo-Pakistan wars of 1948, 1965, and 1971. Closely linked to the Kashmir front, and also with the Bangladesh war of independence in 1971

Insurgency in Punjab
Sikhs here want a greater degree of self-rule

Border dispute
China claims part of Arunachal Pradesh. Conflicts in 1962, 1969, and 1978

Naga–Naxalite insurgency
Since 1967, a large-scale tribal uprising among the Nagas spread to Assam in 1989. With no political solution in sight, it involves considerable Indian forces

Tamils and Sri Lanka
Large-scale Indian intervention in Sri Lankan civil war, in a peacekeeping role, but seen as supporting Sri Lankan government forces

⊞ Operations

The Indian army's operational deployment is dominated by the need to respond quickly and decisively to any attack by Pakistan and/or China.

Russian T72 main battle tank operating in the foothills of the mountain frontier with Pakistan.

Armored cavalry

The armored corps provides the prime operational element of the Indian army. In the 53 years since Independence many fine armored units have been raised, but pride of place is still taken by the old cavalry regiments, such as the famous "Gray's Horse" which now rides to war in powerful T72 main battle tanks.

The Western Command Headquarters

The Western Command HQ at Chandigarh has two corps, the 10th and 11th, based in the Punjab, and a third, the 2nd Strike Corps, held in reserve for highly mobile armored warfare operations. Its tank and mechanized infantry formations, supported by heavy concentrations of mobile artillery, air defense, and combat engineers, are tasked to defeat any attempt by the Pakistan army at repeating the armored thrusts of the 1965 and 1971 campaigns across the arid deserts of Rajastan and from Lahore.

The Northern Command Headquarters

The Northern Command HQ at Udhampur deploys its three corps across inhospitable mountain ranges on the Kashmir cease-fire line and the Chinese border—the 14th is based in Ladakh, the 15th in Kashmir, and the 16th in Jammu. Here, they face the extremes of weather, terrain, insurgency from the Azad-Kashmiri para-military, Pakistan army regulars, growing instability in Nepal, and the constant threat of conventional war with China. Considerable numbers of special forces and intelligence gathering units are attached to this command.

The Eastern Command Headquarters

The Eastern Command HQ in Calcutta also faces extremes of terrain and a wide variety of threats; its 3rd Corps contends with insurgency in Nagaland, the 4th in Assam, and the 33rd deals with the threat of Chinese incursion across the Himalayas. There are a large number of mountain divisions and special forces committed in this area.

The Central Command Headquarters

The Central Command HQ at Lucknow holds its only corps, the 1st Strike, as a strategic reserve in support of the Eastern Command.

The Southern Command Headquarters

The Southern Command HQ at Poona (Pune) stations its 21st Strike Corps in Rajesthan, its 12th Corps is tasked for security operations in southern India and, if necessary, is available for further operations in Sri Lanka.

Other deployments abroad

In keeping with its long-standing commitment to peacekeeping operations, the Indian army currently has forces serving with the United Nations in the Democratic Congo (MONUC), Iraq-Kuwait border (UNIKOM), Lebanon (UNIFIL), and Sierra Leone (UNAMSIL).

The long range M46 130mm heavy field gun was originally developed from a naval weapon.

Weapons and units / overview of an army

Army units

The present organization has

5 regional commands	
4 field armies	
12 operational corps	
Combat units include	
3 armored divisions	
4 Rapid divisions	
18 infantry divisions	
9 mountain divisions	
1 artillery division	
7 independent armored brigades	
5 independent infantry	
2 mountain brigades	
1 airborne/commando brigade	
4 air defense brigades	
14 air defense brigades (cadre only) to be reinforced and brought up to combat readiness in wartime	
3 engineer brigades	

The Indian army is 1,100,000 strong, with some 800,000 personnel available to combat formations.

With its long tradition of cavalry operations, the Indian army maintains a large armored corps (with 59 tank regiments) and has a degree of mobility atypical of non-Western armies. This will soon be enhanced further with the delivery of 310 state-of-the-art Russian T90 main battle tanks. There is also a large, highly effective artillery corps of approximately 190 regiments, including one surface-to-surface missile regiment, two multiple launching rocket systems (MLRS), and 14 self-propelled regiments. These are complemented by the infantry, with 355 battalions, including 25 mechanized, eight airborne, and three commando. Supported by combat engineers, extensive medical facilities, and a major logistics infrastructure, this gives the Indian army a real and well-tried war fighting capability.

Infantry small arms

9mm FN Browning automatic pistols	5.56mm INSAS automatic rifles
9mm Sterling Mk4 sub-machine guns	5.56mm M16 automatic rifles
9mm MP5 sub-machine guns	7.62mm Dragunov sniper rifles
303 Lee-Enfield Mk-4 bolt action rifles	7.62mm L4A4 machine guns
7.62mm IA/C automatic rifles	7.62mm IB machine guns
7.62mm AKM automatic rifles	5.56mm INSAS-LM machine guns
7.62mm MAG GP machine guns	12.7mm M2 HB heavy machine guns

Impressive Indian designed and built ARJUN main battle tank armed with a 120mm gun—in production since 1999.

Average allocation Armor, artillery, and helicopters within each brigade

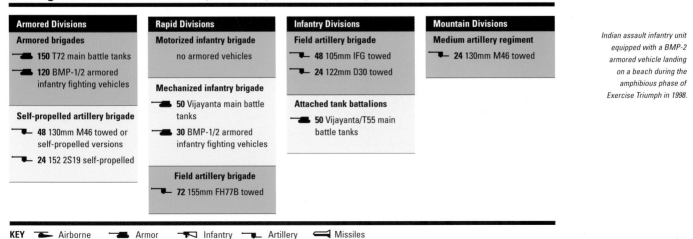

Armored Divisions	Rapid Divisions	Infantry Divisions	Mountain Divisions
Armored brigades	**Motorized infantry brigade**	**Field artillery brigade**	**Medium artillery regiment**
150 T72 main battle tanks	no armored vehicles	**48** 105mm IFG towed	**24** 130mm M46 towed
120 BMP-1/2 armored infantry fighting vehicles		**24** 122mm D30 towed	
	Mechanized infantry brigade		
Self-propelled artillery brigade	**50** Vijayanta main battle tanks	**Attached tank battalions**	
48 130mm M46 towed or self-propelled versions	**30** BMP-1/2 armored infantry fighting vehicles	**50** Vijayanta/T55 main battle tanks	
24 152 2S19 self-propelled			
	Field artillery brigade		
	72 155mm FH77B towed		

Indian assault infantry unit equipped with a BMP-2 armored vehicle landing on a beach during the amphibious phase of Exercise Triumph in 1998.

KEY ➤ Airborne   ➤ Armor   ➤ Infantry   ➤ Artillery   ➤ Missiles

Firepower   The cutting edge

Airborne	Armor	Infantry	Artillery	Missiles

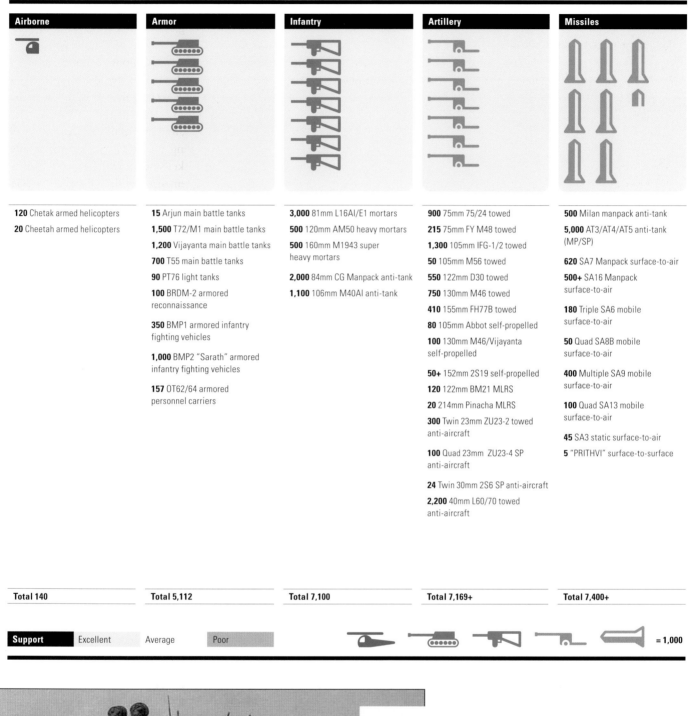

Airborne

120 Chetak armed helicopters
20 Cheetah armed helicopters

Armor

15 Arjun main battle tanks
1,500 T72/M1 main battle tanks
1,200 Vijayanta main battle tanks
700 T55 main battle tanks
90 PT76 light tanks
100 BRDM-2 armored reconnaissance
350 BMP1 armored infantry fighting vehicles
1,000 BMP2 "Sarath" armored infantry fighting vehicles
157 OT62/64 armored personnel carriers

Infantry

3,000 81mm L16AI/E1 mortars
500 120mm AM50 heavy mortars
500 160mm M1943 super heavy mortars
2,000 84mm CG Manpack anti-tank
1,100 106mm M40AI anti-tank

Artillery

900 75mm 75/24 towed
215 75mm FY M48 towed
1,300 105mm IFG-1/2 towed
50 105mm M56 towed
550 122mm D30 towed
750 130mm M46 towed
410 155mm FH77B towed
80 105mm Abbot self-propelled
100 130mm M46/Vijayanta self-propelled
50+ 152mm 2S19 self-propelled
120 122mm BM21 MLRS
20 214mm Pinacha MLRS
300 Twin 23mm ZU23-2 towed anti-aircraft
100 Quad 23mm ZU23-4 SP anti-aircraft
24 Twin 30mm 2S6 SP anti-aircraft
2,200 40mm L60/70 towed anti-aircraft

Missiles

500 Milan manpack anti-tank
5,000 AT3/AT4/AT5 anti-tank (MP/SP)
620 SA7 Manpack surface-to-air
500+ SA16 Manpack surface-to-air
180 Triple SA6 mobile surface-to-air
50 Quad SA8B mobile surface-to-air
400 Multiple SA9 mobile surface-to-air
100 Quad SA13 mobile surface-to-air
45 SA3 static surface-to-air
5 "PRITHVI" surface-to-surface

Total 140	Total 5,112	Total 7,100	Total 7,169+	Total 7,400+

Support	Excellent	Average	Poor						= 1,000

Arjun Mk-1 Main Battle Tank

Country of origin India
First entered service 1996 with Indian army
Main armament 120mm rifled gun (44 rounds)
Max. road speed 42 mph (72 km/h)
Max. range 300 miles (500 km)
Crew 4
Over 120 built so far

▲ Fighting structure

The Indian army has a wide variety of demands made upon its forces, especially considering India's varied and difficult terrain. The structures of the army's main combat formations clearly reflect these problems. Dedicated mountain infantry divisions face the Pakistan or Chinese forces in the freezing mountains of Kashmir, and the armored and mechanized divisions are prepared for major tank battles in the arid desert conditions of Rajasthan. Indian special forces and jungle warfare trained infantry brigades are to be found fighting counter-insurgency campaigns across the hills and densely wooded valleys of Assam and Nagaland, while the infantry divisions regularly provide combat units for the UN's operations in Sierra Leone and elsewhere. The structure of Indian units is complex and often varies according to deployment; an example would be the oversized 16th Corps of six divisions in Kashmir.

Fighting Structure Overview

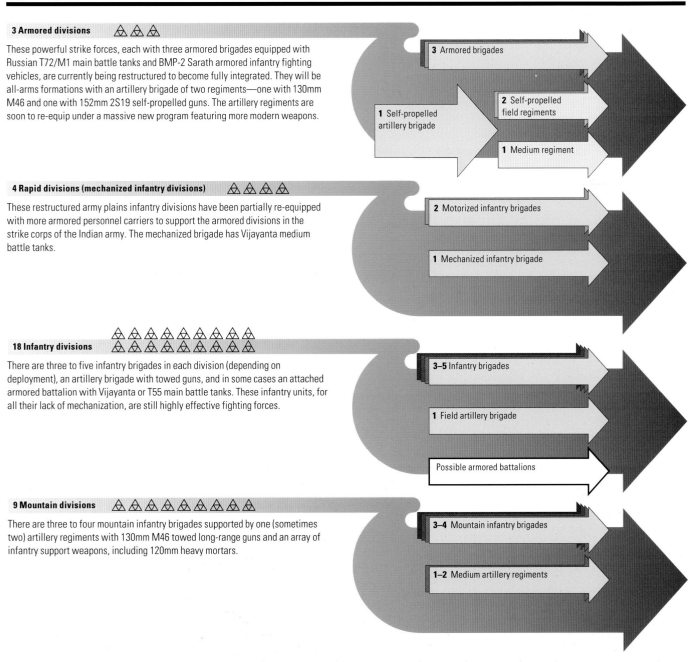

3 Armored divisions △ △ △

These powerful strike forces, each with three armored brigades equipped with Russian T72/M1 main battle tanks and BMP-2 Sarath armored infantry fighting vehicles, are currently being restructured to become fully integrated. They will be all-arms formations with an artillery brigade of two regiments—one with 130mm M46 and one with 152mm 2S19 self-propelled guns. The artillery regiments are soon to re-equip under a massive new program featuring more modern weapons.

3 Armored brigades
1 Self-propelled artillery brigade
2 Self-propelled field regiments
1 Medium regiment

4 Rapid divisions (mechanized infantry divisions) △ △ △ △

These restructured army plains infantry divisions have been partially re-equipped with more armored personnel carriers to support the armored divisions in the strike corps of the Indian army. The mechanized brigade has Vijayanta medium battle tanks.

2 Motorized infantry brigades
1 Mechanized infantry brigade

18 Infantry divisions △ △ △ △ △ △ △ △ △ △ △ △ △ △ △ △ △ △

There are three to five infantry brigades in each division (depending on deployment), an artillery brigade with towed guns, and in some cases an attached armored battalion with Vijayanta or T55 main battle tanks. These infantry units, for all their lack of mechanization, are still highly effective fighting forces.

3–5 Infantry brigades
1 Field artillery brigade
Possible armored battalions

9 Mountain divisions △ △ △ △ △ △ △ △ △

There are three to four mountain infantry brigades supported by one (sometimes two) artillery regiments with 130mm M46 towed long-range guns and an array of infantry support weapons, including 120mm heavy mortars.

3–4 Mountain infantry brigades
1–2 Medium artillery regiments

Special forces

The Indian army has a tradition of providing special forces of considerable quality. During World War II, Indian commandos operated with great success against the Japanese in both mountain and jungle terrain. The growing problem of insurgency since 1945 and the demanding geography of India has ensured that this tradition continues.

The para-commandos

The para-commandos are India's premier special forces. They were formed after the 1965 Indo-Pakistan War, which highlighted the need for an elite special operations capability. The first two battalions, the 9th and 10th, first saw major conflict during the 1971 war, when they took part in the invasion of East Pakistan, now Bangladesh. Both units also played a part in the ill-fated peacekeeping operation in Sri Lanka in 1988, during the height of the civil war with the Tamil separatists. More units have since been added—the late 1970s saw the formation of the 1st Punjab, and in 1990 the 21st Maratha Light Infantry, which now form the Red Devils Parachute Unit (special forces).

Since 1978–79, the para-commandos have been trained in HALO (High Altitude Low Opening) parachute techniques. With their trademark black jumpsuits, wrist altimeters, square canopy, and leaf-pattern parachutes, armed with modern automatic weapons, grenades, and a jackknife, this unit provides the Indian army with a powerful and adaptable special forces capability, deployable for a wide range of counter-insurgency and anti-terrorist missions.

The para-commandos' tasks include provision of elite infantry battle groups, the establishment of special forces superiority within a battle-zone, and clandestine operations— sabotage and intelligence-gathering behind enemy lines. Their training is of the highest quality, and includes combat shooting, marksmanship, heliborne-insertion, combat swimming, explosives ordnance disposal, mountain warfare techniques, prisoner-of-war rescue, surveillance, HAHO (High Altitude High Opening), and HALO (High Altitude Low Opening).

They regularly cross-train with special forces from other armies, and personnel are sent on specialist courses abroad. They have available the wide range of standard issue Indian army weapons for counter-insurgency operations. For clandestine operations, they have access to specially acquired small arms, such as the 9mm Israeli UZI and 9mm German MP5A2/3 sub-machine guns, 5.56mm U.S. M16A2 assault rifles, and a range of specialist sniper rifles including the 7.62 mm PSG-1/MSG-90 and the SSG-2000. They are equipped with a wide range of specialist communications and GPS.

Fierce and loyal

When the old British Indian Army was broken up in 1948 along religious lines between India and Pakistan, an exception was made for the Gurkhas. While the majority of units joined the British army, three Gurkha regiments stayed with the Indian army where they have played a leading role as elite light infantry in special forces operations ever since.

A special forces soldier armed with a 7.62mm Mauser SP-66 specialist sniper rifle, which uses a short-throw bolt action to limit the movement required of the firer.

Pakistan

The Pakistani army, like the Indian army, was born out of the division of the old British-Indian army. However, unlike India, Pakistan received little or no modern equipment, and had to play the game of catch-up for years following its independence in 1947. However, fierce military pride, dedicated professionalism, and a determination not to be overshadowed by India have now created a tight, highly motivated fighting force.

While distracted by a desire to play a political role in governing the country, the Pakistani army has nonetheless proven itself a force to be reckoned with. It succeeded in forcing India to commit considerable parts of its huge army to achieve a limited victory in the border war of 1965. However, after underestimating the strong anti-Pakistani feeling among the Bengali people of East Pakistan, the Pakistani army found itself grossly overstretched in the war of 1971. This led to a humiliating defeat in the Eastern region that later became known as Bangladesh.

The Pakistani army then launched a major campaign against Indian forces in the West Pakistan border, with the intent of taking pressure off the hard-pressed army units in East Pakistan. After some initial advances by Pakistani forces, the Indian army quickly developed a highly mobile, armored warfare offensive, and left a rather chastened Pakistani army firmly on the defensive.

In the years since, the Pakistani army has been restructured and rearmed (within the constraints of a limited budget), but it remains an army of considerable ability and proven qualities. However, although the army has improved, by the late 1990s it had been outmatched by improvements in the Indian army. Pakistan has had to face the fact that even with increased levels of foreign aid and additional funding from the hard-pressed national budget, it would not be able to seriously match the superiority of the Indian army.

Flashpoints and deployments

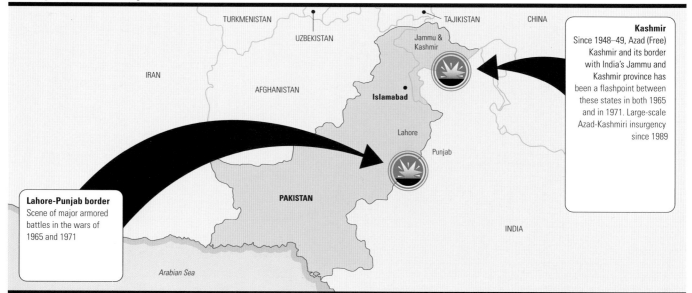

Kashmir
Since 1948–49, Azad (Free) Kashmir and its border with India's Jammu and Kashmir province has been a flashpoint between these states in both 1965 and in 1971. Large-scale Azad-Kashmiri insurgency since 1989

Lahore-Punjab border
Scene of major armored battles in the wars of 1965 and 1971

☐ Operations

The Pakistani army's operations cover a wide range of geographic and climatic extremes. The hot, low-lying Rann of Kutch in the south was the scene of major tank battles in the Indo-Pakistan war of 1965; the dusty desert borders of Lahore and Rajasthan are where major fighting occurred during the war with India in 1971; and the bleak, bitterly cold high mountains of Kashmir saw hand-to-hand combat in 2000.

The army is also responsible for counter-insurgency operations in Baluchistan, and securing the borders with Iran and Afghanistan. Most of the main combat units are permanently dug in along the borders with India, preparing for the fourth major war between the two nations since 1947.

Current deployments

The present operational deployment of the army has the 7th Infantry Division opposite Dras-Kargil in Kashmir.

10th Corps, in Kashmir with
- 12th Infantry Division, a reinforced unit with 6 brigades at Muzzafarabad
- 19th Infantry Division at Rawalkot
- 23rd Infantry Division at Mangla

30th Corps on the northeast front with
- 8th Infantry Division at Sialkot
- 15th Infantry Division at Sialkot

4th Corps on the northeast front with
- 10th Infantry Division
- 11th Infantry Division

31st Corps on the central front with
- 37th Infantry Division at Sukkar
- 33rd Infantry Division at Bhawalpur

5th Corps in the central area with
- 16th Infantry Division at Rahim Yar Khan
- 18th Infantry Division at Hyderabad

11th Corps Army Reserve Center with
- 9th Infantry Division at Mardan
- 7th Infantry Division at Baltstan

2nd Corps on the eastern front with
- 1st Armored Division at Multan
- 14th Infantry Division at Multan
- 40th Infantry Division at Okara

1st Corps northern front reserve with
- 6th Armored Division at Mangla
- 17th Infantry Division at Kharia
- 35th Infantry Division at Gujranwala

12th Corps on the western area with
- 41st Infantry Division at Quetta

Other deployments abroad

Pakistani military personnel are presently serving abroad on United Nations peacekeeping operations in Croatia (UNMOP) since 1995, East Timor (UNTAET) since 1999, Georgia (UNOMIG) since 1995, Iraq/Kuwait (UNIKOM) since 1992, Sierra Leone (UNAMSIL) since 1999, and Western Sahara (MINURSO) since 1994.

The Kashmir problem

The major stumbling block to better relations between Pakistan and India is the major ongoing operations in Kashmir. In 1948, the pro-Pakistan, majority Muslim population of Kashmir revolted after the ruling Hindu Mararajah opted to join India. After a bitter campaign, a cease-fire line was established between the areas occupied by the two armies. It is along this line that conflict has continued ever since.

Pakistani soldiers have served in UN peacekeeping operations in a number of areas, including East Timor, Georgia, and Kuwait.

Weapons and units / overview of an army

The strength of the Pakistani army presently stands at 550,000, with some 400,000 personnel available for main combat units. While the army is heavily equipped with armor, much of it is obsolete. Attempts have been made to improve this situation, including the purchase of 320 T80UD main battle tanks from Ukraine. However, this still leaves the mechanized infantry desperately short of armored personnel carriers, and financial constraints are likely to continue, so the problem may not be addressed in the near future.

Elite infantry units are trained to operate in a wide range of extreme weather conditions and difficult terrain. Here in the mountains of Kashmir, they are equipped with high-altitude breathing apparatus and modern automatic weapons.

Army units

There are 9 corps headquarters, with
9 attached artillery brigades
2 armored divisions
19 infantry divisions
1 area command (divisional strength)
3 armored reconnaissance regiments
7 independent armored brigades
9 independent infantry brigades
3 special forces battalions
8 air defense brigades
7 engineer brigades
17 aviation squadrons

Average allocation Armor, artillery, and helicopters within each brigade

Armored Division	Infantry Division	Artillery Division
440 T80UD/Type-85/Type-69/Type-59 main battle tanks	**48** 122mm Type-54/60 and 130mm Type-59 towed artillery	**48** 122mm Type-54/60, 155mm M114/M198, or 203mm M115 towed
200 M113 armored personnel carriers		
72 155mm M109A2 self-propelled artillery	**Those with attached armored brigades have**	
24 AZAR multiple rocket launchers	**140** Type-59/M48A5 main battle tanks	
	60 M113 armored personnel carriers	

M198 Towed/Airportable Artillery

Country of origin U.S.
First entered service 1982 with U.S. army
Main armament 155mm Gun-Howitzer
Max. range 14 miles (23 km) rocket-assisted shell 18 miles (30 km)
Rate of fire 4 rpm (max.) 2 rpm (sustained)
Crew 9
Thousands built, in service with over 20 armies

KEY ⬤ Airborne　⬤ Armor　⬤ Infantry　⬤ Artillery　⬤ Missiles

Firepower   The cutting edge

Airborne	Armor	Infantry	Artillery	Missiles

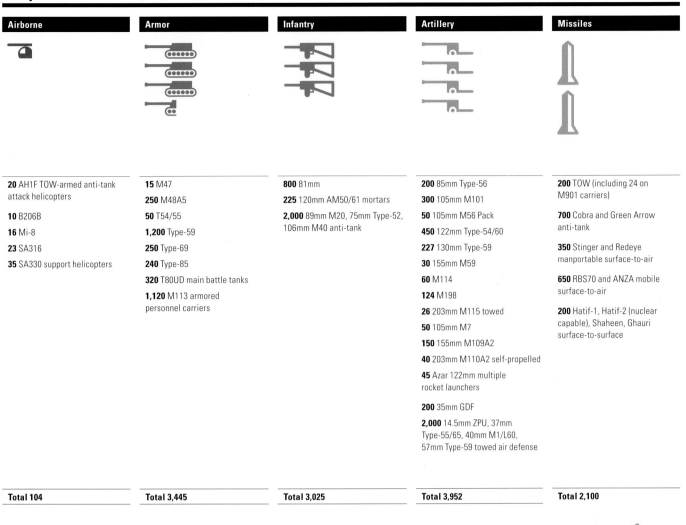

Airborne
20 AH1F TOW-armed anti-tank attack helicopters

10 B206B

16 Mi-8

23 SA316

35 SA330 support helicopters

Armor
15 M47

250 M48A5

50 T54/55

1,200 Type-59

250 Type-69

240 Type-85

320 T80UD main battle tanks

1,120 M113 armored personnel carriers

Infantry
800 81mm

225 120mm AM50/61 mortars

2,000 89mm M20, 75mm Type-52, 106mm M40 anti-tank

Artillery
200 85mm Type-56

300 105mm M101

50 105mm M56 Pack

450 122mm Type-54/60

227 130mm Type-59

30 155mm M59

60 M114

124 M198

26 203mm M115 towed

50 105mm M7

150 155mm M109A2

40 203mm M110A2 self-propelled

45 Azar 122mm multiple rocket launchers

200 35mm GDF

2,000 14.5mm ZPU, 37mm Type-55/65, 40mm M1/L60, 57mm Type-59 towed air defense

Missiles
200 TOW (including 24 on M901 carriers)

700 Cobra and Green Arrow anti-tank

350 Stinger and Redeye manportable surface-to-air

650 RBS70 and ANZA mobile surface-to-air

200 Hatif-1, Hatif-2 (nuclear capable), Shaheen, Ghauri surface-to-surface

---

Total 104   **Total 3,445**   **Total 3,025**   **Total 3,952**   **Total 2,100**

Support   Excellent   Average   Poor   = 1,000

Infantry small arms

9mm Browning HP automatic pistols
9mm MP5 sub-machine guns
7.62mm G3 automatic rifles
7.62mm Type-56/AK automatic rifles
5.56mm M16 automatic rifles
.30 M1919 machine guns
7.62mm PK machine guns
12.7mm M2 HB heavy machine guns

Large numbers of Type-69 main battle tanks now equip armored units alongside the older variant, the Type-59. Both vehicles are of Chinese design.

◭ Fighting structure

The Pakistani army has spent much of the last 50 years organizing and arming itself for war with India. Armored and mechanized infantry were trained, equipped, and deployed for the fluid situations that developed in the wars of 1965 and 1971 in the battle zones of Lahore, Punjab, and Rajasthan. Highly trained mountain infantry and Azad (Free) Kashmiri forces operate in the high mountains and bitterly cold glaciers of Kashmir, where the demands on equipment and manpower are considerable. The Pakistani army has restructured its formations in recent years to try to counter India's manpower advantage. A sizable reserve has been created that can be deployed quickly to give parity or even short–term superiority in local areas. Also, some infantry divisions have been strengthened with independent armored brigades.

The Baluchi infantry regiment stand guard outside state buildings in Islamabad. They are armed with a non-standard issue German MG42/MG3 machine gun.

Fighting Structure Overview

2 Armored divisions ◭ ◭

The armored brigades have T80, Type-85, and M48A5 main battle tanks. The infantry brigade has M113 armored personnel carriers, and the artillery brigade has both 155mm M109A2 and 203mm M110A2 self-propelled guns. Infantry support is well-equipped and includes 81mm and 120mm mortars and TOW anti-tank guided weapons. Air defense is provided by Stinger and RBS70 surface-to-air missiles. AH1F TOW armed attack helicopters provide close air support for the armored divisions.

3 Armored brigades

1 Infantry brigade

1 Artillery brigade

19 Infantry divisions ◭◭◭◭◭◭◭◭ ◭◭◭◭◭◭◭◭◭◭◭

The infantry brigades are still largely motorized with perhaps only one company in each having M113 armored personnel carriers. The artillery brigade has 105mm M101 and 122mm Type-54/60 towed field guns. Some infantry divisions now have an attached independent armored brigade with T54/55 and Type-59 main battle tanks.

3 Infantry brigades

1 Artillery brigade

Some have armored brigades attached

1 Artillery division ◭

The nine independent artillery brigades support the armored and infantry divisions and can concentrate considerable firepower with 122mm Type-54/60, 130mm Type-59, 155mm M114 and M198 and 203mm M115 towed field guns and howitzers.

9 Independent artillery brigades

⚜ Special forces

In 1954, the Pakistani army created an elite commando unit with U.S. army assistance. In order to disguise its operational tasks, it was given the cover title of the 19th Battalion Baluch Regiment. Today, this unit has become the cornerstone of a much enlarged special forces community.

The SSG (Special Service Group)

The present SSG (Special Service Group), effectively the enlarged 19th Baluch Regiment, has been based at its headquarters in Cherat for more than 45 years. But in March of 1964, a U.S. army training team helped set up the airborne training school at Peshawar. All members of the 19th Baluch have to be qualified in airborne techniques, and training includes both basic and jumpmaster courses. The SSG now has some 24 companies, each of which has specialized units in desert, mountain, ranger, underwater warfare, and intelligence-gathering operations.

The Musa Company

In 1970, a genuine anti-terrorist role was added, with responsibility being given to the independent Musa Company, which formed in the same year (originally as a combat swimmer unit). The Musa Company has now become a dedicated counter-terrorism unit and since 1981 has received training by SAS advisors. A wide range of skills is now considered necessary, including heliborne insertion, combat shooting, and parachute techniques including HAHO (High Altitude High Opening) and HALO (High Altitude Low Opening). It has a wide variety of weapons available for use including standard army issue as well as black market 9mm Israeli UZI and German MP5 sub-machine guns, U.S. M16A1 automatic rifles, and PSG1 sniper rifles.

The SSG has conducted deep penetration operations within India and disputed areas of Kashmir, and helped train Sri Lankan army commandos for operations against the Tamil Tiger insurgents. It has also conducted covert missions into Afghanistan, and provided air-marshals for airliners carrying VIPs. Indeed, one of its most notable operations to date was the successful rescue of hostages during the storming of a hijacked civil airliner at Lahore Airport in September 1981. The SSG is presently organized into three special forces battalions, each of four companies, with two based at the Cherat headquarters, and one on operations along the borders with India or at strategic locations such as nuclear research facilities, or at the Terbella Dam. In addition, there are 12 more independent special forces companies, including the enlarged Musa Company, which now provides Pakistan with a dedicated, genuine counter-terrorism capability.

An airmobile infantry squad dismount quickly from a hovering SA330 Puma assault helicopter. There are 35 of these versatile machines operational with the Pakistan army.

The SSG, or Special Service Group, practice close protection of VIPs in hostile environments at the special forces headquarters at Cherat, near Attock City.

Birth of a nation

In March 1971, the 3rd Commando Battalion of the special forces was ordered to suppress the growing political unrest among the Bengali population in East Pakistan. On the night of March 25–26 they launched Operation Searchlight, when a unit of the 3rd Battalion raided the home of Sheikh Mulibar Rahman, the leader of the pro-independence Awami League, and captured him alive. By that evening civil war had broken out. Eight months later, and after Pakistani special forces had made numerous raids into India to cut off the supply of arms to the Bengali "freedom fighters," India invaded, and shortly afterward the independent state of Bangladesh was born.

China

China's army is a vast force, much of which is under-trained, poorly equipped, and of uncertain quality, yet it remains loyal to the current Communist regime (at least for the immediate future). China has made great efforts to produce units that are better equipped, trained, and tasked for major flashpoints, such as the borders with India, Vietnam, Russia, and Taiwan. However, most units remain old-fashioned and unwieldy corps-sized formations, made up of many different divisions that are far too large to be of real combat value.

Many of China's most serious problems lie within its own borders—namely the ever-present risk of civil revolt against the Communist government. This has been simmering since the Tiananmen Square revolt in 1989, when only a politically loyal army prevented the government from being ignominiously overthrown (as happened to Russia).

The Chinese army is also faced with the threat of a confrontation with the growing number of indigenous religious groups among the Chinese working masses. But most importantly, a real threat is emerging from the largely ignored ethnic insurgents and Islamic terrorists who inhabit much of western and southern China. There, the ethnic population is not only seeking the right to practice their religion openly, but increasingly to throw off Chinese control altogether. As the revolts spread, the danger increases that countries such as

New century, new weapons

China no longer regards conventional fighting forces as the only way to combat U.S. military supremacy. Chinese strategists now consider "unrestricted warfare" as a means to target the United States—they are intent on exploring the use of computer viruses, information warfare, and stock market manipulation in addition to the use of traditional weapons, such as missiles, tanks, and rifles.

A Chinese army mechanized infantry unit on maneuvers in central China with a Type-62 light tank.

Flashpoints and deployments

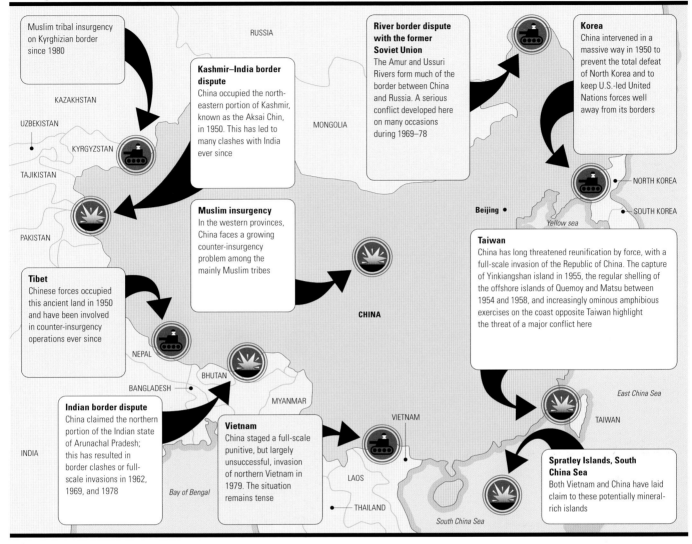

Muslim tribal insurgency on Kyrghizian border since 1980

Kashmir–India border dispute
China occupied the north-eastern portion of Kashmir, known as the Aksai Chin, in 1950. This has led to many clashes with India ever since

River border dispute with the former Soviet Union
The Amur and Ussuri Rivers form much of the border between China and Russia. A serious conflict developed here on many occasions during 1969–78

Korea
China intervened in a massive way in 1950 to prevent the total defeat of North Korea and to keep U.S.-led United Nations forces well away from its borders

Muslim insurgency
In the western provinces, China faces a growing counter-insurgency problem among the mainly Muslim tribes

Tibet
Chinese forces occupied this ancient land in 1950 and have been involved in counter-insurgency operations ever since

Taiwan
China has long threatened reunification by force, with a full-scale invasion of the Republic of China. The capture of Yinkiangshan island in 1955, the regular shelling of the offshore islands of Quemoy and Matsu between 1954 and 1958, and increasingly ominous amphibious exercises on the coast opposite Taiwan highlight the threat of a major conflict here

Indian border dispute
China claimed the northern portion of the Indian state of Arunachal Pradesh; this has resulted in border clashes or full-scale invasions in 1962, 1969, and 1978

Vietnam
China staged a full-scale punitive, but largely unsuccessful, invasion of northern Vietnam in 1979. The situation remains tense

Spratley Islands, South China Sea
Both Vietnam and China have laid claim to these potentially mineral-rich islands

RUSSIA
KAZAKHSTAN
UZBEKISTAN
KYRGYZSTAN
TAJIKISTAN
PAKISTAN
MONGOLIA
Beijing •
NORTH KOREA
SOUTH KOREA
Yellow sea
CHINA
NEPAL
BHUTAN
BANGLADESH
MYANMAR
VIETNAM
INDIA
Bay of Bengal
LAOS
THAILAND
South China Sea
East China Sea
TAIWAN

Afghanistan (now under the militant Taliban), and perhaps Iran will become involved by supplying weapons and trained insurgents to these groups.

The Chinese army first occupied Tibet in 1950, and has been fighting a limited, low-level war against a revolt by native Tibetans ever since. These campaigns have been noted for their brutality, but not their military efficiency. In Nepal, Maoist terrorists now control much of the country and have thereby created yet another potential flashpoint for the Chinese with their Indian neighbor.

A Chinese artillery unit firing a heavy 152mm Type-54 field gun on the Himalayan border with India.

⚑ Operations

The operational deployment of major Chinese formations is set to change dramatically over the next five years and the divisional structure will be replaced by several hundred smaller, more flexible and mobile brigades. The present basis of the Chinese army is the Army Group, twelve of which are deployed to protect the capital, Beijing, and the industrial north of China from internal unrest or from any unlikely external attack from Russia, Japan, or Korea. Five armies currently face the National Chinese in Taiwan and the remaining four are all dual-tasked.

Chinese infantry practice an attack on a defensive position with copies of the Russian LPO 50 flamethrower, during a training exercise.

Amphibious threat to Taiwan

China's decision to stage a massive amphibious warfare exercise off Dongshan Island in the Taiwan Straits in mid-2001 is a cause of great concern. The 160 amphibious vessels and transports involved are capable of moving a full mechanized infantry division, and with China's ability to launch an assault with two full airborne brigades, a full-scale invasion of Taiwan is a distinct possibility.

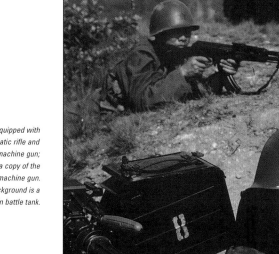

Chinese infantry equipped with Type-56 automatic rifle and Type-54 heavy machine gun; the latter is a copy of the Russian DSHK machine gun. In the background is a Type-59 main battle tank.

A Chinese PLA mechanized infantry unit stages a massed attack training exercise, equipped with a Norinco YW-531E armored personnel carrier.

Vietnam hits back

Not all of China's military operations have been successful. The Chinese invasion of Vietnam began on February 17, 1979 with infantry units heavily supported by tanks and artillery. Although the towns of Cao Bang and Lang Son fell by March 4, the Chinese had been severely mauled by Vietnamese home guard units. China quickly withdrew by March 16, as a large number of Vietnamese regulars advanced.

Conflict with Taiwan

The simmering dispute with Taiwan has continued since 1949 with occasional outbreaks of conflict. From August 1954 to May 1955, the Communists shelled the offshore islands of Quemoy and Matsu, and during this period China successfully launched a seaborne invasion and captured the island of Yijiangshan, 210 miles north of Taiwan. The Chinese army currently deploys five armies in that region, each with a minimum of three divisions, plus supporting armor and artillery. And while the Chinese have greatly increased their amphibious warfare capability, it is doubtful whether it has reached a stage where success is likely.

Dispute with Russia

The Chinese attack on the Russian garrison on the disputed island of Demansky in 1969 led to a massive Russian counter-attack, in which the Chinese suffered large numbers of casualties. China also learned a severe lesson in just how far its army had fallen behind those of the superpowers since the Korean War of 1950–53. By 1971, the Russians had 44 divisions, 500,000 men, and over 1,800 main battle tanks close to China's vulnerable northern frontier. Therefore, it is not surprising that China deploys some twelve Category A and B armies in defense of its main population centers, its industrial heartland, and massive road and rail infrastructure.

Other deployments abroad

The Chengdu military region (in southwest China) is host to two of the remaining armies and these are dual-tasked—their range of responsibilities includes the occupation of Tibet and the border conflict with India and Vietnam. Two additional armies are serving in the Lanzhou military region (in western China) and are tasked to guard the borders with Mongolia. But, most importantly, they are tasked to deal with the growing ethnic and Muslim resistance to Communist rule in the vast expanses of western China. The Lanzhou military region now has the largest number of independent special forces units, as the Chinese army struggles to come to terms with what could soon become the world's most ferocious insurgency problem.

Weapons and units / overview of an army

The Chinese army has a strength of 1,750,000 with over 1,400,000 personnel available for front-line service. But the army is struggling to continue its massive program to reduce and restructure its forces, while at the same time modernizing the fighting abilities of a shambling mass of soldiers, (800,000 of whom are becoming increasingly unwilling conscripts). So far, only three infantry divisions at national level, and eleven at regional level have been improved sufficiently to have a rapid-reaction capability. This is mainly for the protection of the ruling Communist regime, rather than for a genuine combat role.

Army units

The present organization has

7 military regions

27 provincial military districts

4 garrison commands which between them command

    21 integrated group armies (scheduled to reduce to 18 by 2002); under their control are a total of

    7 mechanized infantry divisions

    37 infantry divisions

    10 armored divisions

    12 armored brigades

    13 infantry brigades

    5 artillery divisions

    20 artillery brigades

    7 helicopter regiments

Type-85 Main Battle Tank

Country of origin China

First entered service 1984–85 with Chinese PLA

Main armament 125mm smoothbore gun (40 rounds)

Max. road speed 36 mph (58 km/h)

Max. range 330 miles (550 km)

Crew 3

Several thousand built, in service with some 4 armies

Independent units

Independent units include

5 infantry divisions

1 armored and **2** infantry brigades

1 artillery division

3 artillery brigades

4 air defense brigades

Garrison, border, and coastal forces include

12 infantry divisions

1 mountain brigade

4 infantry brigades

87 infantry battalions

Average allocation Armor, artillery, and helicopters within each brigade

10 Integrated Group Armies

3 Infantry divisions

- **93** T-59/69 main battle tanks
- **130** T-63/77/891/92/86 armored personnel carriers

Tank division

- **319** T-69/79/85 main battle tanks
- **260** T-92/86 armored personnel carriers

Artillery brigade

- **108** T-70/701/89 105mm self-propelled guns
- **108** T-83 155mm self-propelled guns
- **108** 130mm M46 towed field guns

Anti-aircraft artillery brigade

- **108** 23mm T-80 and 57mm T-59 towed
- **62** HN5A/B/C manportable surface-to-air missiles

9 Integrated Group Armies

2 Infantry divisions

- **31** T-62/63 light tanks

Tank brigade

- **93** T-59/69 main battle tanks
- **46** T-63/77 armored personnel carriers

Artillery brigade

- **108** 130mm M46 towed field guns
- **108** 152mm T-66/83 towed field guns

Anti-aircraft artillery brigade

- **108** 23mm T-80 and 37mm T-65/74 towed
- **26** HN5A/B/C manportable surface-to-air missiles

Airborne Assault Corps

3 Airborne divisions

Reconnaissance battalion

- **40** BMD-3 armored infantry fighting vehicles (IFV)

Infantry small arms

7.65mm Type-67 automatic pistols

7.65mm Type-50 sub-machine guns

7.65mm Type-79 sub-machine guns

7.65mm Type-64 silenced sub-machine guns

7.62mm Type-56 carbines

7.62mm Type-56 assault rifles

7.62mm Type-68/73 assault rifles

7.62mm Type-53 machine guns

7.62mm Type-56 machine guns

7.62mm Type-57 machine guns

7.62mm Type-58 machine guns

7.62mm Type-67 machine guns

12.7mm Type-54 heavy machine guns

Support troops include

6 combat engineer regiments

46 engineer regiments

50 signal regiments

KEY ⬛ Airborne   ⬛ Armor   ⬛ Infantry   ⬛ Artillery   ⬛ Missiles

Firepower   The cutting edge

Airborne	Armor	Infantry	Artillery	Missiles

8 SA342/HOT anti-tank missile armed helicopters

24 Mi-17

30 Mi-8TB

30 Mi-171

3 Mi-6

4 Z8A

73 Z9

20 S70C2

10 SA319

20 Z11 support helicopters

5,500 Type-59-1/11

150 Type-69-1

550 Type-79

500 Type-85B

400 Type-85C

100 Type-98 main battle tanks

700 Type-62/621, Type-63 light tanks

100 BMD-3 armored infantry fighting vehicles

1,800 Type-63A/1/11

100 Type-77 (BTR50PK)

1,300 Type-891/11

2,000 WZ523, Type-92, Type-86/86A armored personnel carriers

16,000 82mm Type-53/67/82/87, 100mm Type-71, 120mm Type-55, 160mm Type-56 mortars

18,000 62mm Type-70, 75mm Type-56, 85mm Type-65/78, 105mm Type-75 anti-tank

1,000 100mm Type-59

6,000 122mm Type-54, Type-60 Type-83

800 130mm Type-59/59-1

4,000 152mm Type-54, Type-66, Type-83

340 155mm Type-88 towed

1,000 122mm Type-70, Type-89

300 152mm Type-83 self-propelled

100 2S23 gun-mortars

1,800 122mm Type-81/89

200 130mm Type-70

400 273mm Type-83

100 320mm Type-96 multiple rocket launchers

700 100mm Type-73/86 towed anti-tank

320 120mm Type-89 self-propelled anti-tank

8,000 23mm Type-80, 25mm Type-87, 35mm Type-90, 37mm Type-55/65/74

3,000 57mm Type-59, 85mm Type-56, 100mm Type-59 towed air defense

1,000+ 37mm Type-89, 57mm Type-80 self-propelled air defense

7,500 HJ73 (AT-3 copy), HJ8 (Milan copy) anti-tank

8,000 HN5 (SA-7) manportable surface-to-air

3,000 QW-1/2, HQ-61A, HQ-7, PL9C, 26 SA15 surface-to-air

Total 222	**Total 13,200**	**Total 34,000**	**Total 29,060+**	**Total 18,500**

Support	Excellent	Average	Poor		= 1,000

◭ Fighting structure

The Chinese army has seen a recent reduction in the number of Army Groups from 21 to 18, and great efforts are now being made to reorganize ten of the remaining groups as Category A. As a result, they will be given increased mobility and more modern and heavier equipment. However, the Chinese are still a long way from producing more than a handful of such formations. When these enhanced groups are fully operational, they are to be deployed either facing the Russian border or on the coast opposite Taiwan. The main combat units positioned along this coastline have already received amphibious warfare training and regularly practice mass airborne assaults. The formations tasked for an invasion of Taiwan will continue to receive much of the best new equipment and have a greater air defense capability.

The major reorganization now underway will also result in the present divisional structure being slowly replaced by smaller brigades, with an enhanced combat capability.

Fighting Structure Overview

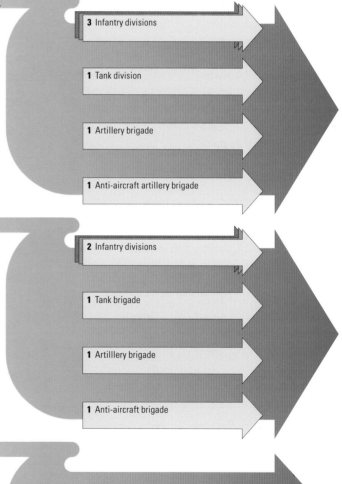

10 Integrated group armies (Category A)

These groups have an enhanced capablility, more modern weapons and mobility, and are based in strategically more important regions. Each has three infantry divisions, and each division has three or four brigades. These units have an inadequate supply of old Type-63, Type-891, or Type 86/86A armored personnel carriers. Their infantry support weapons include 82mm and 120mm mortars, anti-tank recoilless weapons, HJ-73 anti-tank guided weapons, and HN-5 (SA-7) shoulder-launched air defense missiles. The integral tank battalion has older Type-59 main battle tanks. The tank division has at least three brigades and will probably have the more modern Type-85 or Type-79 main battle tanks, with 122mm Type-70/701 self-propelled guns in support. The artillery brigades will have 130mm Type-59 long-range field guns and a battalion of 152mm Type-66 or 83 heavy guns, and 122mm or heavier multiple rocket launchers. Air defense is still largely a range of towed anti-aircraft weapons ranging from 23mm up to 57mm, with the occasional mobile surface-to-air battery.

3 Infantry divisions

1 Tank division

1 Artillery brigade

1 Anti-aircraft artillery brigade

9 Integrated group armies (Category B)

These formations are based in less important regions and will eventually either be moved and raised to Category A, or disbanded, as the Chinese army is gradually restructured. These units will largely be motorized infantries, with just a few leading units having Type-62 armored personnel carriers. Small arms are fairly standard, as are infantry support weapons, but integral tank units will have only Type-59 main battle tanks or Type-63 light tanks. Again, the tank brigade will have two or three battalions of older Type-59 main battle tanks. The artillery brigade will have a mix of older towed 122mm Type 54/60 and 152mm Type-54 field guns, and a battalion of 122mm multiple rocket launchers. This also applies to the anti-aircraft brigade, where the shortage of modern air defense is very obvious.

2 Infantry divisions

1 Tank brigade

1 Artilllery brigade

1 Anti-aircraft brigade

1 Airborne assault corps

Manned by the Air Force, this corps comes under army control and comprises three full divisions. However, the air lift capability of the Chinese armed forces would find it difficult to move one division, let alone the entire corps. But these divisions do get the pick of new infantry equipment and would normally act as elite infantry in combat.

3 Airborne divisions

⚕ Special forces

China is short on trained personnel, specialist weapons, technical expertise, and support, but nevertheless has a growing need for special forces and has now embarked on a program to provide the army with the required units by 2010.

Immediate Action Units (IAU)

The Chinese counter-terrorist units are known as Immediate Action Units (IAU) and their operations are controlled by the State Security Police. Personnel are mainly from special operations units, and the army provides all the training, weapons, and support.

Significant terrorist activity is dealt with by a regional Immediate Action Unit that is supported by the army when required. These units are not comparable to Western special forces as they concentrate largely on martial arts and the elimination of the threat— the intent is to kill rather than capture. Little emphasis is placed on clandestine operations, capturing terrorists, preventing incidents, or hostage rescue.

Long-Range Operations Group

In the fall of 1999, China formed the first of a new, intensely trained Long-Range Operations Group for airborne, reconnaissance, and amphibious warfare. Its personnel were drawn from the 6th Special Warfare Group, 8th Special Warfare Group, and the 12th Special Warfare Group's own Special Forces Detachment. Based in the Guangzhou Military Region (in southern China), it has been nicknamed the "Sword of Southern China." This group has advanced equipment, command, control, global position system (GPS), and a wide range of weapons, including some specially purchased in Western Europe. The officers are all staff college trained, and it is believed that approximately 60 percent of serving members have university degrees.

This new generation of Chinese special forces is cross-trained and multi-disciplined. The brigade-sized unit would provide the initial clandestine elements in any invasion of Taiwan. But with its multiple-role capability, it can be used as a mobile counter-insurgency or counter-terrorism "fire-brigade." The fact that the cities of China and its hinterland are now beset by growing ethnic, tribal, and religious conflict provides the immediate need for more such units, and it is believed that up to five more Long-Range Operations Groups are in the initial stages of development.

One of the new breed of Chinese army elite special forces, a para-commando in balaclava and parachute harness.

Electronic warfare

Chinese special operations also specialize in electronic warfare and intelligence gathering, both before and during the battle-phase. They are adept at close-range signal interception and jamming techniques, often getting to within 550 yards of the target, thereby having a propagation (signal) loss of at least 10,000 times lower than traditional methods. Though dangerous, these missions are seen as one way of counteracting the serious shortcomings caused by the technical and financial inadequacies of the Chinese army's technical services.

Chinese special forces personnel training in unarmed combat techniques.

Securing a bridgehead

Chinese military doctrine has a primary special forces role for its airborne troops in support of an amphibious assault. Troops inserted by parachute and helicopter are first deployed to seize vital defensive positions and suppress local air defenses. However, the most vital mission is to capture key points along the coast and inland early in the operation in order to prevent defenders from counter-attacking the landing zones.

Japan

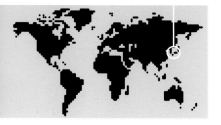

Japan has been a major military force for over 100 years—the Japanese army has resoundingly defeated the huge armed forces of both Imperial China and Imperial Russia in well-planned and well-executed campaigns. The Japanese army also proved highly capable and remarkably adaptable in its brutal conquest over a vast area of Asia, from 1930 through to its eventual defeat in 1945.

The Japanese army *(Rikujo Jieitai)*, or the Ground Self-Defense Force (JGSDF), re-formed in 1952, and found itself acting more or less as a night watchman for the U.S. bases that had been established in the post-war years. It was not until 1954 that the Japanese forces were given the responsibility of defending the nation's security.

Major military exercises have involved the regular rehearsal for the only operational role likely for the Japanese JGSDF, the defeat of major seaborne or airborne invasions by Russian forces based on the island of Sakhalin, just north of Hokkaido.

The Japanese army is constantly falling short of the financial support needed for the creation of a truly effective modern force, and lacks the firm foundation to play a traditional and integral part in the future of the nation. But despite these problems, today's Japanese army has succeeded in producing well-armed and trained combat units, though still, of course,

without a real military role to play. Indeed, only when Japan once again starts to take a role in Asian affairs befitting its economic superpower status, will the army achieve a genuine importance in the minds of the Japanese people and recover much of its self-respect and confidence.

As it stands, it still lacks the training and logistical support for overseas deployment, and considerable restructuring and new investment will be needed before the Japanese army can once again prove itself capable of a major international role.

Flashpoints and deployments

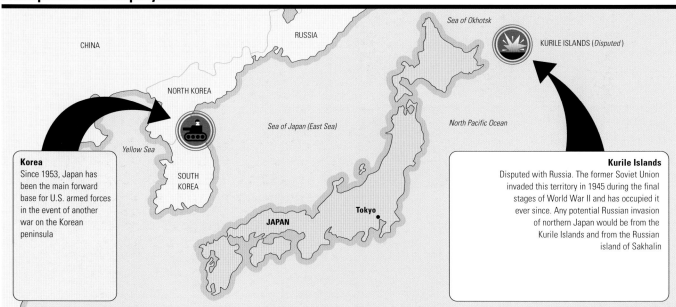

Korea
Since 1953, Japan has been the main forward base for U.S. armed forces in the event of another war on the Korean peninsula

Kurile Islands
Disputed with Russia. The former Soviet Union invaded this territory in 1945 during the final stages of World War II and has occupied it ever since. Any potential Russian invasion of northern Japan would be from the Kurile Islands and from the Russian island of Sakhalin

Operations

The Japanese army is responsible for the defense of Japan's main islands, including the offshore group known as the Ryukyus. Its operational role is to provide a combat force capable of defeating a small, localized amphibious or airborne invasion independent of any additional international force. However, in the event of a major invasion, it must be able to delay an attacking force long enough for its U.S. allies to bring their far greater firepower. But the operational parameters for the Japanese forces are strictly limited; both by geography as an island nation and by political constraints still imposed on the use of Japanese combat formations outside of national borders.

It is expected that following the change of government in Japan in 2001, there will be political moves to change the constitution to allow for the creation of a true Japanese army, free of its current constraints. This would then allow combat units to be deployed abroad.

However, the Japanese army also has a growing internal security responsibility due to the rise of internal extremist groups, such as the religious fanatics who nerve-gassed the Tokyo subway in 1995–96. And, as with all major nations, there is the threat of international terrorism. On top of all that, the army also plays a major role in providing disaster relief and civil action in a nation so often battered by earthquakes, typhoons, and other weather extremes.

Regular operational deployments

The present operational deployment of the Japanese army is fairly conventional and is based on the following:

Northern Army headquarters in Sapporo on Hokkaido with
• 2nd Mechanized Infantry Division headquarters in Asahikawa
• 5th Infantry Division headquarters in Obihiro
• 11th Mechanized Infantry Division headquarters in Makomania
• 7th Armored Division headquarters in Higashi-Chitose
• 1st Artillery Brigade headquarters in Kita-Chitose

Northwestern Army headquarters in Sendai on Honshu with
• 6th Mechanized Infantry Division headquarters in Jimmachi
• 9th Infantry Division headquarters in Aomori
• 2nd Artillery Brigade headquarters in Sandai

Eastern Army headquarters in Ichigaya on Honshu with
• 1st Airmobile Brigade headquarters in Nerima
• 12th Infantry Brigade headquarters in Somagahara
• 1st Airborne Brigade headquarters in Narashina

Central Army headquarters in Itami on Honshu with
• 3rd Mechanized Infantry Division headquarters in Itami
• 10th Infantry Division headquarters in Moriyama
• 13th Infantry Brigade headquarters in Kaitaichi
• 2nd Combined Brigade headquarters in Zentsuji

Western Army headquarters in Kengun on Kyushu with
• 4th Mechanized Infantry division headquarters in Fukuoka
• 8th Infantry Division headquarters in Kumamoto
• 1st Combined Brigade headquarters in Naha on Okinawa

Other deployments abroad

Japanese military personnel are deployed abroad in support of United Nations peacekeeping operations, including the Golan Heights-Syria/Israel since 1996. They also took part in mine-clearing operations in Cambodia 1992–93, humanitarian relief operations in the Goma area of Zaire in 1994, and in Mozambique 1993–95.

The U.S. MLRS, or multiple launch rocket system, has added greatly to the operational versatility of Japan's main artillery units.

Fighting withdrawal

In the event of a major invasion of northern Hokkaido by Russian airborne and amphibious forces based on the island of Sakhalin, Japanese forces are intended to make a fighting withdrawal inland, if it proves impossible to defeat the initial attack. A determined defense would then be made of the mountain-ringed Sapporo plain and the city of Sapporo itself, with the intention of holding out until major support arrived from Japanese and U.S. forces.

🪖 Weapons and units / overview of an army

The strength of the Japanese army is 148,500, with some 70,000 personnel available to the combat units. Although well supported by engineers and medical facilities, the Japanese army has developed only a limited logistic infrastructure, needed to fight a campaign with internal lines of supply, and therefore has no capability to project or maintain its forces outside national territory.

Army units

The present organization has

5 army regional commands based on the main islands, controlling

1 armored division, **11** infantry divisions, **1** infantry brigade

2 composite brigades (mixed armor and infantry)

1 airborne brigade

In addition there is

1 artillery brigade

2 artillery groups (battalions)

2 air defense brigades and **3** air defense groups (battalions)

5 engineer brigades

1 helicopter brigade (support)

5 attack helicopter squadrons

Type-90 Main Battle Tank

Country of origin Japan

First entered service 1993 with JGSDF

Main armament 120mm smoothbore gun (40 rounds)

Max. road speed 42 mph (70 km/h)

Max. range 240 miles (400 km)

Crew 3

Over 200 built so far

The Japanese designed and built Type-90 main battle tank. This 120mm smoothbore gun/armed vehicle is the mainstay of the armored regiments.

The CH47 Chinook is a twin rotor heavy lift support helicopter. It is the workhorse of many infantry operations.

The 90 AHIS missile armed helicopter is often used to give Japanese forces close anti-tank air cover.

Average allocation Armor, artillery, and helicopters within each brigade

Armored Division

🔫 **450** Type-74 and Type-90 main battle tanks

🔫 **300** Type-89 armored infantry fighting vehicles and Type-73/82 armored personnel carriers

🔫 **20** Type-87 armored reconnaissance

🔫 **75** Type-75 155mm self-propelled artillery

🔫 **25** 227mm MLRS multiple rocket launchers

Infantry Divisions

Infantry divisions (5)

🔫 **50** Type-74 main battle tanks

🔫 **100** Type-60/73 armored personnel carriers

🔫 **10** Type-87 armored reconnaissance

🔫 **25** Type-75 155mm self-propelled artillery

Infantry divisions (6)

🔫 **25** 155mm FH70 towed artillery

Army Headquarter Troops

🔫 **300** Type-61/74 main battle tanks

🔫 **100** Type-60/73 armored personnel carriers

🔫 **90** AH1S attack helicopters

🔫 **40** CH47 support helicopters

🔫 **100** UH1H/J support helicopters

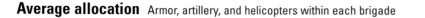

KEY 🚁 Airborne 🔫 Armor 🔫 Infantry 🔫 Artillery 🔫 Missiles

Firepower   The cutting edge

Airborne	Armor	Infantry	Artillery	Missiles
90 AH1S attack helicopters	**20** Type-61	**720** 81mm	**470** 155mm FH70 towed	**150** Type-64
40 CH47JA	**860** Type-74	**270** 107mm	**200** 155mm Type-75	**250** Type-79
160 OH6D and	**190** Type-90 main battle tanks	**310** 120mm mortars	**90** 203mm M110A2 self-propelled	**300** Type-87 manportable anti-tank
150 UHIH/J support helicopters	**90** Type-87 armored reconnaissance	**1480** 89mm	**60** Type-75 130mm	**320** Stinger
	70 Type-89 amored infantry fighting vehicles	**2,720** 84mm Carl Gustav and	**60** 227mm MLRS multiple rocket launchers	**110** Type-91
	220 Type-60	**260** 106mm M40/Type-60 anti-tank	**30** Twin 35mm towed and	**60** Type-93 and
	340 Type-73 and		**50** Type-87 35mm self-propelled air defense	**70** Type-81 manportable surface-to-air
	250 Type-82 armored personnel carriers			**200** I-Hawk towed/static surface-to-air
Total 440	**Total 2,040**	**Total 5,760**	**Total 960**	**Total 1,460**

Support	Excellent	Average	Poor

= **1,000**

Infantry small arms

9mm P220 automatic pistols

9mm M3A1 sub-machine guns

7.62mm Type-64 automatic rifles

5.56mm Type-89 automatic rifles

7.62mm Type-62 machine guns

12.7mm M2 HB heavy machine guns

The Japanese designed and built Type-81 quad launcher carries a 6-mile range air defense missile.

◮ Fighting structure

The JGSDF is structured and equipped to defeat a massive sea-borne or airborne invasion by Russian forces. In reality, this is extremely unlikely to occur, even though Japan is in dispute with Russia over the sovereignty of the Kurile Islands, seized by Soviet forces in 1945. However, it does mean that the Japanese have created a well-equipped and organized combat force consisting of 12 divisions.

A change in the Japanese constitution to allow its armed forces to be deployed on combat duty outside national borders would most likely lead to a more effective army available for major international peacekeeping operations, rather than its present small-scale UN involvement. This is assuming that the political sensibilities arising from memories of Japanese actions during World War II can be successfully overcome.

Fighting Structure Overview

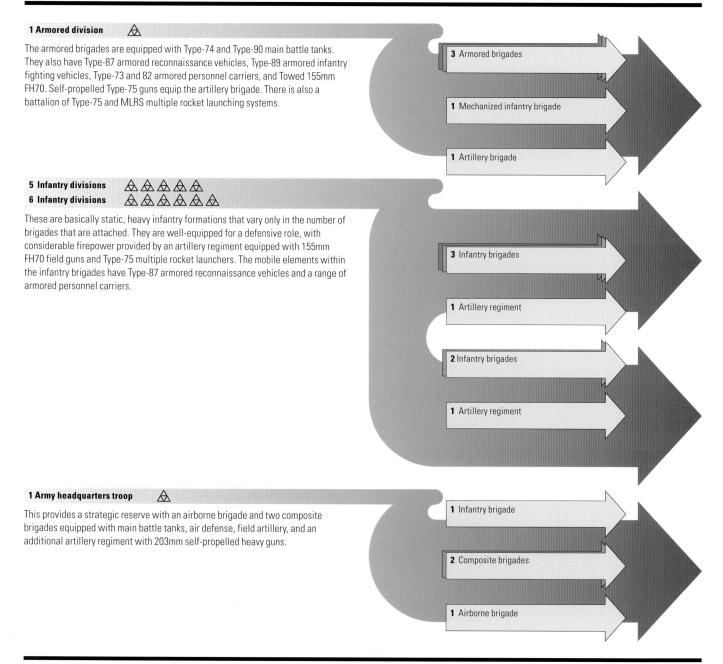

1 Armored division

The armored brigades are equipped with Type-74 and Type-90 main battle tanks. They also have Type-87 armored reconnaissance vehicles, Type-89 armored infantry fighting vehicles, Type-73 and 82 armored personnel carriers, and Towed 155mm FH70. Self-propelled Type-75 guns equip the artillery brigade. There is also a battalion of Type-75 and MLRS multiple rocket launching systems.

3 Armored brigades
1 Mechanized infantry brigade
1 Artillery brigade

5 Infantry divisions
6 Infantry divisions

These are basically static, heavy infantry formations that vary only in the number of brigades that are attached. They are well-equipped for a defensive role, with considerable firepower provided by an artillery regiment equipped with 155mm FH70 field guns and Type-75 multiple rocket launchers. The mobile elements within the infantry brigades have Type-87 armored reconnaissance vehicles and a range of armored personnel carriers.

3 Infantry brigades
1 Artillery regiment
2 Infantry brigades
1 Artillery regiment

1 Army headquarters troop

This provides a strategic reserve with an airborne brigade and two composite brigades equipped with main battle tanks, air defense, field artillery, and an additional artillery regiment with 203mm self-propelled heavy guns.

1 Infantry brigade
2 Composite brigades
1 Airborne brigade

Special forces

In the past, the Japanese army has had little need for highly specialist counter-terrorist forces since their creation in the 1950s. However, with the advent of indigenous extremism and the rise of international terrorism, the Japanese have created a combination of civil and military response units.

Initially, all counter-terrorist operations within Japan were handled by specialist departments of the Metropolitan Police Department of Tokyo and the Osaka Prefectural Police Headquarters. But it eventually became clear that specialist units were needed to deal with growing extremist behavior, such as the eight deadly attacks by members of the Japanese Red Army on the Tokyo subway in 1972, and the *Aum Shinri Kyo* religious group that used Sarin nerve gas in an attack that killed 12 and injured 5,500 Tokyo subway passengers in 1995. The latter attack resulted in 26 stations and two complete subway lines being shut down, which basically saw the subway grind to a halt. The National Police, who had to commit around a third of their available manpower to the incident for several weeks, responded in April 1996 by forming the Special Assault Team.

Special Assault Team

This para-military force is organized into 10 platoons, each of 20 personnel, and is trained to the highest possible military standards by, among others, the French GIGN *Gendarmerie* special operations unit. The Special Assault Team is considered very skilled and proficient in a wide range of techniques from heliborne insertion, combat shooting to hostage rescue, counter-terrorism, anti-hijacking, with a particular interest in buses, subways, and close-quarter battle situations. In addition, there is a small, and very discreet, special hostage rescue unit for highly delicate operations. These extremely fit and well-trained personnel are known as the "modern ninja."

Special Operations Warfare Center

In 1999 and 2000, and continuing today, the Japanese Defense Ministry has begun to give its land forces a genuine anti-terrorist and counter-insurgency capability. The first step has been to create a special operations warfare center, and provide training by personnel from the U.S. Delta and SEAL units.

Initially, new units will be created within the existing structure of the Japanese forces Airborne Brigade. However, over the next five years, it is expected that the Japanese will have a considerable special forces capability for both domestic use, as well as being additionally tasked to carry on the fight against terrorism well beyond national borders.

Expanded capability

Japanese special forces face a particular problem with fanatical religious terrorists operating out of Japan's major cities, who appear to have a total disregard for human life. The difficulties of dealing with nerve gas attacks on crowded public subway systems and the politically related terrorism of groups like the Red Army, has prompted the Japanese government (elected in 2001) to begin a major reorganization of its counter-terrorist forces. The army is to have a vastly expanded special forces command that will be capable of operating both at home and abroad in defense of Japanese targets.

Elite assault unit abseiling down the outside of a modern city office block during a hostage rescue exercise—an increasingly necessary skill for today's special forces.

North and South Korea

I n 1950, the North Korean army, heavily armed and equipped by Russia and Communist China, crossed into South Korea and began a conflict that created a holocaust of death and destruction across the peninsula. It lasted for three years, and evolved into a minor world war involving Allied forces who fought under the United Nations flag.

Flashpoints and deployments

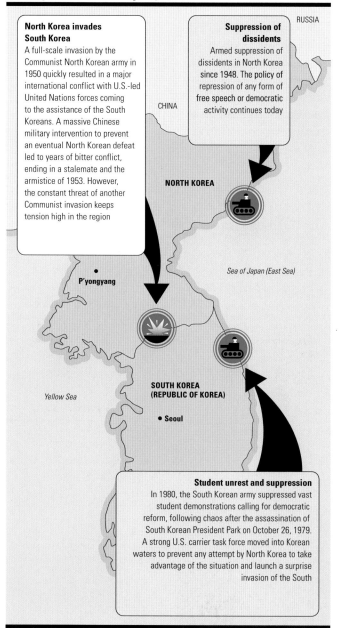

North Korea invades South Korea
A full-scale invasion by the Communist North Korean army in 1950 quickly resulted in a major international conflict with U.S.-led United Nations forces coming to the assistance of the South Koreans. A massive Chinese military intervention to prevent an eventual North Korean defeat led to years of bitter conflict, ending in a stalemate and the armistice of 1953. However, the constant threat of another Communist invasion keeps tension high in the region

Suppression of dissidents
Armed suppression of dissidents in North Korea since 1948. The policy of repression of any form of free speech or democratic activity continues today

RUSSIA

CHINA

NORTH KOREA

P'yongyang

Sea of Japan (East Sea)

SOUTH KOREA (REPUBLIC OF KOREA)

Yellow Sea

• Seoul

Student unrest and suppression
In 1980, the South Korean army suppressed vast student demonstrations calling for democratic reform, following chaos after the assassination of South Korean President Park on October 26, 1979. A strong U.S. carrier task force moved into Korean waters to prevent any attempt by North Korea to take advantage of the situation and launch a surprise invasion of the South

After ferocious battles across the frozen landscape of central Korea, the Allied forces eventually pushed the invading army back across the demarcation line and deep into North Korea, only then to be faced by several hundred thousand Communist Chinese troops who poured across the northern frontiers of Korea to decisively intervene and rescue China's client state from total defeat. A stalemate of World War I proportions was to settle across the original border between North and South Korea for a further 2½ years of bloody conflict.

The cease-fire that finally fell across the peninsula in 1953 has been maintained ever since with some considerable difficulty in the face of constant provocations and even small-scale invasions of the South by Northern forces. The large North Korean army has remained poised for action along the international cease-fire line, forcing South Korea, with many internal problems of its own, to remain on constant war alert for some 48 years. South Korean forces are strengthened by a substantial U.S. army garrison that has been permanently deployed there in support of its Korean allies.

The North Korean army is well-trained and heavily equipped, but with largely obsolete weaponry. It also faces a growing doubt about its motivation and, ultimately, its loyalty given the widespread starvation, poverty, and economic collapse of the Communist regime. It now also has to face a highly capable South Korean (or Republic of Korea) army that is well-armed with the latest modern weapons.

The South Korean forces were not created or intended for an invasion of the North, being an entirely defense-oriented force. However, such is their level of military proficiency, supported as they are by mobile artillery and swarms of attack helicopters, that they would probably be able to defeat a North Korean invasion. Then, with additional U.S. reinforcements, they should prove quite capable of carrying the war decisively back into the very heart of the Communist regime.

⊞ Operations

North Korea

North Korea's operational deployment is straightforward and very direct, with a large percentage of the armored, elite infantry, and artillery units with huge stocks of munitions positioned on, or near, the Demilitarized Zone (DMZ), or cease-fire line. An assault would be launched by huge numbers of special forces commandos, many of them using the large maze of tunnels built under the front-line (in place since the end of the Korean War of 1950–53), who would attempt to overrun many of the South Korean and U.S. defensive positions. Once these had been knocked out, a massive wave of North Korean armor would punch through what was left of the main front-line. They would then quickly expand the gap for the following infantry, and then race south to the capital, Seoul, and beyond in the hope of achieving a victory before large-scale U.S. reinforcements could arrive.

1st Operational echelon

The present deployment has the 1st Operational echelon ready for initial Offensive action with the
- 1st Forward Army Corps
- 2nd Forward Army Corps
- 4th Forward Army Corps
- 5th Forward Army Corps

2nd Operational echelon

The 2nd operational echelon ready for offensive exploitation has the
- 806th Mechanized Corps
- 815th Mechanized Corps
- 820th Tank Corps

Strategic reserve

This force is ready with the
- 108th Mechanized Corps
- 425th Mechanized Corps

Rear echelon

This force is ready with the
- 3rd Rear Army Corps
- 6th Rear Army Corps
- 7th Rear Army Corps
- 8th Rear Army Corps

Each corps is made up of several divisions each of between 8,000–10,000 personnel.

Covert infiltration

On September 17, 1996 a small North Korean transport submarine became stranded on the South Korean coast as it landed 26 members of North Korean special forces on a covert infiltration operation. Dressed in South Korean uniforms and armed with U.S. M16 rifles, this force was part of many aggressive operations initiated by the Communist regime. It was mid-November before all the Northern infiltrators were finally either killed or captured by the South Koreans.

South Korea

South Korea's operational deployment has been simply to prevent any initial invasion force from overcoming its front-line defenses, or to effectively counter-attack any successful North Korean breakout. South Korea is now confident that it possesses the forces capable of achieving this, and its army has proved itself in past campaigns both at home and abroad. Its most notable success was in Vietnam in the late 1960s, when the Korean divisions deployed there in support of the U.S. were highly effective against both the Vietcong guerrillas and the regular North Vietnamese army.

Present operational deployments

The present operational deployment of the South Korean forces has two army groups covering the area south of the cease-fire line. They occupy well-fortified positions stretching southward from the DMZ for a total of some 30 miles (48km), behind that are deployed the three mechanized divisions tasked for a counter attack: 1st ROK Army (FROKA) covers the eastern sector 3rd ROK Army (TROKA) is responsible for defending the prime invasion routes of the Munsan, Ch'orwon, and Tongduch'on corridors. The 1st and 3rd Armies are to merge by 2002 creating one major front-line command with improved control and communications.

The 2nd ROK Army (SROKA) will continue to be responsible for the defense of territory from the front-line to the coast. This rear area command is vitally important due to the large numbers of North Korean special forces capable of deep penetration raids or coastal landings. It is therefore also responsible for coastal protection and defending ports, lines of communication, and the mobilization of both reserves and materials.

Other deployments abroad

South Korean personnel have been working with the UN as military observers in East Timor (UNTAET) since 1999.

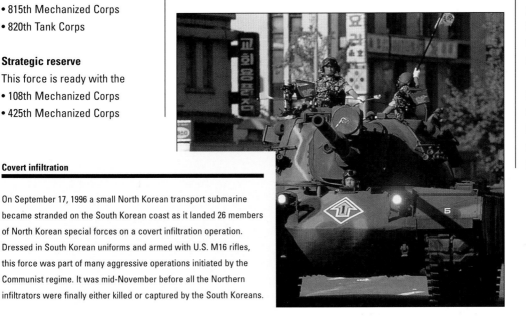

A column of M48A5 main battle tanks move through the streets of Seoul. Until the introduction of South Korea's own Type-88, the M48 was the most effective tank in South Korea's armed forces.

💣 Weapons and units / overview of an army

North Korea

The North Korean army has some 950,000 personnel, with at least 800,000 available for front-line service.

The North Korean army is basically a "one-throw-of-the-die" force, with limited logistics infrastructure, and primitive medical and support services. Should the first all-out assault fail to be decisive, then there is little capability for a sustained conflict or for defense against an effective counter-attack.

South Korea

The South Korean army is 560,000 strong, with some 400,000 personnel available to the main combat units.

The South Korean army is tasked to absorb and then defeat the massive blitzkrieg-style assault that would be launched by the North in any future conflict. With a heavy emphasis on modern armor and anti-tank capability, command and control, and attack helicopters, the South Korean army with prompt support by U.S. forces is probably more than capable of achieving this aim.

NORTH KOREA Infantry small arms

9mm DP51 automatic pistols

9mm M3 sub-machine guns

9mm MP5 sub-machine guns

5.56mm K1/K2 automatic rifles

5.56mm M16 automatic rifles

7.62mm M24 sniper rifles

7.62mm PSG-1 sniper rifles

7.62mm M60 machine guns

12.7mm M2 HB heavy machine guns

NORTH KOREA Army units

There are 20 operational corps with

27 infantry divisions

15 armored brigades

14 infantry brigades

The North also has a massive artillery capability with

14 field brigades

6 heavy brigades with both towed and self-propelled guns and additional multiple rocket launchers

9 dedicated multiple rocket launcher brigades

1 Scud surface-to-surface missile brigade, with an additional FROG (free-range over ground) short-range, surface-to-surface missile regiment

The Special Purposes Forces Command

10 specialist sniper brigades

12 light infantry brigades

17 reconnaissance battalions

Average allocation Armor, artillery, and helicopters within each brigade

NORTH KOREA

Armored Corps

Infantry division

🔫 **300** BTR60/80A armored personnel carriers

Armored brigades

🔫 **1080** Type-59/T54/T55 main battle tanks

🔫 **120** M1985/PT76 light tanks

Artillery brigades

🔫 **144** 122mm M1985 and 152mm M1977 self-propelled artillery

Rocket launcher (MLRS) brigades

🔫 **350** 122mm BM21/M1992/M1993, and 240mm M1989/91 multiple rocket launchers

SOUTH KOREA

Mechanized Infantry Divisions

🔫 **450** Type-88/T80U/M48 main battle tanks

🔫 **580** KIFV and M113 armored personnel carriers

Reconnaissance regiment

🔫 **40** BMP3 armored infantry fighting vehicles

Artillery regiment

🔫 **120** 155mm M109A2 self-propelled

🔫 **20** 227mm MLRS multiple rocket launchers

SOUTH KOREA infantry small arms

7.65mm Type-64/68 automatic pistols

7.62mm Type-49 sub-machine guns

7.62mm Type-63 carbines

7.62mm Type-58/68 automatic rifles

7.62mm Type-91/30 sniper rifles

7.62mm Type-64 machine guns

SOUTH KOREA Army units

There are three army groups (one to be disbanded by 2002) with 11 operational corps (two to be disbanded by 2002) with

3 mechanized infantry divisions

19 infantry divisions

2 independent infantry brigades

7 special forces

3 counter-infiltration brigades

In addition there are

3 surface-to-surface missile battalions with improved versions of the elderly Honest John system

3 air defense artillery brigades

31 air defense missile battalions

1 aviation command

KEY 🔫 Airborne　🔫 Armor　🔫 Infantry　🔫 Artillery　🔫 Missiles

Firepower   The cutting edge

NORTH KOREA

Airborne	Armor	Infantry	Artillery	Missiles

All helicopters are operated by the North Korean air force

3,500 T34/85, T54, T55, T62, Type-59 main battle tanks

560 PT76, M1985 light tanks

2,500 BTR40, BTR50, BTR60, BTR152, Type-531, M1973, BTR80A armored personnel carriers

7,500 82mm, 120mm, 160mm mortars

1,700 82mm anti-tank

3,500 122mm, 130mm, 152mm towed

4,400 122mm, 130mm, 152mm 170mm self-propelled

2,500 107mm, 122mm, 240mm multiple rocket launchers

11,000 14.5mm, 23mm, 37mm, 57mm, 85mm, 100mm towed air defense

5,000 AT-1, AT-3, AT-4, AT-5 anti-tank

11,000 SA-7, SA-16 manportable surface-to-air

30+ SCUD/No-Dong

24 FROG-3/5/7 mobile surface-to-surface

Total 0	Total 6,560	Total 9,200	Total 21,400	Total 16,054+

SOUTH KOREA

60 AH1F/J
45 H-500MD
12 BO105 attack helicopters
18 CH47D
130 H500
20 UH1H
116 UH60P support helicopters

1,000 Type-88
80 T80U
400 M47
850 M48 main battle tanks
40 BMP-3 armored infantry fighting vehicles
1,700 KIFV
420 M113
140 M577
20 BTR80 armored personnel carriers

6,000 81mm, 107mm mortars
7,000+ 57mm, 75mm, 90mm, 106mm anti-tank

1,700 105mm
1,800 155mm/203mm towed
1,040 155mm M109/K9 and **40** 175mm M107
13 203mm M110 self-propelled
156 130mm "Koor Yong"
29 MLRS multiple rocket launchers
700 20mm, 30mm, 35mm, 40mm towed air defense
50 90mm M36 self-propelled anti-tank

6,000+ TOW2A, AT-7 anti-tank
350 Javelin
60 Redeye
130 Stinger, SA16 manportable surface-to-air
170 Mistral mobile
110 I-Hawk
200 Nike Hercules static surface-to-air
12 NHK-1/11(Honest John) surface-to-surface

Total 401	Total 4,650	Total 13,000+	Total 5,528	Total 7,032+

Support	Excellent	Average	Poor		= 1,000

◬ Fighting structure

North Korea

The North Korean army, for so long organized along Soviet and Chinese lines, has, since the early 1990s modified both its tactics and structure according to its own evolving military doctrine.

Recent restructuring has created not only massive armored and mechanized corps, but has also seen the disappearance of the armored divisions to be replaced by increased numbers of independent tank brigades. Most armored units with mechanized infantry, massed artillery, and multiple rocket launcher support are deployed close to the border with South Korea. However, a major weakness in North Korean restructuring is the obvious lack of sufficient mechanized or motorized infantry, as well as a dramatic lack of mobile, effective, air-defense missile systems, leaving the armor in particular vulnerable to air attack and devoid of support from infantry units able to keep up with the pace of advance.

South Korea

South Korea has recently restructured its combat formations into highly effective and integrated heavily armored units capable of responding quickly to any assault from the North. Having brought the enemy to a halt, these units are structured to turn defense into an offensive counter-attack with minimum delay. A heavy emphasis has been placed on command and control, with a great improvement in the gathering and use of tactical and strategic intelligence.

The massive restructuring needed to acquire this level of mobile offensive capability required the mechanization of most major combat units and the introduction of large numbers of modern tanks, self-propelled artillery, attack helicopters, combat engineers, and logistic support.

Fighting Structure Overview

NORTH KOREA (Main strike force) 1 Armored corps ◬

With 9 armored brigades, each with 3 tank battalions of Type-62 and T55 main battle tanks and PT76 and M1985 light tanks, this is the army's main strike force. There is also an infantry division equipped with BTR40/50/60/152, Type-531 and the more modern BTR80 armored personnel carriers; the integral tank battalion has T54/55.

North Korea also has 2 brigades with 6 artillery battalions of 122mm, 130mm, 152mm, and 170mm self-propelled guns. The corps includes 5 full brigades, some 15 battalions of 122mm, and 240mm multiple rocket launchers. Finally, they have large numbers of SA7/16 manportable surface-to-air missiles and massed conventional towed anti-aircraft guns.

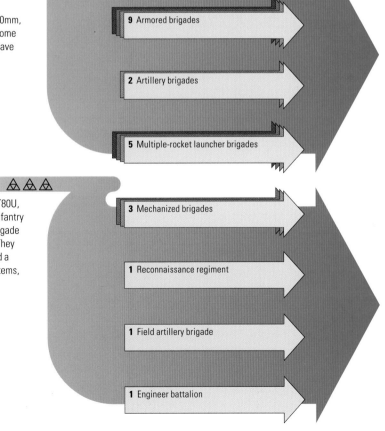

1 Infantry division

9 Armored brigades

2 Artillery brigades

5 Multiple-rocket launcher brigades

SOUTH KOREA (Main defensive forces) 3 Mechanized infantry divisions ◬ ◬ ◬

The mechanized brigades each have 3 tank battalions with modern Type-88, T80U, or older U.S. M47 and M48 main battle tanks. They also have KIFV armored infantry fighting vehicles and M113 armored personnel carriers. The Field Artillery Brigade has 155mm M109A2, 175mm M107, and 203mm M110 self-propelled guns. They also have multiple rocket launchers, large numbers of anti-tank weapons, and a potent air defense capability provided by self-propelled guns and missile systems, making these divisions highly effective and integrated combat formations.

3 Mechanized brigades

1 Reconnaissance regiment

1 Field artillery brigade

1 Engineer battalion

Special forces

Both North and South Korea maintain special forces, but of a very different nature. Those of the North are basically offense-oriented assault commandos, while those of South Korea are tasked to defeat large-scale incursion and sabotage, and have a more traditional anti-terrorist role.

North Korea

North Korea maintains a huge capability with some 80,000 soldiers in 22 commando brigades under the 8th Special Operations Corps. These forces are trained more in the style of U.S. Rangers, and elite light infantry than as true special forces in the style of the British SAS or U.S. Delta units. However, they are highly capable fighting formations, trained in amphibious and mountain warfare, parachuting, and underwater warfare techniques. They also have the pick of weapons and personnel, many of whom serve for up to seven years, thus developing a high degree of proficiency. However, they lack modern weapons, high technology, command and control, and mobility and logistics backup.

South Korea

The South Korean army has a considerable special forces capability in the form of seven special forces (airborne brigades), trained in U.S. Green Beret-style operations. Each serving member of the special forces is trained to a very high standard in a wide variety of techniques, but must also be trained in karate and tae kwon do. Within these brigades are a number of long-range reconnaissance and patrol (LRRP) units.

707th Special Mission Battalion

However, the main counter-terrorist unit is the 707th Special Mission Battalion and part of the South Korean army's special forces command, formed in April 1958. Ten years after the tragic events of the Arab terrorist attack on Israeli athletes at the 1972 Munich Olympic Games, South Korea, in anticipation of hosting the 1988 Games, formed the 707th Battalion in 1982. This unit, based in Songham, southeast of Seoul, is organized into two companies, each with four 14-man operations squads and supported by specialist women-only weapons, demolitions, and intelligence teams. Counter-terrorism training, often provided by the German GSG9, is extremely tough, with some six months of developing advanced fitness, weapons, and infantry skills. This is followed by a further six months of training in close-quarter combat skills, special warfare training, underwater warfare, and parachute techniques. Mountaineering and cold weather warfare are also very important to a unit often called upon to operate in sub-zero conditions. The 707th uses a wide variety of foreign and domestically produced weapons, including the 9mm Daewoo automatic pistol, 9mm MP5 sub-machine guns, 5.56mm CAR15 carbines, Daewoo K1/2 assault rifles, and PSG-1 and U.S. M24 sniper rifles. The 707th has already seen considerable and successful action in operations mounted against North Korean infiltrators.

Strategic disruption

South Korea faces an immense threat from North Korea's huge special forces capability. With some 100,000 elite troops and over 1,500 covert agents already in place, the North has plans for its special forces to breach South Korea's "flankless" defenses, create a "second front" behind the lines, disrupt U.S. reinforcements, conduct wide-scale sabotage and assassination, and gather intelligence. The ultimate aim is to create strategic disruption.

The MIM-23 Hawk towed/airmobile surface-to-air missile system. This very effective weapon has seen combat with many armies, and, with its constant upgrades, will see service well into this century.

North Korean special forces have a large number of tank-killer units. Some of these are equipped with Chinese YW531 armored carriers usually fitted with AT3, AT4, or AT5 anti-tank missiles.

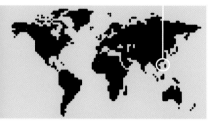

Taiwan

The Taiwanese army was created out of the remains of Chiang Kai-shek's defeated Chinese Nationalist armed forces when they were finally forced to retreat to the island of Formosa in 1949, by Mao Tse Tung's victorious revolutionary Communist Red Army or People's Liberation Army as it was soon renamed.

Flashpoints and deployments

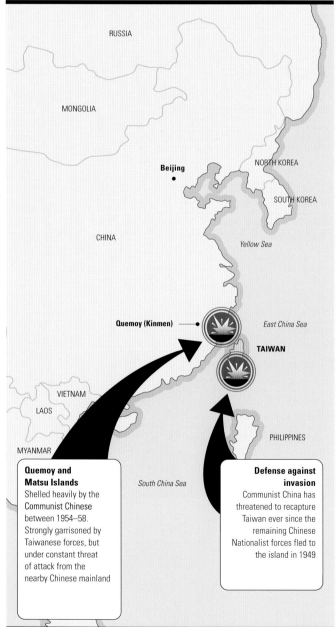

RUSSIA

MONGOLIA

Beijing

NORTH KOREA

SOUTH KOREA

CHINA

Yellow Sea

Quemoy (Kinmen)

East China Sea

TAIWAN

VIETNAM

LAOS

PHILIPPINES

MYANMAR

South China Sea

Quemoy and Matsu Islands
Shelled heavily by the Communist Chinese between 1954–58. Strongly garrisoned by Taiwanese forces, but under constant threat of attack from the nearby Chinese mainland

Defense against invasion
Communist China has threatened to recapture Taiwan ever since the remaining Chinese Nationalist forces fled to the island in 1949

The early years, under constant threat of invasion, saw immense Communist Chinese artillery bombardments of the garrisons on the offshore islands of Matsu and Kinmen (Quemoy). The present army still faces the prospect of defending both the offshore and the main islands of Taiwan against either amphibious or airborne invasions by the Communist Chinese forces massed on the opposite coastline. These forces are continually upgraded and re-equipped and, with growing Chinese naval and air force capabilities, the threat of invasion still exists, despite recent diplomatic suggestions to the contrary.

It is known that Chinese special forces units trained in the art of capturing and securing a beachhead, and other large formations, regularly practice amphibious landings and airborne operations that can only relate to a possible operation against Taiwan. There is little doubt that the major exercises in the Taiwan Strait in November 1996 and again in June 2001 were conducted with the intention of accurately assessing the ability of the Chinese armed forces to carry out a successful invasion. Many analysts would agree that only a lack of sufficient amphibious capability, adequate logistic backup, and the uncertainty of a major U.S. military response have prevented the Chinese from carrying out their threats to invade and defeat their old enemy.

The Taiwanese army began a restructuring campaign of its forces in 1997. The aim was to upgrade its combat effectiveness, to emphasize rapid reaction capabilities against a defended beachhead, to defeat an airborne invasion, and to infiltrate using special forces. The operational intention behind these changes is to provide the ability to concentrate considerable forces quickly whenever and wherever there is a threat either inland or on the coast.

The Taiwanese army faces an uncertain future. The next ten years or so could bring a change in the balance of power that would allow Communist China to exert increasingly more severe pressure, and it is vital for the future survival of this small country that the United States defense umbrella survives intact.

Operations

The Taiwanese army's operational deployments are totally dictated by the need to defend the main island of Taiwan, as well as the numerous offshore island groups, from a growing risk of a determined combination of Communist Chinese amphibious and airborne invasions or clandestine operations.

Armored defense

Taiwan's army has lacked combat experience since its retreat from the mainland in 1949. With the exception of the defensive role played out under Communist fire on the offshore islands, much of its operational efficiency is based on highly realistic exercises carried out on a regular basis. A fast armored response to any amphibious or airborne invasion is vital for the defense of Taiwan, and such exercises form a very important part of its strategic defense.

M48A5/H main battle tanks move out in a column. Some 550 of these vehicles still serve in the Taiwan Amored Corps.

Current deployment of operational units

There are three army groups and one airborne special operations headquarters. Major garrisons are to be found on the islands of Kinmen (Quemoy), Matsu, P'enghu, Hualien-T'aitung, and the smaller Tungyin Island and Chukuang Island commands.

The Kinmen and Matsu garrisons close to the Chinese mainland have been the scene of several bitter periods of conflict or heightened tension. The first was in 1954–55, when the islands were heavily shelled by the Communists, again in 1958–59, and most recently

in 1995–96. As a result, both islands are now exceptionally well defended, and also have very modern air defense systems.

The present deployment of the Taiwanese army is being radically altered in the period 1998–2002, by restructuring the divisions into 30, smaller, more mobile, specialist brigades.

Remaining in overall command are the three army headquarters covering the main island of Taiwan, with the divisions remaining only as overall command and administrative structures.

Operational combat control will pass to the brigade which will remain under

Northern area, headquarters based on T'ai-pei
• 3 independent armored brigades
• 2 independent mechanized infantry brigades
• 6 independent infantry brigades
Central area, headquarters based on T'ai-chung
• 4 independent armored brigades
• 2 independent mechanized infantry brigades
• 6 independent infantry brigades
Southern area, headquarters based on Kao-hsiung
• 1 independent armored brigade
• 4 independent infantry brigades

Airborne Special Operations headquarters, based on T'ai-chung
• 2 airborne brigades

The Taiwanese army garrisons on the offshore islands will retain the divisional command structure that suits the needs of static defense; therefore on Kinmen (Quemoy) there are
• 4 infantry divisions
• 1 armored group

On Matsu there remains one infantry division.

Weapons and units / overview of an army

The strength of the Taiwanese army is now 200,000, with around 140,000 personnel available for front-line service. The Taiwanese army has long been caught between having a sufficiently strong defense to effectively deter a Communist Chinese invasion, while not appearing to have a force strong enough to be seen as a threat. The balance that has existed for many years is now being altered by the Chinese armed forces as a result of their gaining a genuine, offensive amphibious capability. In response, Taiwan has opted to streamline its army, with a reduction in strength from 240,000 in 1999, the introduction of smaller, more mobile combat units, and a determined effort to enhance the other major elements of the armed forces.

Army units

The present organization has

3 army special operations headquarters
1 airborne special operations headquarters under which are
10 infantry divisions
2 mechanized infantry divisions
2 airborne infantry brigades
6 independent armored brigades
1 tank group
2 air defense missile groups (brigade sized)
2 aviation regiments

M220 TOW Anti-Tank Missiles

Country of origin U.S.
First entered service 1970 with U.S. army
Tube launched BGM-71 Missile, rate of fire 3 rpm
Max. range 2.4 miles (4 km) can penetrate over 23 in (60 cm) of armor
Crew 2
Tens of thousands built, in service with over 40 armies

The AH1 Super-Cobra provides a deadly anti-tank capability and gives Taiwan an enhanced defense against any mainland Chinese assault.

Average allocation Armor, artillery, and helicopters within each brigade

Army Headquarters	Army Reserve	Airborne Special Operations
300 M48/M60 main battle tanks	**150** M48/M60 main battle tanks	**100** V150 commando armored personnel carriers
150 M113 armored personnel carriers	**450** M113 armored personnel carriers	**50** AH-1S attack helicopters
50 155mm M114 towed artillery	**100** 155mm M109 self-propelled artillery	**110** UH-IH support helicopters
		30 TH67 support helicopters

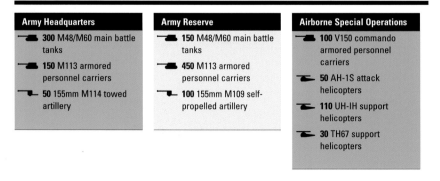

The U.S. Avenger: highly mobile surface-to-air missiles provide air cover for the Taiwan armored forces.

KEY 🛬 Airborne 🛡 Armour 🔫 Infantry 🎯 Artillery ◁ Missiles

Firepower   The cutting edge

Airborne	Armor	Infantry	Artillery	Missiles

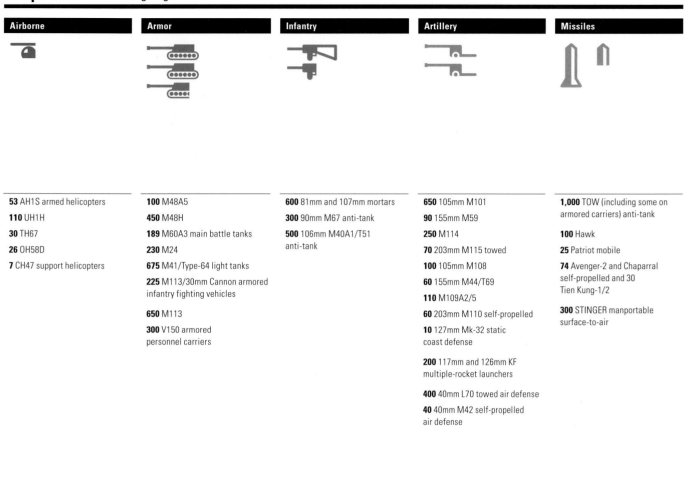

Airborne

53 AH1S armed helicopters
110 UH1H
30 TH67
26 OH58D
7 CH47 support helicopters

Armor

100 M48A5
450 M48H
189 M60A3 main battle tanks
230 M24
675 M41/Type-64 light tanks
225 M113/30mm Cannon armored infantry fighting vehicles
650 M113
300 V150 armored personnel carriers

Infantry

600 81mm and 107mm mortars
300 90mm M67 anti-tank
500 106mm M40A1/T51 anti-tank

Artillery

650 105mm M101
90 155mm M59
250 M114
70 203mm M115 towed
100 105mm M108
60 155mm M44/T69
110 M109A2/5
60 203mm M110 self-propelled
10 127mm Mk-32 static coast defense
200 117mm and 126mm KF multiple-rocket launchers
400 40mm L70 towed air defense
40 40mm M42 self-propelled air defense

Missiles

1,000 TOW (including some on armored carriers) anti-tank
100 Hawk
25 Patriot mobile
74 Avenger-2 and Chaparral self-propelled and 30 Tien Kung-1/2
300 STINGER manportable surface-to-air

Total 226	Total 2,819	Total 1,400	Total 2,040	Total 1,499

Support Excellent   Average   Poor   = 1,000

Infantry small arms

9mm Browning HP automatic pistols
9mm Type-37 sub-machine guns
5.56mm Type-65/M16A1 automatic rifles
5.56mm Type-68 automatic rifles
7.62mm Type-57/M14 automatic rifles
7.62mm Type-57/M60 machine guns
12.7mm M2 HB heavy machine guns

The CM31 is one of a new range of armored vehicles that will play an increasingly important role in the restructured Taiwanese army.

▲ Fighting structure

The army of Nationalist China is based purely on survival: the defense of the island of Taiwan from amphibious and airborne assault by the forces of the People's Republic. And there is a vital need for effective coastal defenses, given the limited number of suitable landing beaches or dropping zones, and a requirement for a rapid response by highly mobile combat groups to any such incursion. These factors have dictated both the weapons and structure of the modern Taiwanese army. A further drain on the army's manpower and resources is the need to maintain and support the four divisions of the heavily armed garrisons on the offshore islands of Quemoy, and one division on Matsu. In an attempt to restructure the army into a smaller, more mobile and effective force, a major reorganization of units into 30 independent combined arms brigades is underway. This will result in a mixture of armored, armored infantry, motorized, parachute, and special forces brigades. The divisional headquarters will be retained to provide tactical control.

The workhorse of many armies throughout the world, the M113 armored personnel carrier has been produced in many variants since its introduction in the late 1950s.

Fighting Structure Overview

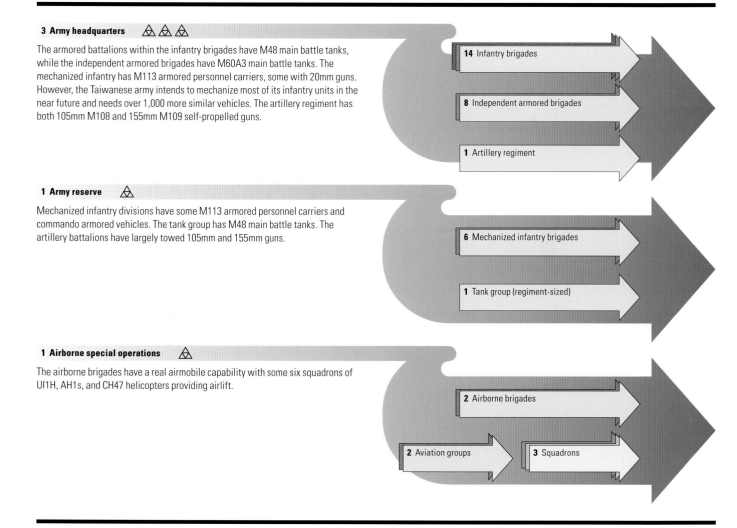

3 Army headquarters ▲ ▲ ▲

The armored battalions within the infantry brigades have M48 main battle tanks, while the independent armored brigades have M60A3 main battle tanks. The mechanized infantry has M113 armored personnel carriers, some with 20mm guns. However, the Taiwanese army intends to mechanize most of its infantry units in the near future and needs over 1,000 more similar vehicles. The artillery regiment has both 105mm M108 and 155mm M109 self-propelled guns.

14 Infantry brigades

8 Independent armored brigades

1 Artillery regiment

1 Army reserve ▲

Mechanized infantry divisions have some M113 armored personnel carriers and commando armored vehicles. The tank group has M48 main battle tanks. The artillery battalions have largely towed 105mm and 155mm guns.

6 Mechanized infantry brigades

1 Tank group (regiment-sized)

1 Airborne special operations ▲

The airborne brigades have a real airmobile capability with some six squadrons of UI1H, AH1s, and CH47 helicopters providing airlift.

2 Airborne brigades

2 Aviation groups

3 Squadrons

🎖 Special forces

The Taiwanese army has a relatively restricted special forces capability, with a limited scope for sabotage missions by the Communist Chinese, no domestic extremism, and little interest from international terrorists. The small scale of potential insurgency from the native Taiwanese against the Nationalist Chinese who fled to the island in 1949 has yet to make an impact on defense policy.

Current special forces structure

The current special forces structure is based on the Airborne Special Operations Headquarters, with two airborne brigades. These units are trained both in limited airborne operations, as elite infantry, and, finally, in the assault commando role. However, each brigade also has a company trained for long-range reconnaissance and patrol (or LRRP). These units would operate behind the lines of the landing zones of any Communist Chinese airborne invasion or the bridgehead of an amphibious invasion. They are also equipped with the pick of standard issue weapons and other equipment. In addition, these LRRP companies train on a regular basis with similar U.S. army units.

It would be in keeping with such units if these Taiwanese special forces trained for the eventuality of clandestine operations on mainland China. For in the event of a serious deterioration in relations between the two states, it would be vitally important for the Taiwanese forces to have a greater understanding of Chinese activities. Information on the overall capabilities and large-scale military movements can often be gathered successfully from either SIGINT (signals intelligence) or satellite surveillance. However, the insertion of deep cover units from the offshore islands of Kinmen (Quemoy) or Matsu, or by the Taiwanese navy, would certainly be within their known capability, and would play a vital part in obtaining the sensitive information needed to predict Chinese intentions. Taiwanese special forces are also known to have stocks of suitable documents, uniforms, and standard Chinese weapons to equip such units, either to gather intelligence or to carry out a spoiling attack with sabotage operations against Chinese forces preparing for an assault on Taiwan or the offshore island garrisons.

Long Range Amphibious Reconnaissance Commandos

In this context, it should be noted that the only other major special forces units are the Long Range Amphibious Reconnaissance Commandos trained for pathfinder operations, as para-commandos, in underwater warfare, and in the beach reconnaissance and sabotage role against enemy bridgeheads. This unit, though not strictly part of the army, is very similar to the U.S. Marine Corps Recon (Reconnaissance), and receives regular training at U.S.M.C. bases.

The remaining special forces formation of note is the Para-Frogman Assault Unit, which is very similar in training, equipment, organization, and operational techniques to the U.S. SEALs. This unit can parachute into the sea in full scuba gear, and carry out underwater reconnaissance or sabotage missions against Chinese coastal positions or warships.

Tough and well-trained, Taiwanese commandos parade before taking part in an operation. They are equipped with M113 carriers armed with .5 Browning M2 heavy machine guns.

Watching the dragon

The National Security Bureau, which is in overall charge of Taiwan's numerous intelligence services, cooperates closely with both the Military Intelligence Bureau and Special Operations Command. Among its many tasks is to oversee the covert infiltration of agents and long-range reconnaissance units into mainland China. Special forces penetration of Communist China has long been of considerable importance to the overall defense of both Taiwan and the United States.

Indonesia

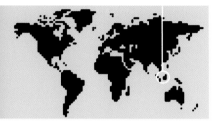

The Indonesian army is beset with major problems that include growing levels of terrorist insurgency and civil unrest as well as the threat of international intervention in situations similar to that of East Timor. But there are also the major problems that stem from the sheer size and diversity of the nation itself. Indonesia comprises some 17,000 islands and the people speak dozens of different languages and dialects. The islands cover a vast area of the Southern Pacific; a distance wider than the North Atlantic.

The magnitude of the logistics, communications, and security problems faced by the Indonesian army is immense. Many of these difficulties were inherited from the Dutch colonial forces after they finally withdrew in December 1949. As a result, much of the army is still effectively an old-style colonial occupation force, with lightly armed infantry battalions supported by wheeled armored vehicles and artillery deployed as garrisons throughout the islands. Better-trained and better-armed mobile units from the Strategic Reserve are available, but only when an insurgency or civil disturbance deteriorates to a point where the local garrison and the para-military police can no longer keep control.

Only on the main island of Java does the Indonesian army deploy anything that remotely resembles a modern, integrated combat force. This organization is the Strategic Reserve, which, apart from supporting regional garrisons that are under pressure, has the prime responsibility of ensuring the safety and survival of the central Indonesian government. The army, through its territorial structure, is represented at every level of government—in every province, district, and subdistrict administration throughout the country—and is particularly strong within the intelligence and security services. This has allowed the army to have a measure of influence in important policy-making decisions and, thus, in the running of the country and the election of its leaders.

Flashpoints and deployments

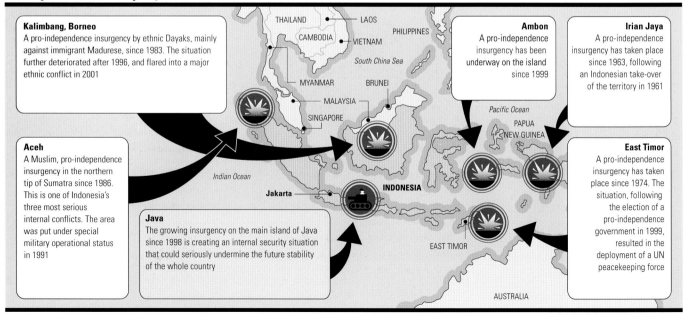

Kalimbang, Borneo
A pro-independence insurgency by ethnic Dayaks, mainly against immigrant Madurese, since 1983. The situation further deteriorated after 1996, and flared into a major ethnic conflict in 2001

Aceh
A Muslim, pro-independence insurgency in the northern tip of Sumatra since 1986. This is one of Indonesia's three most serious internal conflicts. The area was put under special military operational status in 1991

Java
The growing insurgency on the main island of Java since 1998 is creating an internal security situation that could seriously undermine the future stability of the whole country

Ambon
A pro-independence insurgency has been underway on the island since 1999

Irian Jaya
A pro-independence insurgency has taken place since 1963, following an Indonesian take-over of the territory in 1961

East Timor
A pro-independence insurgency has taken place since 1974. The situation, following the election of a pro-independence government in 1999, resulted in the deployment of a UN peacekeeping force

Operations

The Indonesian army's operational requirements has created a two-tier system of deployment. The upper tier comprises two specialist military commands, the KOPASSUS, or the Army Special Force Command, and KOSTRAD, or the Army Strategic Reserve Command. Both commands form the only true professional fighting forces available to the army. The lower tier is formed by KODAM, a military administration for the colonial-style occupation of much of Indonesia, with large numbers of strategically placed garrisons.

The KOPASSUS special forces and the strategic reserve, KOSTRAD, are based permanently on Java, and are deployed to other islands only when any of the lightly armed local garrisons are at risk of losing control in a rebellion. KODAM, however, is constantly struggling to cope with the growing threat of civil unrest, separatism, and insurgency.

KODAM

KODAM is operationally deployed throughout the 17,000 islands that make up Indonesia and comprises:
• *KODAM-1* Special region of Aceh and Sumatra
• *KODAM-2* Jambi, Bengkulu, Sumatra, Selatan, and Lampung
• *KODAM-3* Jawa Barat province
• *KODAM-4* Jawa Tengah and the special region of Yogyakarta
• *KODAM-5* Jawa Timur province
• *KODAM-6* Kalimantan
• *KODAM-7* Sulawesi
• *KODAM-8* Maluku and Irian Jaya
• *KODAM-9* Bali, Tenggara Timur, and Timor Timur
• *KODAM-10* Jaya Jakarta, the special capital city region
   Most operational deployments by KODAM are of infantry battalion strength or less. One notable exception was the assault on Timorese

separatists in then Portuguese East Timor on December 7, 1975. An Indonesian force of ten battalions occupied the eastern half of the island, killing 60,000 civilians. But, more often, civil unrest is suppressed because of the all-pervasive security system run in the towns and villages by KODIM Military District Command. A combination

of informants, surveillance, and torture regularly allow the Indonesian army to conduct nothing more than limited low-intensity operations to suppress any local opposition successfully.

KOREM

Each KODAM unit is divided for operational purposes into a KOREM, or military garrison command, and a KODIM, or a military district command. Each KOREM unit has control of one or two light infantry battalions, while the KODAM has one or two extra battalions with light armored support attached to the headquarters, including one para-commando unit as a quick reaction strike force.

Other deployments abroad

The Indonesian army sent 14 of its personnel as observers to Croatia (operation UNMOP) in 1996, to Georgia (operation UNOMIG) in 1997, and to Sierra Leone (operation UNAAAMSIL) in 1999.

Violence in paradise

In early 1999, violence broke out between the Christian and Muslim populations in the Spice Islands, in the Moluccas, and within weeks around 1,700 people had been killed. The local command, KODAM-8, had only lightly armed infantry battalions available, which were soon unable to maintain security. Heavily armed forces from KOSTRAD and KOPASSUS (special forces) were deployed in their support and the fighting slowly decreased as the forces took control of security. However, the islands remain highly unstable and violence is still continuing in 2001.

A Russian-designed and built BMP.2 armored infantry fighting vehicle (AIFV). Eleven similar vehicles serve with the Indonesian army.

Weapons and units / overview of an army

The Indonesian army's present strength is 230,000, with some 160,000 personnel available for front-line duty. The majority of combat units are based on light infantry and light armored cavalry. They are mobile and self-sufficient. However, a move toward creating heavily equipped combat formations is being forced on the army as the many different insurgent groups become better armed.

Average allocation Armor, artillery, and helicopters within each brigade

KOSTRAD HQ (Integrated)

2 Infantry divisions
No permanently attached heavy weapons

3 Infantry brigades
- 20 AMX-VCI armored personnel carriers
- 20 Stormer/BTR-40 armored personnel carriers

3 Airborne brigades
- 20 BTR-50PK/BTR-40 armored personnel carriers

2 Field artillery brigades
- 72 105mm M101 towed field guns

Air defense artillery brigade
- 72 S60 57mm towed
- 48 Rapier/RBS70 surface-to-air missiles

2 Independent armored battalions
- 50 Scorpion/AMX-13 light tanks
- 5 BMP-2 armored infantry fighting vehicles

2 Independent artillery battalions
- 40 105mm M56/M101 and 155mm FH-2000 towed field guns

KODAM

2 Infantry brigades
No armored vehicles

5 Airborne battalions
No armored vehicles

8 Cavalry battalions
- 30 AMX-13 light tanks
- 6 Ferret reconnaissance
- 8 Saladin reconnaissance
- 10 Commando armored personnel carriers

60 Infantry battalions
No armored vehicles

KEY — Airborne — Armor — Infantry — Artillery — Missiles

Army units

The present organization has	
1 Strategic Reserve (KOSTRAD) with	
	2 infantry divisions
	3 infantry brigades
	3 airborne brigades
	2 field artillery regiments
	1 air defense regiment
	2 armored regiments
11 Military Area Commands (KODAM) with	
	2 infantry brigades
	5 airborne
	60 infantry
	8 cavalry
	11 field artillery and air defense battalions
The special forces (KOPASSUS) has	
	5 battalion-sized groups

One of five FH2000 155mm howitzers built by CIS of Singapore for the Indonesian army. This is an upgraded version of the FH88 towed artillery piece.

RBS-70 Surface-to-Air Missiles

Country of origin Sweden

First entered service 1982 with Swedish army

Manportable whole air defense system can be assembled and deployed in 30 seconds

Max. vertical range 1.8 miles (3 km)

Max. range 3 miles (5 km)

Crew 2

Thousands built, in service with at least 8 armies

Firepower   The cutting edge

Airborne	Armor	Infantry	Artillery	Missiles
30 B205A	**275** AMX-13	**800** 81mm and	**100** 76mm M48	**40** RBS-70 manportable surface-to-air
17 BO-105	**30** PT-76 and	**75** 120mm Brandt mortars	**10** 105mm M56	**51** Rapier towed surface-to-air
28 NB412 and	**50** Scorpion-90 light tanks	**750** 89mm LRAC (manportable anti-tank rocket launchers)	**170** M101 and	
15 H300C helicopters	**69** Saladin	**90** 90mm M67	**5** 155mm FH-2000 towed	
	55 Ferret and	**30** Twin 35mm towed and	**125** 20mm	
	18 BL armored reconnaissance	**45** 106mm M40A1 anti-tank	**90** 40mm M60/70 and	
	11 BMP-2 armored infantry fighting vehicles		**200** 57mm S60 towed air defense	
	200 AMX-VCI			
	45 Saracen			
	60 Commando			
	22 Commando Ranger			
	80 BTR-40			
	14 BTR50PK and			
	40 Stormer armored personnel carriers			

Total 90	**Total 969**	**Total 1,790**	**Total 700**	**Total 91**

Support	Excellent	Average	Poor					= **1,000**

Infantry small arms

9mm FN HP automatic pistols

7.62mm G3 automatic rifles

7.62mm AK47 automatic rifles

7.62mm BM59 automatic rifles

5.56mm M16A1 automatic rifles

5.56mm FNC automatic rifles

9mm M45 sub-machine guns

9mm Beretta M12 sub-machine guns

9mm UZI sub-machine guns

.30 Madsen MK-11 machine guns

.30 M1919A4 machine guns

Some 50 British Scorpion-90 light tanks equip KOSTRAD's two armored battalions. One is seen here during a deployment in Sumatra, on a counter-insurgency operation.

◭ Fighting structure

The structure of the Indonesian army is quite complex with the main combat force, KOSTRAD (Army Strategic Reserve), based almost entirely on the island of Java, with two divisional headquarters that have a mix of infantry, airborne, and artillery units. It is a force primarily involved in maintaining the power of the generals or the government of the day; it has little or no viability as a military force. The National Army of Indonesia (TNI) is largely a counter-insurgency force operationally controlled by ten KODAM (Regional Military Commands) that each has a number of light tank, infantry, airborne, or artillery battalions attached, according to the area they cover. Most of these units are lightly equipped, with no war fighting ability, and are of use only for suppressing civil unrest or for limited counter-insurgency duty.

Fighting Structure Overview

1 KOSTRAD (Army Strategic Reserve) (Main combat force) ◬

KOSTRAD has two operational infantry division headquarters in Java, and three infantry and three airborne brigades equipped with the most modern infantry weapons available to the Indonesian army. The two artillery brigades have six battalions with 105mm M101 howitzers and two independent battalions with more 105mm M101 and some 155mm FH-2000 long-range artillery pieces. The Indonesian army's only effective air defense units are two battalions equipped with 57mm S60 anti-aircraft guns as well as both Rapier and RBS-70 surface-to-air missiles. The two armored battalions have Scorpion and AMX-13 light tanks, BMP-2 armored infantry fighting vehicles and Commando wheeled armored personnel carriers.

1 KODAM (11 Military area commands) ◬

With some 66 light infantry battalions tasked to control counter-insurgency and civil unrest throughout the thousands of inhabited islands that make up Indonesia, KODAM is effectively a colonial police force. The infantry, airborne, and cavalry battalions are equipped with AMX-13 light tanks, Saladin and Ferret armored cars, and Saracen and Commando armored carriers, while the attached artillery batteries have 76mm M48 and 105mm M56 pack howitzers. Infantry support weapons include 82mm and 120mm mortars.

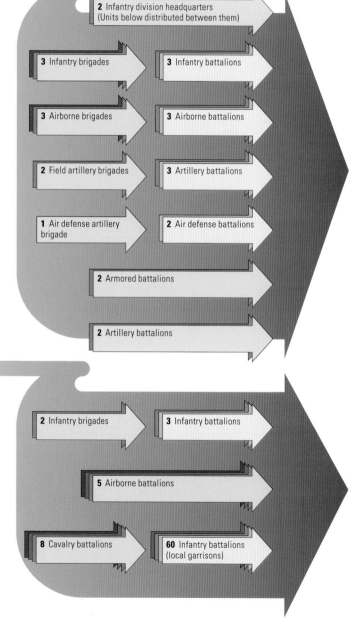

Special forces

Special Forces have played an unusually important part in the Indonesian army for nearly 50 years. This is the result of the severe difficulties of operating conventional forces in such an ethnically and territorially diverse nation, and partly because the nature of the military problems facing the army lend themselves to special operations. The Indonesian Special Operations Command, or KOPASSUS, now has five groups and a Presidential Guard Group, or PASPAMRES, with about 6,000 personnel whose headquarters are at Cijantung, Jakarta, and Java. These units have a reputation for toughness, but with a brutal disregard for the civil rights of their own citizens.

KOPASSUS (Special Operations Command)

KOPASSUS is a strike force whose main missions are counter-insurgency and anti-subversive operations. This force, often known as the Red Berets, has seen the scope of its operations expanded recently to cover all the main areas of Indonesia that are vulnerable to foreign intervention, such as Borneo and Irian Jaya.

It conducts missions such as infiltration, reconnaissance, intelligence gathering, and militia training, behind the lines, in areas liberated by anti-government insurgents or where there may be possible intervention by a foreign power. Its training methods are of a high commando standard, but fall well short of the multiple-role capability expected of Western elite units. KOPASSUS receive the best of new weapons, and have an interesting array available including French FNC SSIV-1, Russian AK47, U.S. M16 assault rifles, Belgian FN MINI light machine guns, and Israeli UZI sub-machine guns.

The stability of the Indonesian government is regularly threatened by the numerous separatist movements. Though most are poorly armed and trained, KOPASSUS has still been called upon to add its support to the local territorial garrisons on many occasions, often with brutal effectiveness.

In June 1996, a major reorganization of KOPASSUS was introduced. Not only was it increased in size with the addition of two extra battalions, but it also returned to the original formation of its establishment in 1952. This was done to simplify its structure and allow better use of manpower, ensuring that at least 25 percent of personnel are on active duty at any one time.

KOPASSUS has long been considered the elite corps of the Indonesian army. It has traditionally emphasized its compact size and rapid strike potential. KOPASSUS operates throughout Indonesia and in clandestine operations in neighboring countries. It has also gained the unfortunate reputation of being closely associated with human rights abuses and "disappearances," as well as being responsible for the arming and training of militias guilty of the mass slaughter of civilians in East Timor and elsewhere.

KOPASSUS

Group-1 Strike para-commando (3 battalions) based in western Java

Group-2 Strike para-commando (3 battalions) based in central Java

Group-3 Training command based in western Java

Group-4 Combat intelligence, squadron-sized based in south Jakarta, Java (This group has the pick of personnel from Groups-1/2/3, and conducts clandestine operations within areas occupied by insurgents or in neighboring countries)

Group-5 Counter-terrorism, battalion-sized, based in south Jakarta, and trained in a wide range of hostage rescue and anti-hijack techniques

Group-Presidential Guards (PASPAMRES) Battalion-sized, based in south Jakarta, provides close protection for the president and senior government ministers

A para-commando unit from the KOPASSUS (special forces unit) prepare to board one of 14 NC-212 twin-engined transport aircraft available for their operations.

 Australia

Australia has been forced to revise its defensive Cold War "fortress" mentality since the 1950s, when it began to feel threatened by Communist China. With the declining influence of the United States in the South Pacific and increasing instability among Australia's neighbors to the north, the Australian government now accepts the fact that it needs to create a defense force capable of deployment throughout the region.

The Australian government also seems more willing to see its military power play an influential part in the future security of this important geostrategic area of the world. Accepting that its aspirations far exceed its present (somewhat limited) capabilities, the government's recent defense policy calls for an increase in combat troop numbers, but an overall decrease in other army personnel.

Along with an ambitious rearmament and reequipment program, Australia now intends to create a force capable of fulfilling the requirements laid down in the "Howard Doctrine," named for Australian Prime Minister John Howard. The objective is for Australia to behave as a deputy, or even replacement, for the United States armed forces in much of the

South Pacific—particularly the many troubled areas just to the north in Indonesia.

Recent events in the South Pacific highlight Australia's need to swiftly pursue its long-term aim to have a more proactive stance in its own backyard. Because of increasing regional instability, Australia may need to fulfill this new role far sooner than originally expected. Therefore, the Australian army is presently at some considerable risk of not being ready for its new geostrategic role when it is most needed.

Flashpoints and deployments

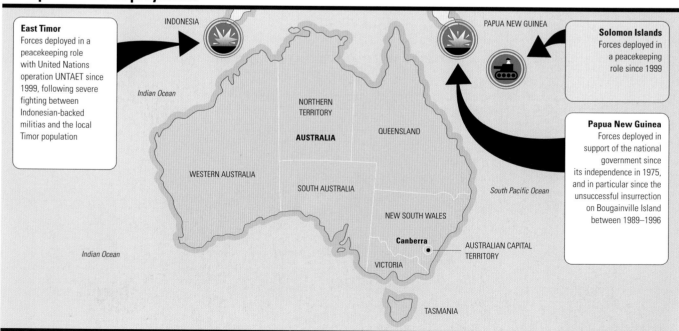

East Timor
Forces deployed in a peacekeeping role with United Nations operation UNTAET since 1999, following severe fighting between Indonesian-backed militias and the local Timor population

Solomon Islands
Forces deployed in a peacekeeping role since 1999

Papua New Guinea
Forces deployed in support of the national government since its independence in 1975, and in particular since the unsuccessful insurrection on Bougainville Island between 1989–1996

INDONESIA

PAPUA NEW GUINEA

Indian Ocean

NORTHERN TERRITORY

AUSTRALIA

QUEENSLAND

WESTERN AUSTRALIA

SOUTH AUSTRALIA

South Pacific Ocean

NEW SOUTH WALES

Indian Ocean

Canberra

AUSTRALIAN CAPITAL TERRITORY

VICTORIA

TASMANIA

🏴 Operations

The Australian army's operational deployment has long been governed by the threat of invasion from the north, a fear that has dominated defense planning since the Japanese army swept south in 1942. At that time, the Japanese got as close as New Guinea, from where their aircraft regularly bombed Darwin. As a result, Australia's main combat units have been sweltering in the northern heat, more than 1,500 miles away from the main centers of population.

The 1st Brigade

The 1st Brigade, also called the 1st Integrated Task Force, based in and around Darwin, falls under the command of the 1st Division in Brisbane. This formation is the trial unit for the organization of the new-style Australian Brigade. Mechanized support is provided by the 1st Armored Regiment based in Palmerston, Northern Territories, with its two regular and one reserve tank squadrons, and the 2nd Cavalry Regiment (also based in Palmerston) with three armored reconnaissance squadrons.

Joint Task Force

Brisbane is also the headquarters of the combat-ready Joint Task Force—Australia's largest combat formation. The 1st Division has four infantry brigades, the 1st in Darwin, with two regular and one reserve brigades, the 3rd in Townsville, the 7th in Brisbane, and the 11th based in Sydney. Mechanized support is provided by the only active remaining armored unit, the B Squadron 3rd/4th Cavalry Regiment, which is based in Townsville.

Other deployments abroad

Historically, the Australian army has been deployed abroad on many occasions, including the Boer War, both world wars, Korea, and Vietnam. It has also seen service in Malaysia, Singapore, and Borneo. Presently there are Australian army personnel in Papua New Guinea, Malaysia, Fiji, Solomon Islands, Thailand, Vanuatu, Tonga, Western Samoa, and Kiribati.

Austalian forces regularly take part in United Nations' peacekeeping missions and are currently serving in Egypt, in Bougainville (New Guinea) with the Peace Monitoring Group, and most importantly in East Timor with UNTAET (United Nations Administration-East Timor). The Australian contingent is led by the 1st Royal Australian Regiment from Townsville. This unit has a long record of serving overseas, including in Vietnam, and it forms part of the Operational Deployment Force (ODF) in the Joint Task Force. At the request of the United Nations, it was deployed in an ongoing operation in East Timor, geared to help bring an end to the bloodbath carried out by pro-Indonesian militias following the election of the separatist movement to power.

The Malaysian emergency

Australia has a history of regularly providing forces for international operations, and not least were those that took part in the Malaysian Emergency of 1956-64. For the best part of a decade Australia maintained an infantry battalion and an artillery battery in Malaysia as part of the 27th Commonwealth Brigade. This unit played a major part in the defeat of the remaining Communist guerrillas, and, as a result, learned some vital lessons in counter-insurgency.

A patrol of the 2nd Cavalry Regiment in the streets of Dili. East Timor is probably the most significant of Australia's current overseas deployments.

AUSTRALIA

🍈 Weapons and units / overview of an army

The present Australian army is 24,100 strong, including 2,600 women, and with some 12,000 personnel being available to the combat units. It is currently in the process of a considerable investment program to provide mobility, logistics, and aviation support necessary to produce a readily deployable force capable of operating throughout much of Southeast Asia.

A Leopard 1 main battle tank of 1st Armored Regiment based in Palmerston, Northern Territory. This unit provides mechanized support to 1st Brigade based around Darwin.

Army units

The present organization has

1 land force HQ, a joint task force HQ

1 task force (integrated) HQ

1 brigade HQ

Combat units include

1 armored regiment (integrated)

2 armored reconnaissance regiments (1 integrated)

1 special air service regiment

6 infantry battalions (2 integrated)

1 commando regiment (integrated)

2 independent armored personnel carrier squadrons (1 integrated)

1 medium artillery regiment

2 field artillery regiments (1 integrated)

1 air defense regiment (integrated)

3 combat engineer regiments (1 integrated)

2 aviation regiments

Average allocation Armor, artillery, and helicopters within each brigade

Task Force

Armored regiment
- 58 Leopard main battle tanks
- 52 M113 armored personnel carrier

Reconnaissance regiment
- 52 ASLAV-25 reconnaissance

2 Infantry battalion
- 50 M113 armored personnel carriers

Amored personnel carrier squadron
- 26 M113 armored personnel carriers

Field artillery regiment
- 32 105mm M2/HAMEL field guns towed

Combat engineer regiment

Air defense regiment
- 16 Rapier surface-to-air missile launchers

Joint Task Force HQ

Reconnaissance regiment
- 52 ASLAV-25 reconnaissance

Medium artillery regiment
- 32 155mm M198 towed guns

Field artillery regiment
- 32 105mm M2/HAMEL field guns towed

Armored personnel carrier squadron
- 26 M113 armored personnel carriers

4 Infantry battalions
- 50 M113 armored personnel carriers

2 Combat engineer regiments

2 Aviation regiments
- 25 UH-1H helicopters
- 35 S70 helicopters

Infantry small arms

9mm Browning L9A1 automatic pistols

9mm FI sub-machine guns

7.62mm L1A1/L2A1 automatic rifles

7.62mm M82 sniper rifles

5.56mm Steyr F88 assault rifles

7.62mm M60 machine guns

12.7mm M2 HB heavy machine guns

An Australian light armored vehicle (ASLAV) of the 2nd Cavalry on operations in Batugade, East Timor against pro-Indonesian militia.

KEY 🛬 Airborne 🛡 Armor 🔫 Infantry 🔫 Artillery ◁ Missiles

An Australian soldier shown below equipped with a 5.56mm Steyr assault rifle outside the INTERFET headquarters in Dili.

INTERFET troops take up positions on the Suai shoreline. Hundreds of troops and vehicles took part in an operation sailing on board Royal Australian Naval vessels from Dili around the coast of East Timor to Suai. After securing the area, the troops moved into Suai to set up WESTFOR, INTERFET's southern command headquarters.

M113 Armored Personnel Carrier

Country of origin U.S.

First entered service 1960 with U.S. army

Main armament 20mm Vulcan or machine guns

Max. road speed 36 mph (61 km/h)

Max range: 288 miles (480 km)

Crew 2+ 11 infantrymen

Over 78,000 built, in service with some 48 armies

Firepower   The cutting edge

Airborne	**Armor**	**Infantry**	**Artillery**	**Missiles**
25 UH1H armed helicopters	**71** Leopard 1A3 main battle tanks	**296** 81mm mortars	**246** 105mm M2A2/L5 towed	**19** Rapier towed surface-to-air
35 S70 helicopters	**111** ASLAV-25 light armored vehicles	**577** 84mm Carl Gustav anti-tank	**104** 105mm Hamel towed	**17** RBS-70 Portable surface-to-air
40 B206 B1 helicopters		**74** 106mm M40A1 anti-tank	**35** 155mm M198 towed	
17 AS350B helicopters	**463** M113 armored personnel carriers			
6 CH47 Chinook helicopters				
Total 123	**Total 645**	**Total 947**	**Total 385**	**Total 36**

Support	Excellent	Average	Poor		= 1,000

◬ Fighting structure

The Australian army has to both protect its vast northern coastline and provide forces for rapid deployment overseas in the Southern Pacific region. This is of increasingly important strategic interest to Australia, particularly as the demands for peacekeeping forces among its many island neighbors are set to increase. A major reorganization to take account of these new demands on Australia's limited military resources was instigated by the government's Defense Review–2000. This review is likely to result in the creation, over the next five years, of an integrated rapid reaction force of six battalions, to include helicopter–borne air mobile infantry and SAS. These units will be split between the Australian Defense Force HQ (Operations) in Darwin and the Deployable Joint Force (7th Task Force) based in Brisbane.

Fighting Structure Overview

1 Task force headquarters (integrated) (brigade-sized force) ⬙

This unit based in Northern Australia has an armored regiment with German Leopard 1A3 main battle tanks and the reconnaissance regiment has the Australian-made ASLAV-25 light armored vehicle (LAV). Two infantry battalions with modern small arms and infantry support platoons have 81mm mortars, 84mm Carl Gustav, and 106mm M40AI recoilless anti-tank weapons. M113 armored personnel carriers equip the armored personnel carrier squadron, while 105mm Hamel field artillery are replacing the older M2A2 in the artillery regiment.

1 Joint task force headquarters (brigade-sized force) ⬙

Also based in Northern Australia, this largely infantry-based unit nonetheless has a reconnaissance regiment with ASLAV-25, a medium artillery regiment of 155mm M198 towed guns, an SAS (Australian Special Air Service) regiment with a strong contingent of combat engineers and two aviation (helicopter) regiments flying a mix of Bell UH-IH Armed & Bell 206B-1 Kiowa.

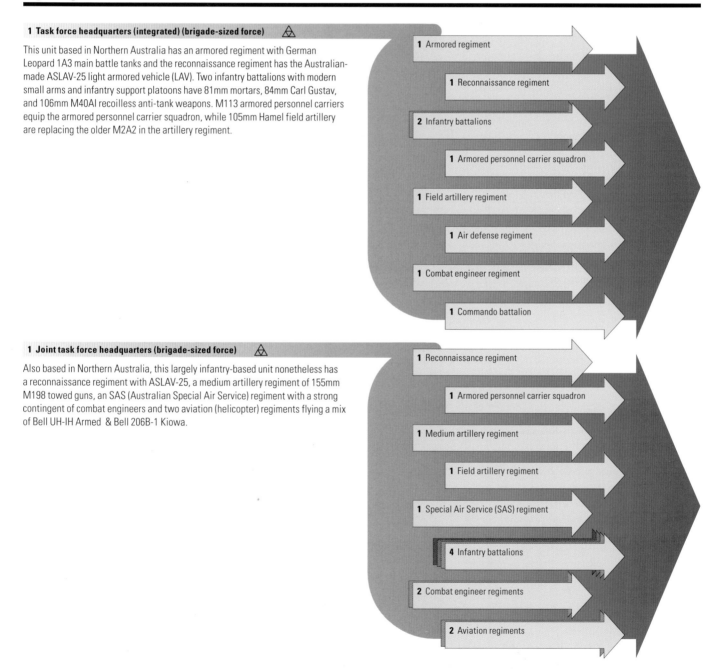

1 Armored regiment
1 Reconnaissance regiment
2 Infantry battalions
1 Armored personnel carrier squadron
1 Field artillery regiment
1 Air defense regiment
1 Combat engineer regiment
1 Commando battalion

1 Reconnaissance regiment
1 Armored personnel carrier squadron
1 Medium artillery regiment
1 Field artillery regiment
1 Special Air Service (SAS) regiment
4 Infantry battalions
2 Combat engineer regiments
2 Aviation regiments

🎖 Special forces

During the run-up to the 2000 Sydney Summer Olympic Games, the threat of a terrorist attack was taken very seriously by the Australian authorities. Every possible action to be taken by the Special Air Service (in cooperation with the Sydney police force) was rehearsed and refined in the weeks prior to the opening of the Games. The Tactical Assault Group (TAG) of the Australian Special Air Service Regiment and its helicopter support unit had been training in and around the Sydney area to familiarize themselves with local operating conditions from road traffic flow to mapping the sewers.

Special Air Service (SAS) and the Tactical Assault Group (TAG)

The Australian Special Air Service was formed in July 1957 as a squadron or company-sized unit. By the 1960s, the time of Australia's involvement in both the Borneo Campaign during the British confrontation with Indonesia, and the Vietnam War, two additional squadrons had been raised, and, along with signals and headquarters units, formed the new 1st SAS Regiment.

By the time the SAS had ceased operations in Vietnam, it had earned a high reputation, racking up an amazing record and firmly establishing itself as a major player in the special operations field. The regiment had a confirmed kill rate of 500 to 1 and had won the highest possible honors for gallantry, with four Victoria Crosses (equivalent to the Congressional Medal of Honor) to confirm its reputation.

Recent years have seen greater attention being paid to the task of countering terrorism. The Tactical Assault Group, part of the SAS, has been Australia's primary counter-terrorist force since 1978, and was the first dedicated unit created for this task. Later, an Offshore Installations Group, with combat swimmers trained to parachute into the sea, in addition to many other other skills, was added. This extra responsibility has placed considerable strain on the limited manpower available to the Australian Special Air Service. In 1996, approximately A$45 million was spent on upgrading the unit's weapons, communications, and command systems to enhance its overall capabilities.

The SAS training, skills, and requirements follow closely those of the leading special forces units. This includes being qualified in HALO (High Altitude Low Opening) and HAHO (High Altitude High Opening), proficiency at heliborne insertion, and familiarity with a wide range of weapons including M16A2 and locally produced F88 (Steyr) 5.56mm assault rifles and Heckler & Koch MP5K sub-machine guns.

Ist Special Air Service Regiment

- 1st, 2nd, and 3rd Squadrons
- 152nd Signal Squadron
- Headquarters Squadron
- Tactical Assault Group
- Offshore Installations Group

Training specialists

Australian special forces have earned considerable respect in Southeast Asia following their involvement in operations there. As a result, a number of countries have sent personnel to take part in joint training exercises in Australia. An example being exercise "Night Crocodile" in October 1998, when members of the Sultan of Brunei's elite Special Combat Squadron trained alongside the 1st Commando Regiment in the sub-tropical areas of northern Queensland.

An Australian paratrooper in defensive posture having just disembarked from an S-70 Black Hawk helicopter during United Nations operations in East Timor.

Index

Numbers in *italics* refer to maps

1st Brigade (Australia) 185
1st Parachute Infantry & Marine
    Regiment (France) 56
11th Airborne Division (France)
    55
13th Commando Regiment
    (Greece) 81
14th Special Forces Division
    (Syria) 121
19th Baluch Regiment (Pakistan)
    151
82nd Para-Commando Battalion
    (Syria) 121
707th Special Mission Battalion
    (S. Korea) 171

A

Achille Lauro hijack 75
Afghan War 131
Algerian War of Independence
    49, 50
Air Assault Brigade (UK) 44, 45
Airborne Brigade (Saudi Arabia)
    87
Al'fa (Special Group A; Russia)
    131
Allied Command Europe (ACE)
    Mobile Force 40
Alpine Commando Unit (Italy) 73
Alpini (Italy) 71, 74
AMAN (Israel) 114
Amazon Military Command
    (Brazil) 33
ARRC (Allied Rapid Reaction
    Corps; NATO) 40, 44, 59, 65,
    71, 75, 77
Australia 184–9

B

Balkans crisis 23, *58*, 70, *70*, 71,
    76
    peacekeeping 40, *58*
Bangladesh: war of
    independence 145, 146, 151
Basque terrorism 48, *64*, 65, 68;
    see also ETA
Black September terrorists 114

BOEL (Special Operations Legion
    Battalion; Spain) 69
Border Guards (Germany) 63
Brazil 32–7
    border disputes *32*
British Army on the Rhine
    (BAOR) 38, 39

C

Canada 26–31
Chechnya 123, *123*, 124, 128
China 7, 123, 152–9
    activity in Nepal 153
    arms to Iran 94
    border dispute with India 140,
        140, 141, 144, 145, *153*, 155
    border dispute with Russia
        153, 155, 158
    dispute with Taiwan 153, 154,
        155, 158, 172, *172*, 173, 177
    intervention in Korea *153*,
        166, *166*
    invasion of Vietnam *153*, 155
    occupation of Tibet 153, *153*,
        155
Cold War 6, 7, 10, 12, 18, 38, 54,
    70, 74, 77, 136, 184
Colombia: civil war 33
Communism, collapse of 6, 38,
    39, 44, 48, 58, 59, 62, 122, 130,
    132
counter-insurgency 8, 14, 76, 92,
    120, 138, 144, 145, 147, 165,
    182, 185
    see also counter-terrorism,
    insurgency, terrorism
counter-terrorism 22, 37, 49, 63,
    68, 69, 75, 87, 114, 115, 121,
    159, 165, 171
    see also counter-insurgency,
    insurgency, terrorism
Counter-Terrorist Detachment
    (Brazil) 37
Cyprus 76, *76*, 132, *132*, 133, 138

D

Delta Force (U.S.) 22–4, 31, 81,
    93, 165
DEW-Line *26*

E

East German army (HVA) 58, 62
East Timor 27, 33, 178, *178*, *184*,
    185
Egypt 7, 88–93, 109
    intervention in Yemen 89
    wars with Israel *88*, 88, 89, 92,
        106, *106*, 109
electronic warfare 7, 8, 159
Entebbe raid 108
ETA (Basque) 48, 64, 65, 68, 69
ETA (*Ediko Tmima Alexiptotiston*;
    Greece) 81
European Rapid Reaction Force
    48, 49, 50, 54, 58, 59, 62, 71, 74

F

Falkland Islands 38, 40
Field Intelligence and Military
    Intelligence (AMAN; Israel)
    114
FLQ (Front de Liberation de
    Quebec) 26, *26*
Folgore Parachute Brigade
    (Italy) 75
FOP (Projection Force; Italy) 71
Foreign Legion 49, 51, 54, 56
France 48-57
    former colonies 49, *49*

G

Germany 39, 58–63
GIGN (Intervention Group of the
    National Gendarmerie;
    France) 56-7, 93, 165
Gibraltar 40, 47, *64*
GOE-11 (Grupo Operaciones
    Especiales; Spain) 69
Golan Heights 89, 106, *106*, 109,
    116, 116, 117, 120, 121
Golani Brigade (Israel) 113
Gray's Horse (India) 141
Greece 76–81
    civil war 76, 77, 81
    dispute with Turkey 76, *76*, *77*,
        80, *81*, 132, *132*, 133, 136
Green Berets (U.S.) 12, 25
Grenada 22

GSG-9 (Grenzchutzgruppe-9;
    Germany) 23, 59, 63, 93, 171
Gulf War 10, 23, 46, 82, 100, *100*,
    101, 102, 105, 117, 122
Gurkhas 145

H

Hama revolt 117
Hamas 115
Hezbollah 95, 115, 121
Howard Doctrine 184
hurricane "Mitch" 15
HVK (Haupt Verteidigungs
    Krafte; Germany) 59

I

Immediate Action Group (NATO)
    27
Immediate Action Units (China)
    159
India 7, 140–5
    border dispute with China
        104, *140*, 141, 144, 145, 155
    invasion of East Pakistan 145
    involvement in Sri Lanka *140*,
        145
    Kashmir conflict 140, *140*, 144,
        146, 147, 150, 153
    wars with Pakistan 140, *140*,
        145, 147
Indonesia 178–83
    East Timor 27, 33, 178, *178*,
        184, 185
    insurgency 12, 38–9, 40, 123, 124,
        177, 140, 145, 152, 178
    see also counter-insurgency,
    counter-terrorism, terrorism
Intifada 107, 109
Iran 7, 83, 94–9
    Kurdish insurgency 94, 95, 98
    Revolution 95
    war with Iraq 94, *94*, 95, 98,
        100, 101, 105
Iran–Iraq War 94, 94, 95, 98, *100*,
    101, 105
Iranian Embassy siege 46
Iraq 7, 83, 86, 88, 100–5, 113, 116,
    120, 121, 133
    Gulf War 82, 100, *100*, 101,

102, 105, 117, 122
Kurdish insurgency 100, *100*,
    101, 105
Shi'ite rebellion 100, *100*, 101
UN sanctions 100, 105
war with Iran 94, *94*, 95, 98,
    100, 101, 105
ISA (Intelligence Support
    Activity; U.S.) 24
Islamic militancy 26, 48, 132
Islamic Revolution (Iran) 95
Islamic terrorism *49, 88*, 89, 93,
    117, 152,
Israel 7, 106–15
    alliance with Turkey 132
    occupation of Lebanon 106,
        106, 117
    Palestinian conflict *106*,
        106–7, 109, 115
    war with Syria 106, 109, 113,
        116, 116, 121
    wars with Egypt 88, 88, 89, 92,
        106, 106
Italy 70–5

J

Japan 160–5
    dispute with Russia *153, 160*,
        161, 164
    JGSDF (Japan Ground
        Self-Defense Force) 160,
        164
Joint Task Force (Australia) 185
Joint Task Force-2 (Canada) 31

K

Kashmir: Indo-Pakistani dispute
    104, *140*, 144, *146*, 147, 150,
    153
KFOR (Kosovo Force) 14
KODAM (Indonesia) 179, 182
KOPASSUS (Indonesia) 179, 183
KOREM (Indonesia) 179
KOSTRAD (Indonesia) 179, 182
Korea 166–71
    Chinese intervention 153, *166*,
        166
    U.S. garrison 166

Korean War 10, 25, 155, 166, *166*,
    167
KRK (Kriesen Reaktions Krafte;
    Germany) 59
Kurdish insurgency: Iran 94, 95,
    98; Iraq 100, *100*, 101, 105;
    Turkey *132*, 133, 138, 139

L

Lebanon: Israeli occupation 106,
    106, 117; Syrian occupation
    116, 116, 117, 120, 121
Long-Range Operations Group
    (China) 159

M

Malaysian emergency 185
Mogadishu 24, 25; hijack rescue
    59
Musa Company (Pakistan) 151
Muslim Brotherhood 89, 117

N

narco-terrorism 32, 33
National Guard (Saudi Arabia) 84
NATO 6, 26, 27, 38, 39, 48, 49, 54,
        62, 64, 65, 66, 70, 74, 76, 77,
        124, 128, 132, 133, 134, 136
    ARRC 40, 44, 59, 65, 71, 75, 77
    Immediate Action Group 27
    peacekeeping 40, 48, 50, 58,
        59, 64, 65, 70, 71, 80
    Rapid Reaction Force 68
Nepal 153
NOCS (Italy) 75
North Africa 64, *64, 65*, 68
North Korea *see* Korea
Northern Ireland 38–9, 40
November-17 terrorists 81

O

OIKB (National Police Jandarma
Commandos; Turkey) 139

P

Pakistan 7, 146–51
    Kashmir conflict *146*, 147, 150
    loss of East Pakistan 145, 146,
        151
    wars with India 140, *140*, 145,
        147
Palestinian conflict *106*, 106–7,
    109, 115
Palsar units (Israel) 114
Panama 23
para-commandos (India) 145
peacekeeping 145, 188
    in former colonies 49
    in former Soviet republics 123
    NATO 40, 48, 50, 58, 59, 64, 65,
        70, 71, 80
    UN 26, 27, 32, 33, 40, 54, 71,
        141, 161, *178, 184,* 185

R

Rapid Deployment Force (Brazil)
    33
Red Brigades *70,* 75
Republican Guards (Iraq) 100,
    101, 104
Revolutionary Guard Corps (Iran)
    95, 96, 99
Russia 122–31, 160
    border dispute with China
        153, 155, 158
    conflict in Chechnya 123, *123,*
        124, 128
    dispute with Japan *153, 160,*
        161, 164
    garrison in Tajikistan *123,* 125
    insurgency in former Soviet
        republics 123, 124

S

SAS (Special Air Service;
    Australia) 188, 189; (UK) 31,
    59, 81
Saudi Arabia 7, 14, 46, 82–7
    border dispute with Yemen
        82, 83, 86
Sayeret MATKAL (Israel) 23,
    114, 115

SEAL 6 (U.S.) 24, 165, 177
Shi'ite rebellion (Iraq) 100, *100,*
    101
Sierra Leone: civil war 39, 41
Six Day War *88,* 106, *106,* 116,
    117
South Korea *see* Korea
Soviet Union 122
Spain 64–9
    involvement in North Africa
        64, *64,* 65, 68
    dispute over Gibraltar *64*
Spanish Civil War 64, 67, 68
Spanish Legion 68, 69
Special Assault Team (Japan)
    165
Special Forces Brigade (Iraq)
    105
Special Forces Command (U.S.)
    12
Special Intervention Unit (Spain)
    69
Special Operations Command
    (Iran) 99; (U.S.) 25
Special Operations Warfare
    Center (Japan) 165
Special Scout Team of the 2nd
    REP (France) 56
Special Security Force (Saudi
    Arabia) 87
Special Warfare Operations
    Department (Turkey) 138, 139
Special Warfare Unit (Saudi
    Arabia) 87
Spetsnaz Special Forces
    (Russia) 105, 121
SSG (Special Service Group;
    Pakistan) 151
Strategic Reserve (Indonesia)
    178, 182
Syria 7, 88, 116–21, 133
    occupation of Lebanon 116,
        116, 117, 120, 121
    war with Israel 106, 109, 113,
        116, *116,* 121

Picture credits

T

Tactical Assault Group
(Australia) 189
Taiwan 172–7
dispute with China 153, 154,
155, 158, 172, *172*, 173, 177
Tajikistan *123*, 125
Tamil separatist movement 145
terrorism: Basque 48, *64*, 65, 68;
see also ETA
Black September 114
Hamas 115
Hezbollah 95, 115, 121
internal 49, 71, 81, 92, 123,
124, 165, 178
international 12, 26, 31, 49,
161, 165, 177
Islamic 49, 88, 93, 152
Maoist 153
Muslim Brotherhood 89, 117
November-17 114
Osama Bin Laden 82
Red Brigades 70, 75
see also counter-insurgency,
counter-terrorism,
insurgency
Tiananmen Square revolt 152
Tibet 153, *153*, 155
Turkey 132–9
alliance with Israel 132
dispute with Greece 76, *76*,
77, 80, 81, 132, 133, 136
Kurdish insurgency *132*, 133,
138, 139

U

Unit-333 (Egypt) 93
Unit-777 (Egypt) 93
United Kingdom (UK) 38–47
Falkland Islands 38, *39*, 40
Gulf War 46
Northern Ireland 38–9, *39*, 40
United Nations (UN) 39, 50
missions 49
operations 64, 144, 166
peacekeeping 26, 27, 32, 33,
40, 54, 71, 141, 161, *178*,
184, 185
sanctions 7, 100, 105

United States (U.S.) 6, 8, 10–25,
132
Gulf War 10, 23, 100, 101
KFOR 14
invasion of Grenada 22
involvement in Korea 10, *166*,
166, 167
Vietnam War 11, 12

V

vertical warfare 8
Vietnam: invasion by China 155;
War 11, 12
Vympel (Pennant Group; Russia)
130

W

War of Attrition 88, *106*, 109
Warsaw Pact 6, 59, 76, 132, 133,
134
World War II 10, 32, 75, 76, 77,
81, 123, 130, 145, 164

Y

Yemen: border dispute with Syria
83, 86
intervention by Egypt 89
Yom Kippur War 88, *88*, 89, *106*,
109, 117, 121

Quarto would like to thank and acknowledge the following for supplying pictures reproduced in this book. All other photographs and illustrations are the copyright of Quarto Publishing plc.

Key

L left, R right, C center, T top, B bottom

Agenzia di Produzione Cinefoto TV Stato Maggiore dell'Esercito: Front Cover, 33Tr, Italy: 72C, 72Bl, 73Br, Greece:79B. **Australia Department of Defence:** 4c, Australia: 185B (by Darren Hilder), 186Tl, 186Br, 187Tr & Tl (Darren Hilder), 189B. **DPL Defence Picture Library:** 6B, United States: 12T, 13, 14B, 15T, 24T, 24c, 25B; United Kingdom: 38c, 38B, 40B, 41T, 41Br, 42c, 43Tl, 45Tl, 46Bl, 47T; France: 49Br, 50c, 55Tr, 56/57, 57Tc, 57B; Germany: 59B, 60Tc, 61Br, 63B; Spain: 65Cl, 38Cl, 66Cl, 66Br; Italy: 71Tr, 75B; Egypt: 89Tr, 89Bl, 90Cr, 90Br, 91B, 92Tr, 93Cr, 93Bl; Israel: 108Tr, 108Bl, 109B, 110Cl, 114Bl, 115T; Turkey: 134Cl, 138B, 139; China: 152B, 153Br, 154Tc, 154Br, 159Tr, 159Bc; Japan: 165B. **Department of National Defence, Canadian Army:** 7Tc, Canada: 27 (Sgt Boies), 28Br (Sgt Mah), 29 (Mcpl Kent), Israel: 114Tr. **F.A.S. Military Analysis Network:** France: 5l. **Christopher Foss (Jane's Information Group):** France: 52Br, Syria:Br. **Japan Ground Self Defence Force:** Japan: 162Cr, 162Cl, 162Br. **Lockheed Martin Missiles and Fire Control:** Japan: 161Bl. **Rex Features:** Brazil: 37B; Saudi Arabia: 83Tr, 83Br, 87Tr; Iran: 95Cr, 96Tr, 99B; Pakistan: 150Tr, 151Br; North & South Korea: 167Bc; Taiwan: 173C, 177Bl. **Rivista Italiana della Difesa:** 7Tr, 8Cl; United States: 10B, 18T, 18B, 19, 20Bl, 22Bl, 22/23; Canada: 28Tr, 31B; Brazil: 33Bl, 34Tc, 35B; France: 48B, 50Bl, 51Tc, 51Br, 53B; Germany: 60Br; Spain: 67Tc, 69Tc; Greece: 77Tc, 78Tl, 80Tr, 81Br; Saudi Arabia: 84B, 85T; Iran: 97Bc; Iraq: 101Tr, 101Br, 102Tr, 103Br, 105B; Israel: 107T, 111Bc, 112C, 112B; Syria:117Tr, 117B, 121Cr; Russia: 122Bl, 124B, 125Tr, 125B, 126Cl, 128Cl, 128Br, 130Tr, 130Bl, 131B; Turkey: 133Tl, 134Cr, 135B, 136Cl, 136Br; India: 141Bl, 142Cr; Pakistan: 147Bl, 148Tr, 149Br, 151Cr; China: 155T; Japan: 163Bc; North & South Korea: 171Tr, 171Br; Taiwan: 174Cl, 174Br, 175Br, 176Tr; Indonesia: 179Cr, 180Cr, 181Bl, 183Br. **Westland Helicopters:** Israel: 113Bl. **www.bharat-rakshak.com The Consortium of Indian Military Websites:** 141Tr,143Bl,145Bl.